1

# Paul's
# Later Letters:
### from promise to fulfillment

# Paul's
# Later Letters:
## From Promise to Fulfillment

*Paul Wrightman*

ALBA · HOUSE     NEW · YORK

SOCIETY OF ST. PAUL, 2187 VICTORY BLVD., STATEN ISLAND, NEW YORK 10314

*Library of Congress Cataloging in Publication Data*

*Wrightman, Paul.*
  *Paul's later letters.*

  *1. Bible. N.T. Epistles of Paul—Criticism, inter-*
*pretation, etc. I. Title.*
*BS2650.2.W743      1984        227'.06        84-11039*
*ISBN 0-8189-0441-0*

*Nihil Obstat:*
*James V. Parker, S.T.D.*
*Censor Deputatus*

*Imprimatur:*
*† Kenneth Steiner, D.D.*
*Auxiliary Bishop of Portland, Oregon*
*May 8, 1984*

*The Nihil Obstat and Imprimatur are*
*a declaration that a book or pamphlet is considered*
*to be free from doctrinal or moral error. It is not implied*
*that those who have granted the Nihil Obstat and*
*Imprimatur agree with the contents,*
*opinions or statements expressed.*

*Designed, printed and bound in the United States of*
*America by the Fathers and Brothers of the*
*Society of St. Paul, 2187 Victory Boulevard,*
*Staten Island, New York 10314, as part of their*
*communications apostolate.*

*1 2 3 4 5 6 7 8 9 (Current Printing: first digit).*

*To the Parishioners of Sacred Heart Church
Medford, Oregon*

# Contents

**Introduction**                                                     IX
Suggestions on How to Use This Book                  IX

**Romans**
Introduction                                                            1
Chapter 1:   Some Key Terms Defined                          3
Chapter 2:   We Stand in Need                                  17
Chapter 3:   Announcement of the Good News          25
Chapter 4:   Of Freedom and Bondage to Sin            34
Chapter 5:   Solidarity with Christ through the
                    Holy Spirit                                         46
Chapter 6:   The "Mystery" of Israel                          57
Chapter 7:   The Moral Side of Theology                    73
Chapter 8:   Concluding Matters                                89

**Philemon**
Introduction                                                          99
Chapter 9:   Paul's Plea for Compassion and
                    Assistance                                          102
**Colossians**
Introduction                                                          107
Chapter 10:  Christ as Lord of Creation and
                    Redemption                                       110
Chapter 11:  Through, With, and In Christ               124

## *Ephesians*
Introduction                                             139
Chapter 12:  The Father's Redemptive Plan in
             the Cosmic Christ                           144
Chapter 13:  The Fulfillment of the Promise in
             Christ                                      154
Chapter 14:  The Church's Call to Unity in the
             Lord                                        165
Chapter 15:  Some Controversial Guidelines              174

## *Philippians*
Introduction                                             185
Chapter 16:  Jesus Christ is Lord!                       189
Chapter 17:  Citizens of Heaven                          203

## *The Pastoral Epistles*
Introduction                                             213

## *Titus*
Chapter 18:  The Call to Correspondence
             Between Faith and Action                    216

## *I Timothy*
Chapter 19:  On Managing the Church                      222

## *II Timothy*
Chapter 20:  Leavetaking                                 231

# Introduction

Embarking on a study of Paul's later letters is to begin a theological and spiritual adventure of major proportions. These letters cover the period of the last nine years in Paul's life and reflect his fully developed theology and spirituality. We see, for example, the rather terse discussion of the meaning of faith in Galatians expand into a full-scale treatise on faith in Romans; we see his provisional concepts on marriage in I Corinthians 7 flower into a profound celebration of marriage in Ephesians 5. It is in these letters that his understanding of the nature of Christ, of Church, and of community reaches its greatest heights and depths.

Paul's personal theological and spiritual adventure in these letters is a journey from promise to fulfillment. As in *Paul's Early Letters: From Hope, through Faith, to Love*, this book will follow a chronological, developmental approach in order to reflect the journey as Paul himself experienced it. We will find along the way that his adventure has become ours, and that his inspired insights have empowered us to further adventures of our own.

I would like to thank Bishop Kenneth Steiner for granting his Imprimatur, Fr. Jim Parker for acting as Censor Deputatus, and Sr. Jeanette von Herrmann, O.S.B. for reading the manuscript.

## SUGGESTIONS ON HOW TO USE THIS BOOK

Although *Paul's Later Letters: From Promise to Fulfillment* will stand as a biblical-theological work in its own right, it is designed to be used as a study guide to the scriptural text. For this reason the following process is recommended:

1. Read the introduction to the biblical book which is up for consideration. For example, read the introduction to Romans on pages 1-4.

2. If possible, read the letter under discussion in its entirety at one sitting. For example, read the entire biblical text of Romans.

3. Then reread the portion of the letter which will be dealt with in a particular section of the study guide. For example, reread Romans 1.

4. At this point read the corresponding section in the study guide, preferably with an *open Bible*, so that you can refer to specific portions of the biblical text as necessary. For example, read chapter 1: "Some Key Terms Defined," pages 4-20.

5. At the end of each chapter of the study guide (with the exception of the last chapter, which has none) answer the "Questions for Personal Reflection, Group Discussion." These questions are most effective if responded to in writing. All chapters have several factual (have I internalized the substance of Paul's thinking?) and several personal (how does what God has to say through Paul apply to me personally?) questions. If answered in a notebook, the answers to these questions will make up a powerful spiritual journal.

Unless otherwise noted, the biblical text quoted in this study guide is that of the *New American Bible*. For ease of reference this translation is recommended.

# Paul's
# Later Letters:
## from promise to fulfillment

# Romans

## Introduction

Paul sojourned in Corinth for eighteen months, and succeeded in establishing an energetic church there. From Corinth he made his roundabout way to Antioch, staying there for approximately a year before moving on to Ephesus, where he spent three years founding a strong Christian community. It was from Ephesus that Paul—vigorously responding to a very mixed report concerning the state of the Corinthian Church—wrote what is now known as his first letter to the Corinthians, probably in the spring of the year 57. The situation further declined and Paul paid a brief, disastrous visit to Corinth. Returning to Ephesus, Paul wrote a heart-wrenching letter to Corinth (a letter which we no longer have, but which Paul refers to in II Cor. 2:3-4), a letter which he hoped would effect a reconciliation.

He is so anxious regarding the outcome of this letter that he leaves Ephesus in the hope of intercepting his messenger, Titus. He meets Titus in Macedonia, and in response to the good news of reconciliation which he brings, composes what we know as the second letter to the Corinthians, in the fall of 57. Paul hopes that this letter will pave the way for a positive visit with the Corinthian Church. Given the fact that one of his reasons for returning to Corinth was to complete the collection that had been started there for the needs of the mother-church in Jerusalem, and considering that this collection was, indeed, successfully accomplished, we can infer that Paul's visit was a successful one.

It was during his three month stay in Corinth, just prior to his journey to Jerusalem with the collection, that Paul wrote his letter to the Christians at Rome, probably early (mid-winter) in 58. Having successfully resolved his differences with the Corinthians, Paul found the comparative "leisure" to compose his longest and most systematic letter. After delivering the collection to Jerusalem, Paul hoped to visit Rome on the way to beginning a new missionary endeavor in Spain.

Paul wrote to the Romans at such length and in such depth for several reasons. First of all, the letter served to introduce himself to the Roman Church, which he had not founded, and which he had not previously visited. Undoubtedly the Roman Christians had already received mixed reports about him. Very likely they were somewhat apprehensive concerning his orthodoxy. The Roman Church was rather conservative, and would probably view some of Paul's ideas—especially his radical notion of "justification by faith" with a great deal of suspicion. This is why Paul goes to such great length in this letter to corroborate his teaching with frequent reference to the Hebrew Scriptures, and why he approaches the topic of the relationship of Judaism to Christianity from as many angles as possible.

Secondly, Paul had by now spent a number of years hammering out his theology in the fierce heat of endless disputation. Now he had the luxury of a relatively relaxed period when he could develop his thought in a serious and systematic way. His letter to the Romans is his most comprehensive statement of "The Gospel According to Paul." Because of its inclusive nature, soon this letter to the Roman Church was being circulated to other churches. It has long been, and continues to be, one of the fundamental teaching documents of the Christian faith.

As we shall see in the commentary, Paul's letter to the Romans is also the most difficult of his letters for contemporary Christians to understand. We need to step back, as it were, and understand where he is coming from when he uses such concepts as "justice," "wrath of God," "predestination," and "judgment" (to name only a few), before we can grasp the depth and beauty of his message.

Romans is not only systematic and difficult, it also contains some of the most soaring passages in the entire Pauline corpus. Chapter 8, for example, which considers the mystery of the empowerment of the Christian by the Holy Spirit and the unbreakable reality of a Christian's relationship with Christ, is unsurpassed in its vision of the believer's participation in the life of the Trinity.

The structure of Romans is rather straightforward. After the lengthiest introduction of any of his letters, Paul makes his theme statement in 1:16-17. Then follows a detailed discussion of how the entire world, Greeks and Jews together, stands in need of salvation (1:18-3:20). Paul develops his doctrine of justification by faith from 3:21-4:25. After this he describes this new life of faith in chapters 5-8 (with the exception of chapter 7, which reasserts the hopelessness of trying to earn one's salvation by following the law). In chapters 9-11 he confronts the problem of why so few Jews have accepted Jesus as Messiah. This concludes the specifically doctrinal section of his letter.

Paul is convinced that sound morality flows out of sound theology, and in the remainder of his letter he considers various aspects of Christian morality. Chapters 12 and 13 consider the "basics;" they are, in effect, Paul's "Sermon on the Mount." In chapters 14-15:13 he looks at a prevalent problem of early Christianity—the tension between "conservative" and "liberal" elements within the Church. Following this he states his credentials, shares his plans, and sends personal greetings (15:14-16).

## Chapter 1: Some Key Terms Defined

*Please read Romans 1.* Ancient letters began with a set form of greeting, prayer, and thanksgiving, a form which is visible in Paul's beginning of this letter, verses 1-6 comprising the greeting, verse 7 the prayer, and verse 8 the thanksgiving. The first part of the letter (1:1-17) is Paul's own "Letter of Introduction" to the Romans. It is by far the most elaborate introduction of any of his letters, serving as it does to not only personally introduce him to a Christian community with which he was not acquainted firsthand, but also to bring up the contents of the main body of the letter in summary form.

Paul opens by acknowledging his servant status to Christ (1:1). The literal Greek for "servant" is "slave." In addition to underlining his dependency on Christ, this word "slave" also links Paul to some of the great heroes (also called "slaves") of Jewish faith—Abraham, Moses, and the prophets. "Called" and "set apart" emphasize God's initiative in Paul's vocation, his designation as "apostle" stresses his authority. Again, in verse 2, Paul makes a linkage with the Hebrew Scriptures, this time in connection with the Gospel. The Gospel, according to Paul, flows directly from God's promises in Scripture (Scripture being, for Paul, what the early Church was eventually to call the "Old" Testament). In referring to Scripture, Paul is highlighting the continuity between the Old Testament and the Gospel. As we shall see, Paul frequently refers to the Hebrew Scriptures in this letter, consistently with the object of presenting this "New" Gospel as the fulfillment of God's "Old" promises.

In verses 3 and 4 Paul briefly sketches in the content of the Gospel. His description of Christ utilizes two categories: "according to the flesh," which relates Jesus to his human ancestors, and "according to the spirit of holiness," which accents Jesus' unique relationship with the Father. Note the emphasis on the Resurrection, the event which for Paul and the early Church makes it possible to proclaim Jesus Christ as Lord.

Paul repeats his status as apostle in verse 5, and in the process of doing so defines apostleship as bringing others to "obedient faith" in Christ, a faith, in other words, which carries with it a change in conduct. "Gentiles" is literally "nations," a designation which would include Jews as well as "Greeks." Verse 6 acknowledges the recipients of this letter as fellow Christians.

In the prayer in verse 7, Paul affirms the high calling of the Romans (literally they are called to be *saints*), and gives them the dual blessing of grace and peace. Grace, signifying undeserved favor, was especially meaningful to the Greeks, while peace, referring to the fullness of life in relationship with God, was a favorite Jewish benediction. By combining grace and peace, Paul was thus taking care to address both Gentiles and Jewish Christians in the Church at Rome.

Paul offers his thanksgiving to God *through* Jesus Christ (1:8); this preposition emphasizes Jesus' position as mediator. Preaching the Gospel is acknowledged as an act of worship in verse 9. It is significant that Paul is able to tell the Roman Christians of his faithfulness in prayer on their behalf. This witnesses to his genuine concern for all the churches, not just the ones that he himself has founded. Verse 10 points to the fact that Paul's desire to visit this church is no sudden whim, but a longstanding hope. "Always pleading" testifies to Paul's persistence in prayer. Obviously he did not allow roadblocks and postponements to erode his hope.

Verse 11 is rather humorous, revealing, as only a dictated letter can do, Paul's initial preoccupation with his own gifts, which he hastily emends in verse 12 to include a mutual gift-giving. Returning to the subject of his own talents in 1:13, Paul refers to the effectiveness of his activity among the Gentiles, an effectiveness which he hopes will be repeated in Rome. Verses 14 and 15 are simply Paul's way of saying that he has been charged to proclaim the Gospel to everyone.

The next two verses, 16 and 17, are among the most important in this letter. They are the theme statement of Paul's epistle to the Romans, and introduce five key theological terms: gospel, power, faith, salvation, and justice.

We all know that "Gospel" means "Good News" and that

this Good News is the proclamation of the life, death, and Resurrection of Christ. What we miss, however, after nearly two thousand years of Christianity, is the real newness of this News. For Paul and the early Church the reality of Jesus is *startlingly* Good News, the most powerful instance of God's breaking into a world filled with suffering and despair and giving it life and hope. The Gospel, then, is not simply the content of the Christian message. This content pulses with life and will not be tied down. Even language cannot contain it; Paul is forced to use a noun in 1:16a, but the noun "gospel" immediately overflows into its verbal characteristic of "power" in 1:16b.

To describe the Gospel in terms of "power" simply means that it is effective, that it is able to accomplish what it claims to be able to accomplish: salvation. As Christians of the Catholic tradition, we are familiar with the efficacious nature of the sacraments; the sacraments, we believe, when received in faith, are able to bring about that which they signify. An important aspect of sacramental theology with which we are not so familiar, however, is the sacramentality of Scripture. This is a theological way of stating what Paul says in 1:16—that God's Word is a *living* Word, a Word capable of effecting nothing less than a personal contact with God.

The word "believes" in verse 16 is literally, in the Greek, "has faith." The term "faith" is the single most important word in the theological vocabulary of Paul. It is pivotal because, without faith, the content of the Gospel is meaningless and its saving power goes unused. Faith is the key to God's promises, the catalyst which empowers them to become effective.

At its deepest level, the meaning of faith according to St. Paul could be described as follows: faith is the response of complete trust in and total surrender to God. The element of human *response* is primary. God reaches out to us in the Good News of the Gospel, which is His personal invitation to relationship. By its very nature, God's initiative requires a response. Either we accept His invitation, or we reject it.

Faith is simply the response of taking God at his Word (the element of trusting belief) and then submitting to the transformation which a real trusting belief in God will inevitably work on our lives (the element of total surrender).

Faith itself is a gift from God; a gift, however, which God does not offer to some while excluding others, but to everyone. Like all God's gifts, it is a gift which does not work "automatically," but has to be accepted in order to be received. Faith, then, is the "bridge" between God and people which makes possible *personal* relationship between them.

There is a definite movement in verse 16, and this movement is from the Gospel through faith to salvation. "Salvation," as St. Paul uses the term, refers to the redemptive dimension of our relationship with God. Our personal relationship with God is what saves us from the self-destruction which would otherwise be our fate. Salvation in its *fullness* is a future reality. It is such a powerful reality, however, that even now we experience hints of future glory. Thus, the word "salvation" for St. Paul embodies both present (a person is "saved" immediately upon entering a faith relationship with the Lord) and future (a person can look forward to the fullness of his or her relationship with God only in the fullness of time) dimensions.

At the end of verse 16 Paul mentions both "the Jew" and "the Greek." Since *all* people fell into either one of these two categories (the "Greeks" representing "Gentiles"), this is his way of saying that salvation is being offered to everyone.

Verse 17 presents us with the difficult word "justice." It is only natural that those of us who have grown up in the environment of English and American criminal law (which features a strict distributive justice) should tend to approach the biblical concept of "justice" from a legal—indeed, often legalistic—perspective. The problem is that the Bible does not consider justice from this viewpoint.

Thus, when we read 1:17 with our usual perspective on law, it simply doesn't make any sense. The sentence begins with the crucial little preposition "for," which indicates that its content is organically connected with the content of 1:16. But how? When we understand justice to mean the "righting of past wrongs," or even "retribution," how can this kind of justice be revealed in the Gospel?

The answer is that it can't. Our legalistic approach to justice turns the Good News of the Bible into the bad news of exacting reparation. The Good News of eternal life becomes, in the rigid context of distributive justice, the bad news of eternal damnation, for which of us can stand blameless before God's law?

The way out of this dilemma is to surrender our "modern" preconceptions of justice and to reapproach this word from a biblical perspective.

When we turn to the Hebrew Scriptures, the Holy Book from which Paul was schooled, we are in for quite a surprise. "Justice," in Old Testament usage, is not synonymous with "evening things out," but with *salvation*! For example, the Psalms, whose major poetic device is to parallel one synonym with another, frequently links justice and salvation. Just a few of many possible instances:

> Your justice is like the mountains of God:
>> your judgments, like the mighty deep:
>> man and beast you save, O LORD.
> (Psalm 36:7; note the triple parallelism between justice-judgments-save.)

> Your justice I keep not hid within my heart;
>> your faithfulness and your salvation I have spoken of.
> (Psalm 40:11; note the triple parallelism between justice-faithfulness-salvation.)

> The LORD has made his salvation known:
>> in the sight of the nations he has revealed his justice.
> (Psalm 98:2.)

In the last instance we find an analogous movement to our text from Romans (1:16-17). In the Psalm salvation is revealed through justice, while in Romans the Gospel of salvation reveals God's justice. "Justice" and "salvation" are apparently interchangeable terms.

A vital linkage between justice and salvation is confirmed in the prophetic literature. The book of Isaiah, for example, states:

Was it not I, the LORD,
  besides whom there is no other God?
  There is no just and saving God but me.
(Isaiah 45:21b.)

So well-substantiated is the connection between justice and salvation that the Septuagint (a Greek translation of the Hebrew Scriptures made in the third century B.C.) translated the Hebrew *sedeq* (the word rendered "justice" in the New American Bible) as "mercy."

All this points to the fact that, when used as an attribute of God, justice points to the reality of God's unconditional faithfulness to His promises. When St. Paul describes God as "just," he is proclaiming the fact that God has, indeed, kept His promise of salvation. To say that "in the gospel is revealed the justice of God" (Romans 1:17) is to say that the Gospel (the life, death, and Resurrection of Jesus, and their proclamation) is the most complete disclosure of God's mercy, of His will to save. The Gospel, in other words, is the ultimate witness to the fact that God has kept His promises, even if we have not kept ours.

The phrase "which begins and ends with faith" (1:17) underscores the crucial role played by faith in the process of God's justice, or salvation, becoming real and effective for us. Faith is really our acceptance of and surrender to God's absolute faithfulness, a movement which the famous biblical commentator William Barclay has captured in his paraphrasing the above phrase as "when man's faith responds to God's fidelity."

The first chapter of Romans is one of the most difficult parts of any of Paul's writings for us to understand. As we have just seen in connection with the word "justice," one major difficulty is that the meaning of certain key biblical words is not necessarily the same as that of modern usage. We are about to encounter a second major difficulty: the fact that Paul persists in using certain stereotyped ways of describing God, ways which are highly problematic for the contemporary reader of the Bible.

1:18 introduces us to the concept of the "wrath of God." In using this kind of imagery as part of his description of God, Paul is following a long-standing Old Testament tradition of portraying God's anger in highly emotional, even vindictive, terms. As might be expected, this kind of imagery is prominent in the prophets:

> Lo, the day of the LORD comes
>    cruel, with wrath and burning anger;
> To lay waste the land
>    and destroy the sinners within it!
> (Isaiah 13:9)

> See the name of the LORD coming from afar
>    in burning wrath, with lowering clouds!
> His lips are filled with fury,
>    his tongue is like a consuming fire.
> (Isaiah 30:27)

> Thus shall my anger spend itself, and
> I will wreck my fury upon them till
> I am appeased; they shall know that I,
> the LORD, have spoken in my jealousy when
> I spend my fury upon them.
> (Ezekiel 5:13)

The advantage of talking about God in this way is that it makes Him very personal and very present. If one takes the prophet's words seriously, one is forced into direct confrontation with this passionate God, an encounter which the prophets know can lead to a "reversal" of God's judgment:

> But if that nation which I have threatened turns
> from its evil, I also repent of the evil which I
> threatened to do.
> (Jeremiah 18:8)

> Now, therefore, reform your ways and your deeds;
> listen to the voice of the LORD your God, so that
> the LORD will repent of the evil with which he
> threatens you.
> (Jeremiah 26:13)

Paul is using the "wrath of God" in this prophetic way in Romans 1:18. His intent is not to announce any kind of *fait accompli* on God's part, but to challenge his readers to repentance.

There is, however, a great disadvantage attached to this kind of talk about God. This is the tendency to take these metaphors literally, and in the process of taking them literally, to put God in the impossible position of performing evil to accomplish good. Some things *are* impossible with God (to act against His nature), and doing evil to attain good is one of them.

The Bible (including the writings of St. Paul) is inclined to make this unconscious contradiction in God's personality because its authors, given the theological limitations of their time, had not yet made a distinction between God's "active" will and His "passive" will.

The writers of the Bible considered God directly responsible for everything. Thus, all good things, like conversion and commitment, life and health and happiness, were credited to God's loving-kindness; all bad things, like hardness of heart, disease and death, were attributed to God's wrath. This neatly accounted for everything, but the neatness of the accounting did a certain amount of violence to God's character.

Are we really to believe, for example, that an all-good God purposefully made Pharaoh obstinate so that he could punish him for his obstinacy (see Exodus 4:21, 7:3, 10:20, 10:27, etc., etc.)? Or is this simply a case of the Bible giving God the undue credit for Pharaoh's *own* hardness of heart?

Contemporary theology would answer the latter question with a strong affirmative. What we might call God's "active" will is always unconditionally loving. In other words, God does not play games with people, expressing love one moment and vengeance the next. His will is *always* to do the loving thing, whether this be trying to open people's hearts (even Pharaoh's), empowering growth through tragedy, bringing wholeness out of brokenness, life out of death.

The single condition to the effectiveness of God's unconditional love is human freedom. God wants to have a real relationship with us, not the relationship of creator to machine, but a love relationship between two persons. For such a relationship to be possible, freedom is a necessity. A person *has* to be able to reject God's offer of relationship if a real relationship with Him is to be a possibility.

If a person exercises his or her freedom in a negative way and rejects God, is this, then, part of God's will? It is certainly not part of God's active will, which is still one of unconditional love toward that person. It is, however, part of God's will in the sense that He respects the person's freedom. Theologians call this aspect of God's will God's "passive" will—those things (like rejection) which He allows to happen as the price required for the possibility of real relationship, or those things (like accidents, sickness, and death) which he allows to happen as part of the now natural order of our broken world.

Modern theology maintains that it is crucial—for the sake of God's integrity—*not* to see God as the direct cause of all the various evils in the world. God effects good, and nothing but good. Evil abounds, but it is not the result of God's doing or willing. It is an expression of the misuse of human freedom or an expression of the broken world order in which we live. Beneath all these expressions of human and natural brokenness, God is there, however, actively seeking to help make the best out of the worst that either we or the world can devise.

But what does all this have to do with "God's wrath?" Simply this: if we truly believe that God is unconditionally loving, and follow the theological consequences of this affirmation through to their conclusion, there can be no such thing as the wrath of God. We must see it for what it is: a biblical metaphor to account for the effects of sin.

There is another strand of biblical theology, a strand which is interwoven with the wrath of God imagery. This strand does not see God as stepping in, so to speak, and wrathfully inflicting punishment and retribution for sin. Rather, it sees sin as containing its own built-in punishment, namely the destructive chain reaction which it sets in motion:

Your own wickedness chastises you,
   your own infidelities punish you.
(Jeremiah 2:19a)

Your conduct, your misdeeds, have done this to you;
   how bitter is this disaster of yours,
   how it reaches to your very heart!
(Jeremiah 4:18)

By the blood which you shed you have been made guilty,
and with the idols you made you have become defiled; you
have brought on your day, so that the end of your years
has come.
(Ezekiel 22:4)

Because they refused to repent,
   their own counsels shall devour them.
.(Hosea 11:6b)

The prophet Hosea summarizes the inherent self-destructive-ness of sin when he observes "When they sow the wind, they shall reap the whirlwind" (Hosea 8:7a). This approach rather corresponds to our observations concerning God's "passive" will.

The problem is that the Bible is not consistent when it comes to assigning causality. On the one hand, at times it attributes the effects of sin to the wrath of God. On the other hand, it often assumes that sin is simply its own punishment.

We can resolve this biblical inconsistency by defining the "wrath of God" as "the destructive consequences of sin which inevitably follow from God's honoring our human freedom to sin." "Wrath," then, is not an "active" attribute of God; it is His "passive" acceptance of the destructive consequences of our own sinfulness. With this definition in mind, we are ready to return to the text of Romans.

Using the concept of the "wrath of God" (1:18) as a prophetic denunciation intended to inspire repentance, Paul describes the moral bankruptcy of the Gentile world (1:19-32), then does the same for the Jewish world (2:1-3:8). His point is to demonstrate that everyone, Jews as well as Gentiles, stands in need of salva-tion. After establishing this universal need (3:9-20), Paul can proceed to preach the good news of salvation through faith in Christ.

In 1:19-21 Paul argues that God can be known, at least to a certain extent, through the very being and structure of the world, since all created realities reflect something of His glory and good-ness. Speaking of the pagan world in general, he maintains that it stands morally condemned because it abused the revelation it had been given.

Probably thinking of his humiliating experience in Athens,

where the Gospel had been ridiculed through the supposed superiority of worldly wisdom (for an account of this experience, see Acts 17:16-34), Paul first indicts senseless speculation (1:21). He goes on to imply a direct connection between "speculating to no purpose" and idolatry in verses 22-23.

Paul, in other words, is claiming that senseless speculation leads to idolatry, and that idolatry, in turn, leads to the moral vices which he mentions in verses 24-31.

When one reflects on the self-centered nature of much of pagan "speculation," the self-centered nature of idol worship (one, after all, prays to an idol in the hope of getting what one wants), and the self-centered nature of the sins mentioned in Paul's list, one cannot help but conclude that he sees the root cause of the moral failure of the Gentile world as willful selfishness.

The litany of vices which Paul cites beginning with verse 24 (remember that he considers these as expressions of the "wrath of God") are not ingenious punishments dreamed up by a vengeful God, but the self-destructive and other-destructive consequences of sin. Notice his use of "delivered them up" in 1:24, which is repeated in 1:26 and 1:28. This phrase literally means "gave them over to" and corroborates our interpretation of God's "wrath" as nothing but His passive acceptance of our human freedom to sin. What did God give them over to? —The destructive consequences of their own actions.

We should never forget, however, that this is only half the story. Love may dictate that God accept the freedom of His creatures, even their freedom to turn against Him. God's own freedom, however, requires that He express Himself, and He does this in the "hidden" but potentially healing way of being present in the midst of human brokenness.

Thus, the pagan world which Paul is describing has indeed been "delivered up" to the results of its own defection. At the same time, however, God stands quietly backstage, ready to help pick up the pieces, should His help be requested.

Writing from Corinth, the headquarters for the deification of sexuality in the Greek-speaking world, it is not suprising that the first example of human brokenness which Paul mentions is homosexuality (1:24-28). He definitely is not of a contemporary school of thought which considers homosexual activity as a perfectly normal expression of sexuality. Rather, he sees it as intimately connected to idolatry, as is clearly indicated in 1:25.

It is not right for Christians to consider homosexual activity as the most horrendous of sins. Neither is it right for Christians to bless it. It is best to consider it from a biblical perspective: an example of human brokenness which, like so many other things human, stands in need of healing.

Paul shifts the angle of his vision from the sexual to the social in 1:29-32. These verses are a devastating description of everyday life in a world which does not know God. They are, unfortunately, just as descriptively accurate of life in today's world as they were in Paul's own day.

## Questions for Personal Reflection/Group Discussion

1. Briefly describe the meaning of the following theological terms as Paul uses them: Gospel, power, faith, salvation.
2. (a) What does Paul (following the tradition of the Hebrew Scriptures) have in mind when he talks about God's justice?
   (b) What is your personal response to the "new" understanding of justice discussed in the chapter?
3. (a) What advantage is there in speaking of the "wrath of God?"
   (b) What disadvantage is there in describing God in this way?
   (c) Do you think we should retain this way of presenting God or drop it? Give reasons for your choice.
4. (a) Summarize the modern theological distinction between God's "active" will and God's "passive" will.
   (b) Do you think this distinction works? Why or why not?

5. (a) Why do you think God allows so much suffering to take place on this planet?
   (b) How is God present in the midst of suffering?
   (c) How have you personally found God to be present in the midst of your own suffering?
6. The Bible seems to be rather inconsistent in places. Why do you think this is so?
7. Paul saw many connections between idolatry and sinfulness in the pagan world of his time. What connections do you see between idolatry and brokenness in our own day?

## Chapter 2:    We Stand In Need

*Please read Romans 2:1-3:20.*    The first verse of chapter two reads like the springing of a trap. Paul is aware of the human tendency toward self-complacency. He knows that Jews, Jewish-Christians, and Gentile-Christians were probably surreptitiously enjoying his denunciation of the sins of paganism; those from a Jewish background feeling superior because of the Law, those from a Gentile background feeling superior because they were no longer part of what Paul was criticizing.

Thus, Paul's sober "That is why *every one of you* who judges another is inexcusable" is calculated to catch one off guard. One begins to see that one is really no better than those whom one is judging, and this is exactly the point which Paul wants to make (vv. 1b-3).

In these verses we meet the concept of "God's judgment," a phrase which closely corresponds to the "wrath of God" which we discussed in chapter one. Again, Paul's use of this kind of imagery is problematic in that it inevitably suggests a God who is more judge than Father.

Many biblical scholars attempt a type of theological tightrope walking by trying to balance God's judgment with His mercy.

They aim to clarify by making such statements as "God is totally just and at the same time totally merciful." This kind of thinking, however, actually leads to more confusion than clarification, often making the typical believer somewhat of an agnostic when it comes to God's nature.

Many Christians fear God's "judgment" because they are afraid that it will be a capricious gesture on His part, an act in which God arbitrarily assigns some to heaven and some to hell. This author thinks it better if we separate God and judgment. Both are real. But it is not God who executes judgment, rather we ourselves. In other words, it is our own acts which will condemn or acquit us, as Paul himself affirms in 2:6.

The "day of wrath," the Last Judgment which Paul refers to in 2:5 is not some awful surprise which God has cooked up to get even with sinners. It is merely the final revelation of the life and death that we ourselves have already chosen.

This author has a real problem with some of Paul's Old Testament imagery, whereby he portrays God as "repaying" (2:6), dishing out "wrath and fury" (2:8), "affliction and anguish" (2:9).

We know from the parables of Jesus that God is a loving Father who would not choose to lose anyone. He actively wills the salvation of everyone. Paul says as much himself in 2:4 when he assumes the reality of God's "kindness" and "forbearance."

But Paul is intent to play the role of the prophet, and goes thundering on in his confusing way about God's judgment. Judgment there is. But if anyone is lost, it is because he or she has consciously and freely rejected God's gift of salvation, not because God wills that person to be lost.

This point having been made in an attempt to clarify some of Paul's confusing terminology, it is important to state that what Paul is trying to do in this particular part of his letter (1:18-3:20) is to prove that absolutely no one can be saved on their own merit. He is careful to mention both "Jew" and "Greek" in 2:9-10, and formally states that "With God there is no favoritism" (2:11).

He continues this line of reasoning in 2:12-16. The "sinners" mentioned in 12a are Gentiles; the ones mentioned in 12b are Jews. Although he does not come right out and say it at this point (he will later), his presumption is that *all* are sinners. The moral standard implied in v. 13 is impossible of fulfillment. No one can keep the law perfectly, whether it be the Gentiles who have the law of conscience (vv. 14-15), or the Jews who have the law of Moses (2:17-29).

He goes on emphasizing the theme of judgment in 2:16. The "day" refers to the Last Judgment, a future certainty for Paul. Again, he is hammering away at the parallel themes of wrath and judgment in a prophetic way to establish the self-destructive nature of a world without Christ. He is in the process of demolishing all human attempts at self-salvation.

So far the Gentiles have been the ones receiving most of the pounding. Now, however, Paul zeroes in on Jewish pretentiousness (2:17-29). This part of his teaching is nothing less than a prophetic denunciation, and would have been certain to outrage Jews and anger Jewish-Christians.

His opening description in verses 17-20 is photographically accurate, and also somewhat ironic. Paul is probably remembering his days as a Pharisee. While there is a lot of truth to their claim of being able to discern God's will, to lead, and to teach through the gift of Torah, there is also a lot of pretense involved. Paul blasts this hypocrisy in verses 21-24, a withering attack similar to Jesus' stinging rebuke of the scribes and Pharisees in Matthew 23.

Paul reserves his ultimate argument, however, for verses 25-29. Many Jews of Paul's day put so much confidence in the "sacrament" of circumcision that they considered it a sure sign of salvation. To their way of thinking, anyone who was circumcised was automatically saved, whether or not they followed the rest of the law.

Paul caustically contradicts this point of view. It is impossible for us to realize the vehemence of Paul's words because circumcision has no religious value for us. Then, however, it was the ultimate sign of being Jewish, the sign which supposedly signified salvation, the sign which enabled the Jews to consider everyone without it as little better than untouchable.

While not mocking circumcision per se, he certainly does mock its salvific power when separated from the observance of the law as a whole (2:25). To fan the flames of anger which this particular style of argumentation is sure to ignite in the Jewish community, he uses the aggravating example of a "good," uncircumcised pagan far surpassing a "bad," circumcised Jew in righteousness (2:26-27).

This example, in turn, clears the way for his powerful observations in verses 28 and 29 concerning the difference between "outward" and "inward" religion. These verses foreshadow his magnificent treatment of the same theme in Romans 8.

The main point which he is trying to make in the opening part of his letter is that *everyone,* Jews as well as Gentiles, stands in need of salvation, because *no one* has been able to successfully fulfill the requirements of whatever law they have been given. Paul's example of the "perfect" pagan in verses 26-27 may be inflammatory, but it is also impossible, and goes against the grain of his argument. Occasionally Paul lets his emotions interfere with his logic.

Paul's harsh criticism of circumcision as an end-in-itself can be a challenge to the ritual presumption which threatens Christianity as well as Judaism. Ritual, or sacramental, presumption is assuming that one can be saved by going through the motions of some rite or sacrament. The action, in other words, is severed from the relationship with God which gives it meaning. We must be careful not to turn Baptism and Eucharist into two more forms of meaningless "circumcision."

Given the truth of Paul's criticism, the inevitable question arises, "What is the advantage, then, of being a Jew, and what value is there in circumcision?" (3:1). This question, and the ones that follow in this section (3:1-20), are raised by an imaginary antagonist whom Paul counters in the popular debating style of his day. The argumentation here is neither developed nor profound; fortunately Paul deals with the important issues at length in depth in other parts of this letter.

Paul's answer to the initial question posed in 3:1 begins with an impressive "much in every respect" (3:2a). His "First of all" in 3:2b leads us to expect a long list of advantages, but in this particular little debate he never gets beyond the fact that "the Jews were entrusted with the words of God." This, indeed, is a significant point, affirming as it does that Israel was the unique bearer of revelation. Paul will dive into the complex question of the relationship between the Jews and Jesus, Judaism and Christianity, in chapters 9-11.

At this point his use of the word "entrust" in 3:2 triggers a new line of thought with the question "what if some of them have not believed?" in 3:3a. In other words, granted the fact that God has entrusted them with His revelation in a unique way, what about those, the majority, who have *not* believed? Does not their unbelief rather make a fool of God: "Will not their unbelief put an end to God's faithfulness?" (3:3b).

Paul's response, "God must be proved true" (3:4a), emphasizes God's unconditional faithfulness to *His* promises ("true" is a synonym for "faithful"). Human beings can and will violate their side of their covenant relationship with God ("even though every man be proved a liar"), but God will never violate His side of the covenant. Thus, Paul is able to use the curious figure in 3:4b of God's being on trial for His supposed unfaithfulness and being acquitted:

> You (God) shall be vindicated in what you say,
> and win out when you are judged.

This affirmation provokes another question from Paul's imaginary antagonist: "But if our wrongdoing provides proof of

God's justice, what are we to say? Is not God unjust when he inflicts punishment?" (3:5). God's "justice" in 3:5a is obviously an equivalent term for God's "faithfulness," mentioned in 3:3b. This corroborates our previous discussion concerning the biblical meaning of "justice."

Paul's parenthetical remark ("I speak in a merely human way") in 3:5c shows that he is painfully aware of the real contradiction contained in the question "Is not God unjust when he inflicts punishment?" According to his own equation between God's justice and faithfulness, it would, indeed, appear that God *is* being unjust when He punishes. For if justice and faithfulness are synonymous with unconditional love, how can God be unconditionally loving and punish at the same time (remember that punishment here refers to all the horrible things earlier ascribed to the "wrath" of God)?

On the basis of our earlier distinction between God's active will and his passive will, we would answer this question about the injustice of God's punishment with a strong affirmative. Paul, who did not have this distinction to work with, and who, like his Jewish predecessors, sees God as directly responsible for everything, (even things that we would call "evil") is forced to exclaim "Assuredly not!" (3:6a)

His reasoning, which to him is obvious—"If that were so, how could God judge the world?" (3:6b)—is to us another indication of the inevitable contradiction to which his limited theological categories have compelled him. We would say that, according to the Bible's own definition of justice as salvation, God simply cannot be just and judge at the same time. The realities of justice and judgment cannot *both* be contained in a God whom we affirm to be unconditionally loving.

We are *not* denying the actuality of judgment, even of a "Last Judgment," as the self-destructive reality of human sinfulness. What we *are* denying, however, is the concept of judgment as some kind of "outside" wrath which God directly inflicts on sinners.

The question posed in verse 7: "If my falsehood brings to light God's truth and thus promotes his glory, why must I be condemned as a sinner?" again points out the unfairness of a God who is conceived of in terms of both justice and judgment. We would simply respond to this question by saying that "God is not condemning you. You are condemning yourself. Don't make God responsible for your condemnation, which is self-inflicted."

The proverbial question of doing evil to achieve good is raised in verse 8. This was a common misrepresentation of Paul's thought ("This is the very thing that some slanderously accuse us of teaching"), and betrays a total misunderstanding of the Christian message. Paul summarily dismisses the question here, but he will, in effect, respond to it in chapters 6 and 8.

Finally, in the next section, 3:9-20, Paul gets to the heart of the matter, and directly makes the point which he has been trying to make since 2:1. Still addressing the Jews, he asks the rhetorical question "Well, then, do we find ourselves in a position of superiority?" (3:9a). His "Not entirely" can also be translated "Not at all." In any case his main point is that *both* Jews and Greeks "are under the domination of sin" (3:9b). This phrase could be paraphrased as "are slaves to sin," and conveys the powerful image of a person who is no longer free *not* to sin. Underlying Paul's understanding of the incredible power of sin is his firm conviction that sin has its source in a greater source of evil than the human heart; we will have occasion to comment on this further in the course of this commentary.

The typical Jew of Paul's time would have been enraged at the accusation that he was as "fallen," as sinful, as his pagan neighbors. Paul relentlessly drives in his point by throwing at them a collage of quotations from the Hebrew Scriptures (3:10-18), the effect of which—through the staccato of the "no," "not even one," "no one," "not one," and the litany of the various "evil" bodily parts: "throats," "tongues," "lips," "mouths," "feet," "eyes,"—is to present a totally devastating picture of fallen humanity, a fallen humanity which definitely includes the Jews.

The emphasis in verse 19 is on the "everything." According to Jewish tradition, a person had to fulfill the law in its entirety to be considered just. Paul has just proven, on the basis of this same tradition, that "There is no just man, not even one" (3:10). Thus, *"every* mouth (including the Jews) is silenced and the whole world stands convicted before God" (3:19b). Because the law is impossible of fulfillment, it cannot possibly provide salvation (3:20a). Hence, its practical effect is to "point out what is sinful" (3:20b), and in the process of doing this, to convince each of us of our need for salvation through something (or Someone) greater than the Law.

Paul has set the stage for his announcement of the Good News.

*Questions for Personal Reflection/Group Discussion*

1. (a) Have you ever been confused by the Bible's talk of God's wrath and judgment?
   (b) Why were you confused and how did your confusion make you feel?
   (c) How did you overcome your confusion if you did?
2. Using the theological distinction between God's "active" will and His "passive" will, reconcile the seeming contradiction between God's mercy and judgment.
3. How might it be possible for a Christian to lose the very real grace of Baptism and Eucharist in the same way that it was possible for a Jew to lose the very real grace of circumcision?
4. How have you personally experienced the law as a dead-end road in terms of salvation?

# Chapter 3:   Announcement of the Good News

*Please read Romans 3:21-4:25.*   The two little words "But now" (3:21) proclaim a totally new revelation as with a trumpet blast. Paul has just finished demonstrating the bankruptcy of law—all law, both pagan and Jewish—as a means for salvation. According to the standards of Gentile and Jew, the situation is hopeless because no one is able to live up to these standards.

Thus, for salvation to be a reality, it must break in from outside the structure of the law. And this is precisely the Good News which Paul announces at this point. God, determined not to be foiled by human sinfulness, has come up with an Other Way, a way of salvation not contingent on human merit, but based solely on His love.

Note Paul's continuing use of the word "justice" (3:21a), which is clearly still being used in the sense of "faithfulness," and as synonym for "salvation." He is quick to assert (3:21b) that both the law and the prophets—in other words, the Hebrew Scriptures as a whole—point to the reality of this "new" way of salvation. Like Jesus in St. Matthew's Gospel, when he says: "Do not think that I have come to abolish the law and the prophets. I have come, not to abolish them, but to fulfill them" (Matthew 5:17), Paul is claiming continuity, not contradiction, between the faith of Israel and the content of the Gospel.

Verse 22 describes Jesus Christ as the fullest expression of God's justice (His irrepressible intent to save). Access to salvation is through faith in this same Jesus Christ. Remember our earlier discussion on the meaning of faith as the personal *response* to God's gifts which makes them effective for us. Faith—personal acceptance of God's promises in Jesus—is thus the only condition for salvation.

Paul restates his previous conclusion of humankind's universal brokenness in verse 23. The "glory of God" is another way of saying "God Himself." In this context to be "deprived of the glory of God" means to lack a saving relationship with Him. In other words, sin cuts us off from a saving relationship with God. And—as Paul has gone to such great length to prove in the previous part of this letter—no law can bridge the gap between God and broken humanity, for no person is capable of completely fulfilling the law.

Verse 23 serves to remind us of the "bad news" of our "natural" state of despair. In verse 24 Paul returns to the triumphant theme of the Good News of salvation in Christ. The word "justified" is another pivotal theological work. It has its roots in the law courts of the day: to be "justified" means to be acquitted. Thus, Paul is telling us in verse 24 that God has given us the gift of justification—acquittal from the otherwise sure conviction of our sinfulness—and that this process of justification has been achieved for us "through the redemption wrought in Christ Jesus."

The word "redemption" comes from the vocabulary of slavery and refers to emancipation. To be redeemed, in Paul's theological use of the term, means to be both saved *from* something and saved *for* something: in this case, to be saved from the self-destructive consequences of sin and to be saved for a life-giving relationship with God. The vehicle, or means, of our redemption is Christ Jesus. "Through Jesus" is the answer to the question "How are we saved?"

Paul gives us a rough sketch of the dynamics of redemption in verse 25. "Blood" refers to Jesus' sacrifice on Calvary. "Expiation" is a synonym for atonement, which can be broken down to mean the state of at-one-ment between God and humanity achieved by Jesus' sacrifice. Thus, 3:25a could be paraphrased "Through his (Jesus') sacrifice, God made him the means of atonement for all who believe."

Paul has been using the images of "justification," "redemption," and "expiation" to express the depth of God's love for a fallen, broken humanity. He is describing the incredible length to which God went to "manifest his own justice" (3:25b); that is,

to prove his faithfulness and love. Thus, Romans 3:25 proclaims
the same reality which St. John will state more poetically in his
Gospel:

> Yes, God so loved the world
> that he gave his only Son,
> that whoever believes in him may not die
> but may have eternal life.
> (John 3:16)

Even though Paul uses words derived from the law court,
the slave market, and the sacrificial altar, the deepest meaning
of what he is talking about is not to be derived from these spheres.
He uses this technical vocabulary to try to break through to the
fundamental reality of relationship with God which only faith in
Jesus can provide. This is why the little phrase "for all who
believe," hidden in the midst of verse 25, is so terribly inportant.
It is the relational phrase, the phrase which acknowledges that
salvation is impossible without a personal encounter, a real meeting, between God and the person in faith.

25b-26 celebrate the amazing extent of God's justice—His
is a justice, a faithfulness, a determination to save—which extends
to the past, through Paul's present, and, by implication, to our
future.

The negative use of "boasting" in 3:27a may be an intentional
slam on the Pharisees, since this, according to Jesus as well as
St. Paul, was one of their favorite pastimes. His contrast of the
"law of works" and the "law of faith" in 3:27b is deliberately
ironic. By "law of works" he means any procedure (in this particular context he is thinking mostly, but not exclusively, of Jewish
procedure) through which human beings can supposedly achieve
their own salvation. The "law of faith" (a paradoxical phrase) is
the attitude of total trust in God's promises as opposed to one's
own achievements.

Paul makes his point theologically explicit in 3:28 when he links the all-important process of justification to faith and not to works ("observance of the law" is literally "deeds of the law"). We should note here that for Paul the contradiction between faith and works occurs only when works are wrongly held to be the *starting point* of the Christian life. Paul maintains that the only true starting point can be faith in God's promises in Christ Jesus; in other words, personal acceptance of the love which God wants to give us. There is no way that we can earn this love. God wants to give it to us not because we could ever do anything to deserve it, but simply because He loves us.

Given the crucial starting point of faith, however, it will naturally overflow into good works. This is only to say that any real relationship with God will inevitably lead to some actual expressions of this relationship. Thus, Paul does not see faith and works as contradictory when works flow from a living faith; when works usurp the place of faith, however, they are irrevocably opposed.

In verses 29 and 30 he tries to argue on the basis of what to him seems obvious, the fact that God is the God of all, not just the Jews, and must therefore be able to save apart from the Jewish rite of circumcision. Paul, of course, affirms faith as the bigger reality through which God is able to express His redemptive will.

The Jews (and probably a lot of Jewish Christians) would not be much impressed by this type of argumentation. They would accuse Paul precisely of that which he so strongly denies in verse 31, that he is "abolishing the law by means of faith." Paul contends that faith does not undermine, but rather upholds, the law. His usage of "law" in this verse includes not just the specifically legal parts of the Old Testament, but the Hebrew Scriptures as a whole. In other words, Paul is maintaining that faith fulfills the true meaning of Scripture. This is a contention which he knows he will have to substantiate much more fully than he has done thus far. He does this with his brilliant interpretation of the story of Abraham in chapter 4.

In choosing Abraham as his model, he could not have chosen a more crucial—or more controversial—example in the entire Hebrew Bible. The Judaism of Paul's day considered Abraham to be *the* great model of a person who won God's favor by meticulously following the law. Aware of the fact that the Torah (that part of the Bible, the first five books, officially known as the "Law") had not yet been written in Abraham's day, popular oral tradition had it that God disclosed the contents of the Torah to Abraham in advance, thus making him the first to follow the Law. Paul rejects this well-known tale by ignoring it and relying totally on Scripture.

He admits that "if Abraham was justified by his deeds he has grounds for boasting" (4:2). The decisive word here is the "if." His whole argument in chapter 4 is intended to prove that this "if" is not so, that contemporary Judaism was dead wrong in its interpretation of Abraham.

Paul puts forward his strongest argument first. He quotes Genesis 15:6, which for him is the pivotal verse in the entire Abraham cycle because it makes the crucial equation between belief (faith) and justice (salvation). For Paul, this text once-and-for-all establishes the fact that Abraham was saved, not by works, but through faith. Thus, God's favor is not something which He owes us because we earn it, but simply the reality of His redemptive love which we receive by trusting in His promise.

Considering that the institutionalized Judaism of Paul's day had largely degenerated into an impersonal system of rule-keeping, Paul's alternative restores the lost dimension of personal relationship between God and his people. In many ways Paul's radical critique of contemporary Judaism was simply a return to the original meaning and vitality of the Hebrew Scriptures themselves.

We Christians must resist the temptation to equate Judaism

with legalism. Certainly at specific periods in its history—Jesus'
and Paul's time was one of them—it stood in drastic need of
reformation. The Christian Churches share this same tendency
toward legalism. In its biblical roots—its foundational message—
Judaism, like Christianity, is based on faith, not works. Paul's
caricature of Judaism as a works-religion is really a polemic aimed
at the devastating legalism of his own day.

His quotation from Psalm 32 in verses 7 and 8 brings one
back to the vitality of early Judaism and highlights the priority
of God's loving, forgiving, relational nature. In this context any
kind of legalistic, works-righteousness approach to God is not
only inappropriate but insulting.

Having just countered the legalism of first century Judaism,
Paul proceeds to challenge its particularism. Circumcision was
seen by the Jews and by certain Jewish Christians as a *necessary*
condition for salvation. The biggest battle in the early Church
was, in fact, fought over the issue of whether or not a Gentile
had to be circumcised in order to be a Christian.

Paul argues against such a requirement as being another
example of "salvation by works" instead of "by faith." The question with which Paul begins 4:9 could be paraphrased as "Is a
real relationship with God possible only for the circumcised, or
is it available to the uncircumcised as well?" The Jews and Jewish
Christians vehemently maintained a particularist point of view:
circumcision, for them, was not optional but required. There
could be no real relationship with God without it.

Again using Abraham as his example, Paul demolishes the
basis of their argument. He does this by cleverly pointing out
that, on the basis of the biblical text, the gift of covenant relationship with God was given to Abraham *before* (some 14 years) he
underwent circumcision (4:10). This can only mean that circumcision is merely the ritual celebration of an already-present faith,
not faith's precondition (4:11a).

According to both Jewish and Christian tradition, what was

true for Abraham is true for his descendants. Paul is quick to make the point that since Abraham believed before he was circumcised, he is the spiritual father of all the "uncircumcised who believe" (4:11b). In other words, Paul has totally turned the tables on the particularism of his opponents. Now Abraham is the spiritual father of believing Gentiles (pagans). Almost as a postscript Paul acknowledges Abraham's spiritual paternity of the circumcised, but only those circumcised who do not let their circumcision stand in the way of their faith (4:12). How Paul's argumentation must have aggravated his opponents!

Once again the Jewish law comes under attack in verses 13-17. In 4:13 the promise to which Paul is referring, God's promise to Abraham that he would "inherit the world" through numerous progeny (Genesis 15:5), was part of the covenant relationship which God established with Abraham *before* he was circumcised.

Even more importantly, Paul is implying that God's promise was His affirmation of Abraham's faith, and not of Abraham's supposed perfection in keeping the law. The promise is thus the result of *relationship*, not of works.

Verse 14 is a poignant statement of the meaninglessness of relationship with God if the law becomes the final word. For to "observe the law," according to Jewish tradition, means to observe the law *completely*. "If only those who observe the law *completely* 'are heirs,' " then faith, indeed, "becomes an empty word and the promise loses its meaning"—simply and tragically because if the standard of salvation is set this high, then no one can be saved.

While a faith-relationship with God can redeem the meaning of law, law, if allowed to exist in proud isolation, can only undermine faith. The law, since it is impossible of fulfillment, in itself can only reveal the inherently self-destructive (wrathful) nature of a broken world and a fallen humanity (4:15). Faith (a relationship of trust and love) is thus the only way we can experience the fullness of God's grace (4:16a). Because of this basic reality of the spiritual life, Abraham, as the father of faith, is the father of *all* faith, be it Jewish or Gentile (4:16b-17a).

The rather lifeless Judaism of Paul's day tended to focus on precision of legal observance as the only sure way to God, and to forget the fact that according to its own scriptures God was hardly limited to the role of a heavenly accountant. There is no room for the elements of spontaneity and surprise in a rigid legalism. These are precisely the characteristics of God (two characteristics of any good lover) which Paul calls to mind when he writes, in 17b: "the God who restores the dead to life and calls into being those things which had not been."

Quite possibly, Paul is reflecting not only on God's gift of fertility and of a son to Abraham and Sarah, but also on God's amazing new act in the Resurrection of Jesus. What kind of legal code or system of works could possibly establish a contract binding on this wild and wonderful God who breaks all the rules in bringing life out of death? Certainly if we are to establish contact with Him, it must be on His terms, not ours. And his criterion, emphasizes Paul, is faith, pure and simple.

He uses the example of Abraham's faith in God's promise of a son to illustrate the true nature of faith (4:18-22). The key phrases are "Hoping against hope" (4:18), "Without growing weak in faith" (4:19), "he never questioned or doubted God's promise" (4:20), "fully pursuaded that God could do whatever he had promised" (4:21). What all these phrases have in common is that they describe total confidence that something will happen which appears to be absolutely impossible. Thus, faith is characterized by its complete trust in God's Word, all appearances to the contrary notwithstanding.

According to the ways of the world, it was impossible for Sarah and Abraham to have a child. But God's reality is stronger and deeper than the ways of the world, and they had their son. According to the strict interpretation of Jewish law, it would be impossible for anyone to be saved. But the business of God is salvation, and He is known for coming up with creative alternatives.

Moreover, Paul implies that Abraham's faith was a crucial factor in God's fulfillment of the promise. Faith was Abraham's response, his personal acceptance of God's Word.

Just as God promised Abraham new life, He promises us eternal life. Our task, as St. Paul points out in verses 23-25, is to make the same faith-response to God's promise of salvation in Jesus as Abraham did to God's promise of a son.

## Questions for Personal Reflection/Group Discussion

1. Define the terms "justification," "redemption," "law of works," and "law of faith" as used by St. Paul.
2. (a) How can faith and works appear to be contradictory?
   (b) What is the proper relationship between faith and works?
3. How does Paul's example of Abraham in chapter 4 serve to illustrate his contention that we are saved through faith, not through works?
4. There seems to be an inevitable tendency for any form of institutionalized religion to tend toward legalism. Much of the anti-Jewish polemic in St. Paul's letters is easier to understand if we realize that he is challenging an extremely legalistic form of Judaism, a form of Judaism which had, to a large extent, lost contact with its own roots. Can you think of some ways in which Christianity shares this same tendency toward legalism?
5. This same dynamic is observable on a personal level as well.
   (a) What are some ways in which your own faith has become rather regimented and impersonal?
   (b) What do you think St. Paul would recommend to counteract this tendency?

6. (a) Describe the nature of Abraham's faith, especially as re-
       vealed in 4:18-21.
   (b) Using Abraham's faith as the standard, how does your own
       faith compare?

## Chapter 4:   Of Freedom and Bondage to Sin

*Please read Romans 5-7.*   An interesting shift occurs with 5:1.
Paul moves from an argumentative style to what we might call
a sermonic style. He is no longer attempting to prove anything,
but to explore the meaning of what has been given. Thus, in 5:1
he assumes the reality of justification in the life of the believer.
Justification produces peace, which Paul uses in the Old Testament
sense of "fullness of life in relationship with God." Both justification and peace are attained *through* Jesus Christ. This preposition brings out the role of Jesus as mediator, or intercessor, in
the process of salvation.

   Paul continues to emphasize the mediatorial role of Jesus in
verse 2. The Greek word for "access" has two connotations:
"introduction," and "approaching safe harbor." Thus Jesus is our
introduction, our means of entry, into the safe harbor of the
Father's love. Faith continues to be the catalyst through which
the whole salvific process, through which "grace," becomes real
for us. The hope to which Paul here refers is an eschatological
hope, a hope which looks forward to a happy outcome concerning
the "last things," including the Last Judgment.

   In verses 2 and 3 Paul is using the verb "boast" in his favorite,
positive sense of being so convinced of the truth of God's promises
that we do not hesitate to "brag" about them to others.

   Apparently his mentioning hope in verse 2 causes him to
recall a supposed contradiction to Christian hope—namely, that
of suffering. He tackles the problem head-on, and traces a vital
connection between affliction, endurance, tested virtue, and hope

(vv. 3-4). Affliction (literally "pressure") provides the occasion for endurance (an active, even joyful, encounter with the situation) which, in turn effects "tested virtue" (character which has been hammered out in the refiner's fire), which gives rise to hope.

Our hope is no vagary, but a sure thing because it is based on the surest thing in the world: the love of God (v. 5). We are already immersed in God's love through the abiding presence of the Holy Spirit, a presence which serves as God's "guarantee" or "down payment" on greater things to come. Paul will develop this theme of the indwelling, transformative presence of the Holy Spirit in the life of a Christian at length in chapter 8.

At this point Paul launches into a celebration of God's redemptive love (5:6-11). "At the appointed time" (5:6), underscores the fact that the gift of Jesus was no whim on the Father's part, but had been carefully planned and prepared for. Theologians refer to this process of preparation, culminating in Jesus, as the "history of salvation."

Note Paul's emphasis on Christ's sacrifical death in verses 6-9. Our salvation, according to St. Paul, is not achieved merely by means of the Incarnation. The Incarnation, of course, is fundamental in that it makes the whole drama of salvation possible. It sets the stage, however, for the more specific redemptive act of God which is Jesus' Crucifixion-Resurrection.

Paul sees a totally united intentionality on the part of the Father, Jesus (and, by implication, the Holy Spirit) concerning Jesus' sacrificial death: the motive is purely and simply love. Father, Son, and Spirit were as one in their commitment to definitively break humankind's bondage to sin and death. And given our world's brokenness, the only way to healing lay through vicarious suffering, sacrificial love. Paul sees the true meaning of sacrifice not in the cheap sense of appeasement, but in the costly sense of freely chosen, personal suffering—the personal suffering through which another person may be made whole and holy.

The incredible thing is that God has taken the initiative and offered His own brokenness as the ultimate expression of sacrificial love: "It is precisely in this that God proves his love for us: that while we were still sinners Christ died for us" (5:8). God's gift is completely unmerited on our part—"we were still (and always would have been) sinners."

"God's wrath" reappears in verse 9, again in the sense of the self-and-other-destructive ways of the world and of ourselves from which Jesus' sacrifice saves us. Paul is using "God's wrath" in a future-oriented way here. Christians have nothing to fear at the Last Judgment because they have already received God's "last" judgment—His final Word of forgiveness, love, and reconciliation—in and through the person and personal sacrifice of Jesus.

Verse 12 is a good example of one of the weaknesses of Paul's particular style of writing letters. His method was to dictate the letter to a secretary. Dictation left plenty of room for digression. Thus, Paul begins a thought, "just as through one man sin entered the world and with sin death," and then goes off on a long digression on death before finally returning to something like his original thought in verse 15.

The concept of sin and death entering the world through one man, Adam, and setting a precedent for all people, was a basic assumption of Judaism. It was based on the notion of solidarity among the people. Thus, Adam's "original" sin was not understood as existing in isolation; its consequences were seen as reverberating through the ages.

This biblical idea of "corporate personality" is somewhat analogous to the modern idea of an ecosystem, in which everything in that system is perceived in terms of interdependence. Just as human choices affect our entire environment, Adam's choice affected all of us.

Based on Genesis 2:17b ("From that tree you shall not eat; the moment you eat from it you are surely doomed to die"), death was seen as an irrevocable consequence of sin. Consequently, Adam's sin involved all future generations not only in sin, but in death as well.

The Judaism of Paul's day was fond of dividing history into three major divisions: the period before the giving of the Law, the period of the Law, and the period of the Messiah. Paul is employing this tripartite division in verses 13 and 14. For him the proof that early humanity was sinful in spite of the fact that it had not yet received the law, is the fact that it was subject to death, an effect of sin.

Paul returns to his main task in verses 15-19, which is to establish a contrasting parallel between Adam and Christ. Just as the principle of solidarity implicated all in Adam's sin, it can also work in reverse, and include all who choose, through faith, the redemptive work of Christ. In these verses Paul stresses the enormity of God's gift because it is so contrary to the destructive nature of our broken world. God's grace, in other words, is immeasurably more powerful than human disobedience. True, the consequences of sin are enormous, but God can take even the death we seem to specialize in and, through Jesus, redeem it for life.

Paul makes his harsh statement about the law in 5:20a, "The law came in order to increase offenses," from the perspective of the *effects,* not the intent, of the law. The intent of the law was to provide a sure pathway to God. The actual effect of the law, however, since broken human beings were not capable of following it in its entirety, was to "increase offenses." This ineluctable increase of offenses dramatically reveals the depth and power of God's "new" way in Christ (5:20b-21).

Given his overwhelming emphasis on God's grace, it was only to be expected that a certain element of Paul's audience would try to use his position for their own ends. This is exactly what happened with the libertine faction of the early Church. This faction, which stood for freedom from all restraint, especially in sexual matters, was a dominant force in Greek culture as a whole. It never really amounted to much in the Church because its teachings were soon seen to be antithetical to real Christianity. The statement which Paul phrases as a question in 6:1, "Let us continue in sin that grace may abound?", was actually one of their slogans, a slogan, moreover, which they claimed captured the essence of Paul's teaching.

When basically the same question had come up in chapter 3 (3:7-8), Paul had given it very short shrift. Here, however, in chapter 6, he provides some substantive teaching on *why* the libertines are wrong. The heart of his teaching is contained in verse 2, "How can we who died to sin go on living in it?" It takes an understanding of the next nine verses (3-11), however, to really comprehend what Paul has packed into this question.

His approach presupposes two things: the first is familiarity with the baptismal liturgy of the early Church. The second is the reality of human solidarity with Christ; in other words, of people being able to participate in a personal relationship with Christ which truly transforms their humanity.

Baptism in the early Church was conferred upon adults who had undergone instruction (the "rule of teaching" which Paul refers to in 6:17), and who had experienced conversion. The actual celebration of baptism was done by total immersion, and was heavy with symbolism. Descending into the water was seen as dying to one's former way of life; rising from the water was seen as a foreshadowing of the believer's future resurrection.

Much more important than the symbolic aspect, however, is the real identification with Christ which happens in the context of this sacrament. Through the believer's relational solidarity with Christ, he or she becomes an actual participant in Jesus' death and Resurrection. This is what Paul is saying in 6:3-5.

Verses 6-11 continue to assume our relational identification with Christ. It is important to realize that when Paul uses the phrase "sinful body" in 6:6, he is *not* intending to say that the body is sinful per se. "Body" is a neutral term for Paul, representing the human person in its aspect of creaturehood. Thus, "body" includes not only a physical dimension, but also an immaterial one, since human beings, as creatures, are composed of both matter and soul.

Because of human solidarity with Adam, we are all affected by his sin. Therefore, since the fall all human beings can be said to possess a "sinful body," a body, in other words, which cannot escape the consequences of sin. When a person responds to the Good News of salvation in Jesus Christ (in our particular context of Romans 6:1-11, Paul is assuming that this happens in the sacrament of Baptism), he or she is in-Spirited; that is, the "sinful body" is transformed and becomes—through its solidarity with Christ and the indwelling presence of the Holy Spirit (which Paul will discuss in detail in Romans 8)—a body which is redeemed and which will participate in Resurrection.

Continuing his baptismal imagery in verses 6-8, Paul argues for a real identification between the death of Christ on Calvary and the "death" of the sinner in the waters of baptism. Baptism (the celebration of a personal, saving relationship with Christ) breaks an individual's slavery to sin. Again, because of the reality of this relationship, we participate not only in Christ's death, but also in His Resurrection.

Jesus' Resurrection definitely broke the reign of sin and death on this planet (6:9-10). Through our relational identification with Him, the reign of sin has been definitively broken in our own lives. A whole new relationship with the Father has been made possible for us through our new life "in Christ Jesus" (v. 11).

There is a certain tension in this chapter (chapter 6) which mirrors a very real tension within the Christian life. On the one hand, Paul spends the first 11 verses on a magnificent description of the definitive, ontological, break which a Christian has made with sin. This break is something which has already happened; it is a present reality.

On the other hand, Paul devotes the rest of this chapter (vv. 12-23) to exhorting Christians to live up to their calling. The necessity of this kind of exhortation obviously presupposes that Christians are still sinning. But we were just told that Christians are "dead" to sin. What is going on here?

Quite simply, the tension between promise and fulfillment,

which is an inevitable part of life in a broken world. The promise
has been given: Christ has, indeed, freed Christians from the
domination of sin and death. But, just as life is developmental,
progressing from one stage to another, so, too, is salvation. Our
fulfillment as Christians is not magically given to us the moment
we accept Christ as savior. It is something which is worked out
in relationship with our Lord, something which we will not experience in its entirety until we taste Resurrection. Thus, in a very
real sense, our salvation is a present reality intended to grow into
greater and greater future fulfillment.

Precisely because the Father has already given us the final
victory over sin and death through the death and Resurrection of
His Son, it is particularly important that Christians act according
to *God's* battle plans, and not those of sin (which Paul understands
as a personified force of evil, as well as individual sinful acts).

Speaking especially to Gentile converts to Christianity—persons who, most likely, before their conversion had participated
in the typically Greek attitude of indulgence toward the body,
particularly in regard to sexual activity—Paul urges them not to
allow themselves to return to their pre-Christian practices (6:12).
The imagery he uses in verse 13 is the imagery of war, underscor-
ing the fact that a real battle is being fought on this planet between
the forces of good and the forces of evil. Since the Christian has
already chosen sides, it is imperative that he or she act accordingly.

The use of the verb *"will"* in verse 14 indicates the futurity
of the Christian's total liberation from sin; nevertheless, grace is
*now* operative, and the Christian has already been freed from the
death sentence imposed on him by not being able to follow the
law completely.

Paul repeats the slogan of the libertines (a slogan which
would have been especially appealing to pagan converts to Christianity) in 6:5, but only to provide the context for his final refu-
tation of this position in verses 16-23.

His argument is blunt and powerful. Again, it would have

special force for many of the Gentile Christians, who had been or were still slaves. Paul maintains that there are two, and only two, moral choices in the world, both of which involve slavery. The key issue is for whom a person chooses to be a slave. One can choose to be the salve of sin or the slave of "obedience" (which, in this context, is synonymous with being a Christian; 6:16). Sin inevitably leads to death, while obedience, just as inevitably, leads to "justice" (salvation).

Paul offers heartfelt thanks for their conversion—their exchanging one slavery for another (vv. 17-18). His parenthetical remark at the beginning of verse 19 indicates that he is a little embarrased at the bluntness of his analogy; nevertheless, he proceeds, imploring them to allow their attitudes and actions to reflect those of their *new* master.

Finally, the crucial difference between the two forms of slavery is outlined in verses 20-23. The supposed "freedom" of sin actually led to the slavery of self-destructive behavior, while the supposed "slavery" of being a Christian leads to the true freedom of a fulfilled humanity. By sanctification (v. 22b) Paul means the developmental process of becoming more and more Christlike.

In Pauline terminology, then, "justification"—being made "right" with God through relational solidarity with Christ—is only the beginning, the birth, of the Christian life. The life itself is the process of "sanctification," growing to be more and more like our creator and redeemer, Jesus Christ.

Verse 23 summarizes much of Paul's teaching in this letter to this point. It presents a stark contrast between two irrevocably opposed approaches to life. On the one hand is sin, whose "wages," meaning just due, is death. On the other hand is God, who offers the *gift* of eternal life in Christ. It seems obvious which is the better choice. But still the choice has to be made in order for the gift to be received.

In chapter 7 Paul shifts the focus of his argument. In chapter 6 he has been addressing himself largely to Christians from a

Gentile background. Now he directs himself mainly to Christians whose background is Jewish. Because many of the Jewish Christians, from Paul's perspective, were still confused about the proper relationship between faith and works—the Law, in his opinion, retaining entirely too much prominence—he is especially harsh on the Law in this chapter.

He begins by using an analogy from marriage law to demonstrate the fact that—just as a woman is freed from her marriage obligations upon her husband's death—in the same way Christians are freed from the obligation to observe the Mosaic Law because they, too, have died (7:1-4). This argument, although a little far-fetched, is a good illustration of the very real, as opposed to symbolic, way in which Paul understands a Christian's identification with Christ. It also shows that he expects Jewish Christians to make a complete break from their dependence on the Law of Moses.

Verses 6 and 7 call for an understanding of Pauline anthropology (the way in which he views the nature of the human person). We have already mentioned that "body," for Paul, is a neutral term, simply denoting the totality of the human person (matter plus soul). The word "flesh" (7:5) refers to human weakness, to humankind's solidarity with sin and death through Adam.

Conversely, the word "spirit" (7:6) refers to humankind's reorientation through Christ. Both "flesh" and "spirit" are dynamic principles, the movement of flesh toward sin and death, the movement of spirit toward love and life.

All human beings, because of their solidarity with Adam, are "in the flesh." It is possible for a person to definitively break his or her identification with Adam, however, and to become "in the spirit" through an identification with Christ which takes place when one accepts Him as Lord and Savior. Even though traces of being "in the flesh" will remain, in Christ the situation is so changed that Paul can speak of a Christian's being "in the flesh" in the past tense. This is what he does in verse 5.

The "sinful passions aroused by the law" describes the futility of the law in the lives of people bound by the "flesh." Rather than empowering its own fulfillment, the law actually has the opposite effect. By "binding" us it actually stirs up our tendencies toward evil much more than it alleviates them.

In verse 6 Paul proclaims that the Christian, by sharing in Christ's death, has been freed from the impossible demands of the law. A new way, the way of life "in the spirit" has been opened up for the person who follows Christ instead of the law.

At the beginning of verse 7, Paul expresses some concern lest those who hear or read this letter accuse him of making a facile connection between law and sin. Basically, he is asking for patience on the part of his audience. The link which he is attempting to describe between sin and the law is a subtle and complex one, a connection which—as is often the case theologically speaking—tends to defy neat categorization.

Paul flatly denies that "the law is the same as sin" (7:7b). At this point, and continuing through the rest of the chapter, he switches into the first person. He is, to be sure, describing his own personal experience. But Paul is an artist as well as a letter-writer, and he uses the first person as a literary device to narrate the personal experience of *all* persons who have struggled with the interconnections between conscience, sin, and the law.

According to Paul, knowledge of the law (he is speaking specifically of the Mosaic Law, although other types of law would be covered by implication)—by pointing out the discrepancy between one's attitudes and actions and the standard of perfection—provides knowledge of sin (7:7c-8). In other words, learning the precepts of the law catapults a person into firsthand experience of his or her sinfulness.

Not only this, but sin, because of its very nature (as an "outside" force of evil willing a person's self-destruction) sets in motion a vicious circle of rebellion against the law: as soon as one learns its precepts, one becomes bound by the law. One also realizes the impossibility of ever living up to the law. This triggers a personal rebellion against the law, a vain attempt to escape from its demands by breaking them.

Paul continues his description of the link between law and sin in verses 9-12. His portrayal is, at the same time, a description of his own experience, and a description of everyone's experience. There is bitter irony in verse 10: "The commandment that should have led to life brought me death." Something (namely, the law) which in itself is good (7:12) and which God meant for our salvation, became, through the power of sin, linked with our destruction.

Paul's wording in verse 11 is intended to recall the story of the fall in Genesis 3. It brings in the dimension of the brokenness of the human person providing the necessary context for the linkage between the law and sin. The problem, in other words, does not reside in the nature of the law, which is "holy and just and good," but in the fallen nature of the human person.

In the same way that he denies an identification between the law and sin in verse 7, Paul now rejects an equation between the law and death in 13a. The connection, rather, is between sin and death. In introducing death into the world (Paul is still following the pattern of the story of the fall in Genesis), sin revealed its true, self-destructive nature (7:13b).

Verse 14 uses the categories of "spirit" and "flesh." The law is part of the spiritual dimension of existence, that part of existence which tends toward life. Paul identifies himself and all people, however, as "weak flesh;" that is, as people tending toward self-destruction because of the power of sin. Sin, in other words, has cancelled out the blessing intended by the law.

Because of their slavery to sin, human beings live in a horrible state of contradiction. Paul forcefully describes this state of contradiction in 7:15-24. This is the most powerful presentation of the hopeless position of a Christless humanity in all of Scripture. Especially worth noting are the following points:

1. The contradiction between humankind's desire to con-

form to the law and its inability to do so proves that the law, in itself, is good (v. 16).

2. Paul continues to see sin as an "outside" force of evil which has "set up camp" within the human person (vv. 17, 20), specifically in the dimension of the "flesh" (v. 18).

3. The "inner self" that Paul mentions in v. 22 is the part of his (and our) human nature that is still created in God's image and yearns to conform to that image.

4. This "inner self" or "law of mind" (what we would call conscience) is engaged in a desperate, losing battle with the "law of sin" (v. 23). Each person is thus in an all-out state of warfare between contradictory parts of him or herself.

5. This war can lead to only one possible conclusion: the destruction of the person. The inevitability of this conclusion leads Paul to exclaim, in verse 24: "What a wretched man I am! Who can free me from this body under the power of death?"

Paul's intent in this section is to underscore the condition of despair in which every person finds him or herself. The state of the "natural" person, according to St. Paul, is one of complete hopelessness.

The joyful proclamation of verse 25, "All praise to God, through Jesus Christ our Lord!" indicates that God has done the impossible, that he has overcome nature with grace and found a way, a new way, to save us from what would otherwise be our inevitable self-destruction. Paul will detail the specifics of this new way in Romans 8, the topic of our next chapter.


*Questions for Personal Reflection/Group Discussion*

1. (a) What is the connection between affliction, endurance, tested virtue, and hope?

  (b) Give an example from your own life in which affliction has led to endurance, endurance to tested virtue, and tested virtue to hope.

2. How does St. Paul understand the redemptive nature of Jesus' death.
3. (a) Describe the biblical notion of solidarity.
   (b) What does it mean to say that humankind stands in solidarity with Adam?
   (c) What are the implications of a person being able to choose relational solidarity with Christ?
4. Define the following Pauline terms:
   (a) "body"
   (b) "flesh"
   (c) "spirit"
5. Define:
   (a) "justification"
   (b) "santification"
   (c) How can it be that Christians have been definitively freed from sin yet go on sinning?
6. According to Paul, what is the link between law and sin?
7. (a) Does Paul's description of the interior battle going on inside each human person (7:15-24) ring true to your own experience? How?
   (b) What is the point of this description; what is he trying to do by describing humankind in this way?

## Chapter 5:  Solidarity with Christ Through the Holy Spirit

*Please read Romans 8.* There is an undeniable element of tension in the Christian life between the "already" of being justified (saved) in Christ, and the "not yet" of perfect sanctification. The Christian has already experienced a taste of eternal life, but the fullness of life eternal is yet to come. What is it that bridges the discontinuity between past and future in the life of a Christian?

Paul answers this question in Romans 8: it is the concrete

experience of our *present* relationship with Jesus Christ through the Spirit. He has mentioned the Spirit only a few times in the first seven chapters. Here, in chapter 8, the Spirit is referred to over twenty times. Romans 8 is the most in-depth and detailed discussion of the role of the Holy Spirit in the life of the Christian which we find in the writings of St. Paul.

Answering the question he raised in 7:24, "Who can free me from this body under the power of death?", Paul focuses on the Christian's saving relationship to God "in Christ Jesus" (8:1). The phrase, "*in* Christ Jesus" is one of Paul's favorite descriptions of the Christian life. It stresses the saving reality of a Christian's solidarity with Christ.

The word "condemnation" is similar to the word "curse" which Paul had used in his letter to the Galatians (see Gal. 3:10,13), and the word "wrath" which he has used earlier in his letter to the Romans. It signifies the self-destructive reality of the person who is not "in Christ Jesus." This person stands self-condemned because he or she is bound by the law, and the law, because of sin, can do nothing but act as the impossible standard against which one's sins become manifest.

In verse 2 Paul contrasts the "law of the spirit" with the "law of sin and death." He is using the word "law" in the sense of "way" or "pattern." The way of the Spirit, in other words, has already released the Christian from his or her previous self-destructive pattern of sin and death. Here, as elsewhere in this chapter, the word "spirit" could (and often is in other versions) be translated with a capital "S". The *New American Bible* reserves this usage for what it considers to be *direct* references to the Holy Spirit.

Returning to his use of "law" as a referent to the Mosaic Law in verse 3, Paul links its ineffectiveness to the "fleshly" part of human nature (the part of the human person which is under the domination of sin), then goes on to summarize the process by which the Christian has been definitively freed from his or her destructive relationship to the law. The aspect of Jesus' ministry which Paul focuses on in v. 3 is the crucifixion, His being a "sin offering." Thus, once again Paul links our redemption with Jesus' sacrifice.

As usual, there is no disparity of intention between Father and Son, "*God* sent his Son..." Paul's statement "in the *likeness* of sinful flesh" is not a denial of Jesus' true humanity, but a reminder that Jesus was not actually sinful. Indeed, his argument in vv. 3-4 depends on the real solidarity of Christ with humanity. It is through His identification with us (in all things save sin) that He was able to stand in our place; it is through our identification with Him that we are able to break out of our self-defeating relationship to the law and live "according to the spirit."

In verses 5-13 Paul elaborates on his earlier contrast between the "law of the spirit" and the "law of sin and death." Here those who follow the "law of sin and death" are those who "live according to the flesh," and those who follow the "law of the spirit" are those who "live according to the spirit" (8:5). One gets the impression that in these verses Paul is addressing himself primarily to the Gentile Christians in the Church at Rome. Because of their pagan pasts, they would be the ones who would have more temptations of the "flesh" to overcome than their stricter Jewish Christian brethren.

The word "intent" in verse 5 could be paraphrased as "centered;" in other words, "Those who live according to the flesh are *centered* on the things of the flesh, while those who live according to the spirit are centered on those of the spirit." This concept of centering (which includes a person's thought, will, and emotion) is important because it is another way of approaching Paul's notion of solidarity. A person who is in solidarity with Christ is a Christ-centered person. Conversely, a person still in solidarity with Adam is oriented to "the things of the flesh."

The word "tendency" in the NAB translation of verse 6 is too weak; the sense is that of "mind" as is "mindset," and describes an outcome which is inevitable or assured. One could paraphrase this verse as "The inevitable outcome of the flesh is death, while the assured result of the spirit is life and peace."

Verses 7 and 8 underscore the opposition between the flesh (as human inclination toward sin) and God. Again, it is crucial to bear in mind the meaning of Paul's term "flesh." He is *not* saying in verse 8, as some medieval commentators would have it, that "those who are in the body cannot please God," but that "those who give in to their propensity to sin cannot please God."

The Good News of salvation is proclaimed in 8:9, with an accent on the decisive role of the Holy Spirit. Note the interchangeability in this verse between "spirit" (which could be spelled with a capital "S"), "Spirit of God," and "Spirit of Christ." Although the Trinity was as yet not an official doctrine, statements like this witness to its biblical roots. The interchangeability of the terms points to the identity of intention between Father, Son, and Spirit. The fact that three different "persons" are mentioned underscores the Mystery of God, which transcends human categories of space, time, and personhood.

The Good News is that Christians can no longer be characterized as being "in the flesh." They can only be described as being "in the spirit," and this because the Spirit actually dwells in them. This concept of the indwelling presence of the Holy Spirit is yet another dimension of Paul's understanding of the Christian's solidarity with Christ. The presence of the Holy Spirit in the life of the Christian is understood to be a real presence, not merely a symbolic one. It is proof positive of one's solidarity with Christ, of one's "belonging" to Jesus.

In verse 10 Paul contrasts two different dimensions in the present experience of any Christian. On the one hand, "the body is dead because of sin;" that is, all human beings are subject to death because of the brokenness of our human condition. On the other hand, "the spirit lives because of justice;" that is, the human person is given a new beginning—a beginning that will never end, and which will eventually involve bodily resurrection, as verse 11 makes clear—through his or her relationship with Christ.

8:11 credits the Resurrection of Jesus to the Father, and affirms the solidarity, or life-giving connection, between His Resurrection and ours. "The Spirit of him who raised Jesus from the dead," the Spirit which this verse assumes to be dwelling in Jesus, and the Spirit which dwells in us are one and the same Spirit. Thus, through the indwelling presence of the Holy Spirit, the Christian not only receives the promise of resurrection, but actually participates in the life of the Trinity.

Verses 12 and 13 are verses of admonishment. Paul implores the Roman Christians not to give in to the temptations of the "flesh," but to combat them through their new life in the Spirit.

At this point Paul plunges into the most profound description of the relationship between the believer and God in any of his letters (8:16-39). While not explicitly Trinitarian (the doctrine of the Trinity was not promulgated until several centuries later), it is implicitly so, founded as it is on the interrelationships of Father, Son, and Spirit. The Trinity, of course, is one of the great Mysteries of our faith—Mystery in this context meaning something of such significance that human concepts, even theological concepts, cannot begin to mine its depth. In these verses, however, Paul largely overcomes the conceptual limitations of theology by focusing on various aspects of the God-person relationship.

The first of these aspects is that of sonship (8:14). Those who allow themselves to be led by the Spirit; in other words, those who accept the gift of a personal relationship with Christ which the Spirit offers, are "sons of God." The Greek word which Paul uses for son is the one with the nuance of legal status—to become a son (or daughter) of God is to enter into a familial relationship with God, with all the privileges and responsibilities which this implies. Paul celebrates the privileges of the Christian's relationship with God throughout the rest of chapter 8. He will discuss the responsibilities in the section of his letter to the Romans having to do with morality, chapters 12-15.

In verse 15 slavery and fear are contrasted with adoption.

The slavery of which Paul is thinking is slavery to law—trying to earn one's salvation by following somebody's set of rules, whether it be the Mosaic Law, or the dictates of astrology, or whatever. Attempting to merit salvation in this way inevitably leads to fear because one can never keep *all* of the rules, and thus there is always some room for doubting one's salvation.

In contrast to a "spirit of slavery" preparing the way for fear, Christians have received a "spirit of adoption," which opens the door to such a personal and intimate relationship with God that fear is banished and one is able to address the Father in the same way that Jesus did. Again, the quality of sonship which Paul is envisioning is real and not merely symbolic. It is so tangible, in fact, that Paul simply refers to actual Christian experience when he talks about using the word "Abba."

This word, the Aramaic equivalent of our "Dad" or "Daddy," was the word which Jesus used to address His Father (see Mark 14:26). It was a word which no one before Jesus would have dared to use to approach God, but which the Holy Spirit, because of the Christian's solidarity with Christ, invites us to use. 8:16 assumes the solidarity of the Holy Spirit with the "spirit" of the Christian—"spirit" meaning that part of the human person, in contrast with the "flesh," which is God-oriented and open to progressive transformation.

Verse 17 brings out one of the legal aspects of being an adopted son or daughter, that of being an heir. Paul uses the word "heir" as a metaphor for salvation. A Christian, because of his or her adoption into God's family, can rest assured of the promise—his or her rightful inheritance—of salvation. Salvation, in other words, is one of the great privileges of being a Christian.

But there are responsibilities as well, and Paul briefly mentions one of them when he talks about suffering with Christ in 8:17b. The willingness to "suffer with him" implies a relationship between the Christian and Christ which is so close that the Christian is willing, so to speak, to help Christ shoulder His Cross.

Paul is not just speaking about the "natural" suffering of things like sickness here, but of the self-chosen, redemptive suffering which comes from a Christian's trying to be the body of Christ in a broken world.

Paul makes another contrast in verse 18, this time between a Christian's present sufferings and the promise of future glory. The "glory" to which Paul refers is not only the glory of an individual's personal salvation, but the glory of the consummation of all things in the Second Coming of Christ. Here we have another example of the creative tension between the "now" and the "not yet" in the theology of St. Paul. From the incredibly expanded perspective of the Parousia (our Lord's Return), our present distress is insignificant.

In verses 19-22 Paul enlarges his vision to include the whole of creation. These verses are amazing because they assume a certain mystical "personality" on the part of creation (vv. 19, 22), and a very real solidarity between humankind and the created world (vv. 20-21). On the one hand, because of its vital connection with humankind, creation shared in the destructive effects of the fall. On the other hand, because of its solidarity with a redeemed humanity, creation will eventually experience its own redemption and fulfillment.

Paul returns to the human condition in verses 23-27. 8:23 expresses once again the tension between the "now" and the "not yet." Although Christians have already received and experienced the gift of the indwelling presence of the Holy Spirit, this is only the "first fruits," or down payment, of what God has in store for us. The gift of salvation is not yet complete, and will not be until Christ returns in His glory, and our bodies experience resurrection (v. 23). The inner groanings of which Paul speaks in this verse are the intense longings for face-to-face relationship with God which every Christian experiences.

The eschatological (future-oriented) nature of hope is acknowledged in verses 24 and 25. Paul does some further reflection on the solidarity between Spirit and Christian in verses 26 and 27. This relationship is so close that the Spirit knows us better than we know ourselves and does not hesitate to intercede for us. "He who searches hearts" (v. 27) is a reference to God the Father.

Romans 8:28, "We know that God makes all things work together for the good of those who love him. . ." is a beautiful expression of God's guiding and sustaining presence in the life of the Christian. The phrase "who have been called according to his decree" (8:28b) parallels the phrase "of those who love him." Like Hebrew poetry, where one phrase often echoes the meaning of another, these two phrases basically mean the same thing. Thus, for St. Paul there is no real distinction between loving God and being called to love God.

This phrase triggers a celebration of God's all-knowing and all-powerful will in verses 29 and 30. Paul's intent in dictating these verses was to provide Christians with a "proof" of the certainty of their salvation. Our salvation is sure because it is part of God's plan.

Once more we need to recall the fact that St. Paul and his contemporaries did not make the modern theological distinction between God's "active" will (which wants everyone to be saved), and His "passive" will (which respects human freedom and allows a person to reject Him). Because Paul did not make this distinction, he considers everything as an active expression of God's will. Thus verses 29 and 30—due to the limitations of Paul's theological categories—give us the impression that God rather arbitrarily chose some and rejected others.

Certainly the overwhelming power of God's choice is descriptively accurate from the viewpoint of Christian experience. Those who enjoy a personal relationship with the Lord often feel that it could not have been otherwise. This feeling is a positive one and witnesses to the depth of the love being expressed in the relationship.

Unfortunately certain fundamentalist Christian bodies have
severed these verses from Paul's original intent, which was descriptive of Christian experience and aimed to provide assurance
of salvation, and set them up as a doctrine in their own right.
This doctrine, while claiming to be literally faithful to Paul's
words, ironically loses his pastoral intent. It also does a great
injustice to the nature of God, emphasizing His power (to choose
or not to choose) at the expense of His love.

The Catholic tradition (and most other mainstream Christian
traditions) has considered it wiser—and ultimately more faithful
to the Bible's real intent—to make the distinction between God's
active will and passive will. In this way the unconditional and
*universal* nature of God's love is conserved.

Paul is simply inconsistent at this point. On the one hand he
uses the inflexible categories of foreknowledge and predestination. On the other hand he does everything he can to encourage
people to enter the Kingdom. He proclaims the Gospel as if God
indiscriminately loves everyone, and that what really matters is
a person's free choice of God's love.

What has happened is that the limitation of his understanding
of God's will (namely, the fact that he conceives of God as
directly causing all things) has forced him into an unnecessary
paradox. There are enough real paradoxes in theology without
hanging onto unnecessary ones. One suspects that Paul himself
would have welcomed the distinction between different aspects
of God's will.

The progression from foreknowledge to predestination, from
predestination to calling, from calling to justification, and from
justification to glorification outlined in verses 29 and 30 was
intended to enable the believer to feel secure about his or her
salvation. The point that Paul was trying to make is that salvation
is not haphazard or fortuitous, but part of God's eternal plan.
Seeing that he or she is part of God's eternal plan, the Christian
can well feel secure.

For Paul, God's eternal plan is the strongest possible proof that He is totally *for* the Christian. Using the Christian's assured place in God's sure plan as his springboard, Paul bursts forth into what might well be called a song of victory and triumph (8:31-39).

When worship of God and observance of law are turned into a simple equation, the person attempting to follow this routine, because of the inability to totally live up to the demands of the law, eventually comes to experience God in terms of opposition. God is felt to be against one since, after all, one *is* guilty. In a religious system such as this, one is never quite sure of one's salvation because one never quite becomes perfect, and the whole system is based on perfection.

We know from his preChristian days that Paul was hopelessly caught up in the vicious circle of trying to earn his own salvation. His personal encounter with Jesus enabled him to see himself as part of God's loving plan which, in turn, empowered him to finally break out of the vicious circle in which he was trapped. For the first time he was able to experience God as *for* him rather than *against* him. This is the background of Paul's exultant proclamation in the form of a rhetorical question (a question whose answer is obvious) in verse 31.

He continues with a whole series of rhetorical questions in verses 32-35. The wording of verse 32 alludes to Abraham's willingness to sacrifice Isaac in Genesis 22 (especially verse 16). If, Paul argues, God loved us so much that He was willing to sacrifice His own son for us, how can we possibly doubt God's love and our salvation? How could we possibly lose our salvation, when it is God Himself who has justified (saved) us—will God break His own promise? (v. 33).

Paul focuses on the believer's relationship with Christ in verses 34-39. Significantly, he sees Jesus' role as savior as still continuing. He has not suddenly reversed roles and become our judge, but in His resurrected state carries on the same ministry of sacrificial love and intercession that He offered to us in His earthly ministry (v. 34).

The triumphal nature of Paul's celebration of God's steadfast love intensifies in the following verses. The list of negative human reactions to the preaching of the Gospel in verse 35—all of which Paul has personally experienced—serves only to make the point that no earthly suffering can separate us from the love of Christ. This point is underlined in verse 36, a quotation of Psalm 44:23, which indicates that a martyr's death was not considered at all unusual for a Christian. These negative reactions to the Gospel— even death itself—are really the consummation ("we are more than conquerors") of a Christian's life (v. 37).

In verses 38 and 39 Paul piles reality upon reality to hammer in the fact that *nothing* can separate the Christian from "the love of God that comes to us in Christ Jesus, our Lord." The "angels," "principalities," and "powers" mentioned in verse 38 refer to forces of good and evil which are more than human. The "height" and "depth" mentioned in verse 39 are astrological terms alluding to the supposed power of the stars to influence, even determine, events.

None of these things, Paul is saying, is able to come between the Christian and God. Note the complete unity between Father and Son in 39b: the Father expresses His love through the gift of His Son. The total effect of these verses (31-39) is to convince the Christian that his or her salvation is actually the surest thing, not only on this planet, but in the entire universe.

## Questions for Personal Reflection/Group Discussion

1. Describe the tension which Paul assumes to be present in the life of a Christian concerning time.
2. What is the unique role of the Holy Spirit in a believer's life?
3. What are some of the privileges of being a Christian according to Romans 8?
4. Several different types of solidarity relationships are assumed in this chapter. List as many as you can and describe them.
5. Why does attempting to earn one's own salvation inevitably lead to fear?

6. (a) What is a Christian really doing when he or she calls God "Daddy" or "Abba"?
   (b) Do *you* feel comfortable addressing the Father as "Abba" or "Daddy"?
   (c) If you are uncomfortable with this, what do you think would help you to overcome your discomfort?
7. Why is it so important that a Christian be willing to suffer for and with Christ?
8. (a) What does Paul teach about a Christian's certainty of salvation in Romans 8?
   (b) Do *you* feel sure of your own salvation?
   (c) If so, why?
   (d) If not, why not? How could you learn to trust God more?

## Chapter 6: The "Mystery" of Israel

*Please read Romans 9-11.* Having argued so forcefully and convincingly for a Christian's assurance of salvation at the end of chapter 8, the question of the relationship of the Jews to the fulfillment of salvation history in Christ surfaces with renewed intensity. This was a question which had already come up in the course of Paul's dictation of this letter. At the beginning of chapter 3 he asks "What is the advantage, then, of being a Jew, and what value is there in circumcision?" (3:1). In chapter 3, however, Paul does not get very far in providing an answer. His developed response occurs here in chapters 9-11.

These chapters, though representing his mature thought on the matter, nevertheless are full of problems. The problems revolve around the unresolved tension between predestination and free will in Paul's thought, a tension which we already noted in chapters 1 and 8. In chapters 9-11 this tension becomes so great as to become unmanageable.

Again, the limitations of Paul's theology—his not distinguishing between different aspects of God's will—force him into a contradictory position. On the one hand, because for him *everything* is an expression of God's will, he sees God as directly responsible for such an ungodly phenomenon as the hardening of Pharaoh's heart (9:17 & 18). According to Paul on this particular issue, God "set up" Pharaoh so that He could punish him, and in His punishment, do something good for Israel. This is tantamount to saying that God does evil to bring about good. Paul himself is aware of this objection, but counters it with a heavyhanded appeal to God's authority (9:19-24).

On the other hand, at the end of chapter 9 (vv. 30-32), and throughout chapter 10, he talks about the rejection of Christ by the Jews very much in terms of their own fault. God, in this context, is *not* presented as stacking the cards beforehand. The Jews have freely chosen to reject the Good News of the Gospel by setting up their own opposing law. Here God is presented as desiring the salvation of everyone, the only requirement for salvation being that a person *accept* this gift (10:11-13).

Finally, Paul again takes a contra-predestination bent when he warns the Gentiles of the possibility of choosing to lose one's salvation in chapter 11: ". . . provided you remain in his kindness; if you do not, you too will be cut off" (11:22b). This statement once again assumes that God has *not* already decided everyone's fate.

We see in these chapters an unresolved battle going on between two conflicting elements in Pauline thought: what we might call God's absolute sovereignty, on the one hand, and the supreme importance of personal choice, on the other. As we have seen, the modern theological distinction between God's active will, which is *always* unconditional love, and His passive will, which respects the freedom of an individual to choose to reject Him, allows us to balance these concerns. *God is sovereign in His love.* Yet it is precisely God's commitment to love which commits Him to grant His creatures real freedom, for it is only a love which is freely chosen which is real love.

Because Paul himself did not make this distinction he creates some problems in these chapters which are not real problems. Since contemporary theology is better able to deal with this particular issue than St. Paul was, we will not hesitate to "complement" his thinking on certain points in these chapters.

This does not mean that we do not consider his writings to be fundamental. What he wrote was inspired by the Holy Spirit. The Holy Spirit, however, respected Paul's freedom, and in this case this meant respecting Paul's use of contradictory theological categories. This same Holy Spirit, through a process which theologians call "the development of doctrine"—the understanding of Scripture and Tradition in increasingly coherent ways—has inspired the Church to a less problematic understanding of the relationship between grace and freedom than Paul himself had.

\*       \*       \*

Paul's solemn opening statement (9:1), the equivalent of an oath, underlines the seriousness with which he is approaching the subject of Israel's failure to respond to Jesus. This failure on the part of Israel was a major problem for the early Church, which took the history of salvation outlined in the Hebrew Scriptures seriously, and saw its unmistakable fulfillment in Christ. Why, then, the lack of response on the part of the Jews?

This was an intensely personal problem for Paul, considering his strong connections with Judaism, and the fact that he probably still considered himself to be a Jew. His bafflement and concern at the failure of his own people to recognize Jesus as Messiah caused him a good deal of personal anguish (9:2), so much, in fact, that, like Moses (see Exodus 32:32), he offers to stand in their place (9:3).

In verses 4 and 5 he cites the highlights of the history of salvation, a history which makes Israel unique in the world. The specific items which Paul singles out are:

1. *Adoption*. God chose Israel for a special relationship, a relationship which can only be described in terms of family:

Thus says the LORD: Israel is my son,
my first-born.
(Exodus 4:22)

When Israel was a child I loved him,
out of Egypt I called my son.
(Hosea 11:1)

2. *Glory*. This refers to the awesome presence of God, a presence which Israel experienced to a singular degree.

3. *Covenants*. Note the plural. A covenant is an expression of committed relationship, and Paul is referring to all the expressions of committed relationship in the Hebrew Bible.

4. *Lawgiving*. Paul is thinking of the Mosaic Law, considered to be the greatest expression of convenant in the Old Testament.

5. *Worship*. The Temple was the center for prayer and sacrifice.

6. *Promises*. God's amazing gifts to his favored people, such as a son to Abraham and Sarah in their old age.

7. *Patriarchs*. For Paul, the great early heroes of the faith who set the stage for the development of the further faith of Israel.

8. *Messiah*. The consummation of all of the above. God's Anointed One who was to bring salvation history to its fulfillment.

Given these incredible blessings, this in-depth preparation, it is truly surprising that more people from the Jewish tradition did not joyfully acknowledge Jesus as their long-awaited Messiah. To outward appearances it looked as if all the years of preparation were for naught, that God's plan to save His people had been foiled.

Paul denies this in 9:6a. He bases his disclaimer on a distinction between true and false Israelites (9:6b). In a similar way to his discussion of Abraham's justification by faith in chapter 4, Paul argues that Isaac alone of Abraham's children is a vehicle of blessing, and this because Abraham had faith in God's promise of a supernatural intervention in regard to Isaac, whereas all his other children were born through merely "natural" means (vv. 7-9). It was Abraham's faith, in other words, which secured for him his heir.

By implication, Paul is making a point against the standard Jewish belief of his time that simply being a son of Abraham (all Jews were considered to be sons of Abraham) was enough to merit salvation. Mere physical descent is not enough. Just as not all Abraham's sons are heirs, claiming him as an ancestor is not enough to make one a true Israelite. A true Israelite, Paul seems to be saying, is one who shares a common *faith* with Abraham. According to this criterion, "not all Israelites are true Israelites."

So far, so good. Paul has simply made the point that a faith response to God is the key to being a true Israelite and that, given this fact, there are not nearly as many true Israelites as it at first appears. The same argument could, of course, be made in connection with Christianity.

Now, however, Paul introduces an argument which needlessly complicates matters (vv. 10-13). Using the story of Jacob and Esau, Paul interprets it in predestinarian terms to mean that even before they were born, God had decided to love Jacob and to hate Esau. To be sure, this was a common Jewish interpretation. It is, unfortunately, a distortion of the original intent of the author of the story, which had nothing to do with predestination, but a lot to do with Jacob's defective character and God's redemption of him almost in spite of himself. Paul has turned a story of God's grace into a story of God's sovereign arbitrariness. His point is that God has the power to make or to break whomsoever He wills, and that the Jews had better be careful not to presume their salvation.

Given the rather rigid mindset of the Judaism of his day, perhaps fighting presumption with predestination was an effective means of evangelization. One, however, has one's doubts. One feels that Paul has lost more than he has gained by this kind of argumentation, and that he would have been safer to stick to the Good News of God's unconditional love which He always offers to everyone, but which a person must accept to receive.

The irony is that Paul senses that he has argued himself into a corner: "What are we to say, then? That God is unjust?" (14a). This *is* the only logical conclusion to be drawn from his interpretation of Jacob and Esau. But Paul stubbornly denies this conclusion (14b), and goes on to offer two more proofs of God's power. These "proofs," the statement to Moses in verse 15, and the treatment of Pharaoh in verse 17, certainly do not prove God's justice; rather, they highlight God's arbitrariness. Sadly, Paul seems to be saying that God is just simply because He has the power to define and to enforce any concept of justice He so chooses. Gone is Paul's earlier equation of justice with God's universal and unconditional love offered to humankind for its salvation. Here "justice" has come to mean little more than luck.

The problem with Paul's proof texts is that they are expressions of an earlier, more primitive theology, a theology which saw God as directly responsible for everything, and thus personally responsible for things like Pharaoh's hardness of heart. We know from the Gospels that Jesus never represents the Father as acting in this manipulative, dictatorial way. What is going on here is that Paul is trying to present an aspect of the Gospel, which is radically *new* news, by using the "old" categories of predestination and power.

His attempt fails because the Gospel cannot be captured in the old categories. His own too rigid logic forces him to reach the unsatisfactory conclusion that "God has mercy on whom he wishes, and whom he wishes he makes obdurate" (9:18). This statement is irreconcilable with the Gospel thrust that God is love, and that this love is available to all.

Paul refused to admit the inadequacy of his approach, and goes on piling one unhappy example on top of another. He is still aware of the normal human reaction to what he has said thus far: "Why, then, does he find fault? For who can oppose his will?" (9:19), but can do no better than an angry and vindictive parent, and attempt to squash any questioning by an appeal to absolute power (vv. 20 & 21).

Verses 22-24 are hopelessly entangled in the inappropriate (from a Gospel point of view) categories of power and predestination. Where, we may ask, is the Paul of his earlier letters, the Paul who had emphasized Jesus' sacrificial love and a person's freedom to choose to become a new creation in Christ? Where?— temporarily hidden behind the smokescreen of an impossible argument.

Returning to his explanation of how it is that many Gentiles have chosen to respond to Christ while most Jews have chosen not to, Paul roughly (he is quoting from memory and is not very exact) quotes two verses from the prophet Hosea (vv. 25 & 26) to the effect that others than those expected will be acknowledged by God as part of His family.

He follows these with a collage of quotations from Isaiah (vv. 27-29) centering around the concept of the remnant—that small group of Israelites who remain faithful while the rest become apostate. Paul's implication is that those Jews who have accepted Jesus as Messiah are part of this faithful remnant, while those who have not are part of the lost majority.

Finally, in 9:30-33, Paul begins to entertain an explanation which is not dependent on the "old" categories of predestination or power, but which develops the Gospel theme of faith. First he states the irony of the situation (vv. 30 & 31), the fact that many Gentiles have found salvation through faith, while many Jews have not found salvation through the law. The crucial contrast, of course, is between faith and law, a contrast which Paul makes clear in verse 32a, where he equates the law with "works." "Works," in this context, is Paul's judgment on the Judaism of his day, whose over-emphasis on law he sees as an attempt at self-salvation. Faith, by contrast, is trust in God, and not one's own achievements.

The "stumbling stone" (32b), in Paul's interpretation, is faith, specifically faith in Christ. Unfortunately this phrase rekindles his fascination with predestination, and he weaves together a couple of quotations from Isaiah in verse 33 which make it sound like God's chief aim in sending Christ was to make people stumble and fall.

Paul's attitude toward the Jews is one of ambivalence. On the one hand, he is angry at them for not responding to the Gospel. As we have seen throughout a good part of chapter 9, his anger triggers in him a harsh, judgmental attitude which erupts in a stance of "you're getting just what you deserve."

On the other hand, he experiences a profound longing that his people may be saved. We saw this at the beginning of chapter 9 (vv. 1-3), and we see it here at the start of chapter 10 (v. 1). Throughout chapters 10 and 11 Paul will alternate between anger and compassionate longing.

This approach may not make much sense theologically, but it certainly does make sense emotionally. Paul's theological inconsistencies seem a little less glaring when we realize that in this whole section (chapters 9 through 11) he largely allows his theology to be directed by his emotions.

10:2 is a good example of Paul's ambivalence in action. He begins on a positive note, "Indeed, I can testify that they are zealous for God," but immediately qualifies this statement by adding "though their zeal is unenlightened." From a rational perspective, Paul is acknowledging the fact that the Jews have a certain passion for God, but insists that this passion is no longer founded on a true knowledge of God.

The word which the *New American Bible* translates as "Un-aware" at the beginning of verse 3 is literally "for not knowing," and has a hint of purposiveness about it; that is, the "not knowing" is not accidental, but intentional, a matter of choice. One could paraphrase the first phrase of this verse as "Rejecting God's justice . . ."

The next phrase, "seeking to establish their own," is Paul's key criticism of the Judaism with which he was contemporary. Instead of accepting the "justice of God," which is the Good News of salvation through faith in Christ, the Jews stubbornly persist in trying to save themselves through rigid adherence to the Law.

Paul goes on to say in 4a that "Christ is the end of the law" meaning that with Jesus a whole new period of salvation history has begun and that the previous period, with its emphasis on law, has been superceded. Salvation (justice) now comes "Through him" (4b); that is, through a personal relationship with Jesus, and no longer through observance of the law. This verse reminds us of what Paul has said earlier to the Galatians:

> Before faith came we were under the constraint of
> the law, locked in until the faith that was coming
> should be revealed. In other words, the law was
> our monitor until Christ came to bring about our
> justification through faith. But now that faith
> is here, we are no longer in the monitor's charge.
> (Galatians 3:23-25)

In verse 5 Paul is thinking of the requirement of the law that in order for it to be a blessing it must be fulfilled in its entirety. He probably had in the back of his mind Deuteronomy 27:26, which reads (concerning the manifold provisions of the Mosaic Law) "Cursed be he who fails to fulfill any of the provisions of this law!" Paul means to imply that there is no such thing as "justice that comes from the law," because it is humanly impossible to completely fulfill the demands of the law.

Paul is not being literally fair in his quotations from "Moses" in verses 6-9. The book of Deuteronomy makes these statements concerning the *law*. Paul strikes law and substitutes *faith*. Although his method of quoting is certainly not fair, it is nevertheless significant, because it shows that he granted a certain compatibility between the law and faith in early Israel, a compatibility which he flatly rejects in regard to the Judaism of his own day. His point in these verses is that faith is not something far away or difficult to attain (like trying to observe the 613 individual commandments of the law), but something which is intensely personal, a personal relationship with Christ.

Verses 9 and 10 are good examples of Paul's use of parallelism—using complementary aspects of the same reality to echo one another. In verse 9, "Believe in your heart" complements "confess with your lips;" "God raised him from the dead" complements "Jesus is Lord." Paul is saying that the public dimension of witnessing, or proclaiming, one's faith is just as important as the personal, or private, aspect of faith. Not only is it just as important, but the parallel structure of this sentence reflects the fact that these two dimensions are so interdependent that you can not really have one without the other.

"Jesus is Lord" is a packed statement, the word "Lord" being used as an honorific title for the emperor and for the Greek (and Roman) gods, and as the Greek translation of the Hebrew word for God's name, YHWH. What is being stated in this simple phrase is the fact that *Jesus*, not some divine emperor, or any other god, is *Lord*; that is, rightful ruler of this world and of the universe. Furthermore, a significant connection is being made here between Jesus and the Father, another indication that the very early Church was implicitly Trinitarian in outlook. "God raised him from the dead" is, of course, a reference to the Resurrection, the central fact and transforming reality of the Christian faith.

The whole of verse 9, "For if you confess with your lips that Jesus is Lord, and believe in your heart that God raised him from the dead, you will be saved" is probably one of the earliest Christian creeds, and may have been used in connection with the celebration of adult conversion in Baptism.

In verse 10, "confession," "lips," and "salvation" are parallel to "faith," "heart," and "justification." This whole verse complements verse 9.

Paul's quotation from Isaiah 28:16 in 10:11 is, again, a rough one from memory. The word "believe" carries with it not just the meaning of acknowledging something to be true, but also the connotations of internalizing, living, and proclaiming this belief.

Verse 12, and Paul's quotation from Joel 3:5 in verse 13, place the responsibility for salvation squarely upon human choice. The fact that God is "rich in mercy to *all* who call upon him," and that "*Everyone* who calls on the name of the Lord will be saved" totally undercuts Paul's earlier emphasis on predestination. Here God is presented as implicitly wanting the salvation of everybody. The only requirement for salvation is not some previous and predestining determination on God's part, but the personal acceptance of the saving relationship which God wants to share with everyone. As we have seen, and as we will see again, Paul is not consistent on this issue.

As Christians we don't *have* to attempt an impossible balancing act between God's predetermining will and our free will any more than we have to somehow balance God's justice with his mercy. It's much truer to the spirit of the Gospels to simplify things and say that God's will is to save everyone and that He is *always* merciful. All we have to do is to *accept* his mercy and salvation. This way we can be sure of our relationship with God and enjoy a security in this relationship which, as we saw at the end of chapter 8, is very dear to Paul's heart. Perhaps we can actually be more true to the spirit of what Paul wants to say by *not* taking him seriously on this matter of predestination rather than by trying to balance it with the *substance* of Jesus' Gospel, and Paul's.

The verb "to call" sparks in Paul's mind a series of thoughts on the urgency of proclamation. Thus, in verses 14 and 15 we find the identification and progression of calling with believing, of believing with hearing, of hearing with preaching, and of preaching with sending. Paul is still speaking from the positive context of his longing for the salvation of his people.

Apparently, his progression of thought takes him to the brink, then over the edge of his patience. For now, suddenly, he remembers that the Gospel has, indeed, been preached to the Jews and that they have, for the most part, rejected it. This realization unleashes his anger, and he concludes chapter 10 with a series of hostile quotations from the Old Testament, quotations intended to point out that Israel has no excuse, for it has both heard and understood the message of the Gospel (vv. 16-21).

The negative reality of these quotations brings him round full circle to his original concern: "I ask then, has God rejected his people?" (11:1a). Again he vigorously refuses to answer this question in the affirmative. He offers himself—a Jew who has come to know Jesus as Messiah and Lord—as an example of God's continuing faithfulness to His people (11:1b). Throughout this chapter he thinks of the Jews as a collective reality. When Paul asks "has God rejected his people?" he is really asking "has God rejected his people *as a whole?*" His own example and, by implication, the instance of all Jewish conversions to Christ, proves that God has *not* rejected his people as a whole.

He briefly pays homage to the notion of predestination (11:2a), then reintroduces the idea of the faithful remnant (2b-6). He uses part of Elijah's story to demonstrate that just as not all Israelites had forsaken their faith in Elijah's time, so too there remain a faithful few in his (Paul's) day—namely, those who have forsaken the way of works (attempting to save oneself by following the law) for the way of grace. Paul strings together another series of hostile quotations from the Hebrew Scriptures to buttress his point (vv. 7-10).

Still speaking of the Jews as a collective entity, he goes on to insist that their "stumbling," their refusal to participate in the saving reality of Christ, is only temporary in nature. In other words, Israel as a people will not remain separate from Christ, but will eventually come to acknowledge Him as Lord and Savior (11:11a).

Paul goes on to give us his personal assessment of the refusal of the Jews to believe in Christ in 11:11b—"by their transgression salvation has come to the Gentiles to stir Israel to envy." On the one hand, as we have seen, Paul is deeply hurt, and sometimes deeply annoyed, that his people as a whole have not accepted Christ. On the other hand, he now sees a positive, or providential, reason for this: it was precisely their unwillingness which opened the door for the proclamation of the Gospel to the Gentiles. Thus, their negative response has had a positive result. And Paul sees the Jews themselves as being stirred to a positive envy because of the great success of the Gospel among the Gentiles, an envy which will eventually bring them round to Christ. He is quite excited at the prospect of Jewish inclusion into the Body of Christ (vv. 12, 15), and regards his ministry to the Gentiles as, in a very real sense, a ministry to the Jews as well (vv. 13-14).

Given the Jewish rejection of Jesus, there was a strong temptation on the part of Christians to despise the Jews. Indeed, what was mostly a temptation in Paul's day became a tragic and destructive reality throughout much of Christian history. If the Church, and individual Christians, had heeded Paul's advice in the next section of this letter, 11:16-24, our supremely unChristian attitudes and actions toward the Jews could have been avoided.

Paul begins by affirming the continuing reality of Israel's special blessing as God's chosen people in verse 16. The "first fruits" he refers to here is the ancient practice of offering the first portion of dough to God—this offering would effectively bless the whole batch. The first fruits in the context of Israel as a people would be the Patriarchs, the great fathers of Jewish (and Christian) faith. Paul maintains that some type of solidarity is still operative between the fathers and the rest of Israel; even if Israel is rejecting the faith of its fathers now, it will not always continue to do so.

Paul switches metaphors in the middle of verse 16, moving from "first fruits" and "whole mass of dough" to "root" and "branches." He will pursue this new mataphor through verse 24, using it as an allegory to describe the relationship of both Jews and Christians to their common root, which is the faith of the Patriarchs.

It is significant that the root and, in fact, the cultivated tree, are specifically *Jewish*. Some of the branches of this cultivated tree have been cut off; these cut off branches represent the Jews who have refused to accept Christ. Gentile Christians, however, are no better than branches from a wild olive tree that have been grafted on to the original. Given their secondary status, they certainly have no grounds of boasting of their superiority: "remember that you do not support the root; the root supports you" (11:18).

In response to the harsh and self-righteous comment of some of the Gentile Christians concerning the Jews, that "Branches were cut off that I might be grafted in"(v. 19), Paul warns them, in effect, not to turn their faith into a "work," and so be cut off in the same way as those they are criticizing (vv. 20-21).

Verse 22 assumes the possibility of choice on the part of the Gentile Christians—to either remain or not to remain in their relationship with Christ—just as verse 23 assumes the possibility of choice on the part of the Jews—to either remain or not to remain in their unbelief. These verses go against the grain of some of his earlier statements on predestination. He concludes this section with another contrast between the primary status of the Jews and the secondary status of the Gentile Christians (v. 24). Again, this is a tactic he adopts in the hope of sparking some humility in those Christians who were already beginning to feel superior.

Continuing his concern for his readers' humility, Paul goes on to describe what he considers to be the "mystery" of the situation (vv. 25-32). "Mystery" refers to something bigger than human words are able to describe. In this case the "mystery" is the fact that God has taken something which is in itself tragic—the repudiation of the Gospel by the majority of the Jews—and used it for the positive purpose of inviting Gentiles into the Kingdom.

The climax of the mystery is yet to come: when "the full number of Gentiles enter in," "then all Israel will be saved" (vv. 25b-26a). The "mystery," in other words, is the grace which God continues to show to Israel; her present defection is only temporary; sooner or later Israel as a whole will be saved. At this point (vv. 26b-27) Paul quotes Isaiah and Jeremiah *in favor* of Israel.

From the larger perspective of its ultimate salvation, Israel's present rejection of the Gospel can be seen in sacrificial terms. The deepest dimension of the "mystery" of Israel is that somehow its very rebellion against God is a sacrifice effective in enabling the Gentiles to come into the Kingdom. As Paul states in v. 28a: "In respect to the gospel, the Jews are enemies of God *for your sake*." There is thus absolutely no ground for the Gentile attitude of pride and superiority toward the Jews; indeed, the Gentiles are, in a very real sense, indebted to the Jews for their salvation.

Although Paul vigorously contested the Jewish presumption which held that a Jew would be saved merely because he was a "son of Abraham," there *is* a sense in which Paul acknowledges some truth to this position. He does this, for example, in verses 28b-29, when he says "in respect to the election, they are beloved by him because of the patriarchs. God's gifts and his call are irrevocable." These verses assume a real, and saving, solidarity between the faith of the Patriarchs and their descendants. If pressed on this point, Paul would probably say that Israel as a collective reality has been permanently elected, or chosen, by God. Individual Israelites, however, can choose to reject their election.

One senses, nevertheless, that there is more going on here

than words are able to capture, that we Gentiles are much more caught up in the saving mystery of Israel than we realize. The saving solidarity of Israel with the Patriarchs spills over into a saving solidarity between Jews and Christians: we have "received mercy through their disobedience" (v. 30); they, in turn, will "receive mercy" (v. 31), perhaps through our intercession (the RSV translates the latter part of this verse as "in order that by the mercy shown to you they also may receive mercy").

A sense of mutual solidarity between Jews and Christians is apparent in verse 32, solidarity not only in disobedience but, more importantly, in God's mercy. Could it be that God uses the suffering of His people Israel in a vicarious way to bring about our mutual redemption? One senses from these concluding verses of Paul's discussion that there is a vital connection between Judaism and Christianity, a vital connection which we Christians would be wise to explore in greater depth.

It is fitting that Paul's insights and intuitions concerning the mystery of Israel should erupt, at this point, into a glorious hymn in praise of God the Father (11:33-36). Throughout these three chapters (9-11) Paul has struggled, and not always successfully, with the concepts of predestination and free will, works and faith, justice and mercy. Now he transcends these theological abstractions in an act of worship which is a profound expression of the mystery of God's relationship with the world and with His people. Paul celebrates the fact that we human beings cannot fully comprehend God's ways (vv. 33-35). Our smallness frees us to worship Him who is, as the *New English Bible* puts it, the "Source, Guide, and Goal of all that is" (v. 36).

## Questions for Personal Reflection/Group Discussion

1. How can it be that St. Paul does not necessarily have the "final" word on everything about which he wrote?
2. What makes Israel so special in terms of the history of salvation?

3. Why was the rejection of the Gospel by the Jews such a big problem for the early Church?
4. Describe the tension between predestination and free will going on in these chapters. How can this tension be resolved in a way that does not do violence to God's nature?
5. What does the early Christian confession "Jesus is Lord" mean to you personally?
6. According to Paul's insights and analogies in chapter 11, what is the relationship of Judaism to Christianity, of Jews to Christians?
7. What are some of the dimensions present in Paul's understanding of the saving mystery of Israel?

## Chapter 7: The Moral Side of Theology

*Please read Romans 12:1-15:13.* As we have seen, chapters 1-8 are a powerful statement of the "Gospel According to Paul." They stress God's initiative in the process of salvation. Chapters 9-11 deal with the problem of the lack of Jewish response to the Gospel. At this point, from 12:1-15:13, Paul concerns himself with the topic of *living* the Good News.

He is following a pattern similar to many of his other letters in beginning with theology, then moving on to its ethical implications. This is a good example of how theology was not an abstract science for Paul or the early Church, but naturally overflowed into the concrete reality of everyday living.

He begins with the fact of God's mercy (12:1). Mercy is simply a shorthand way of summarizing God's gift of salvation in Christ. God has made the opening move. Now it is up to us to respond in an appropriate way. This appropriate way, according to Paul, is to offer ourselves to God as a "living sacrifice."

The notion of a *living* sacrifice is profound and beautiful. It picks up the Old Testament idea of sacrificial offering and runs with it. No longer is the offering seen as something essentially outside oneself (such as an animal), and involving death, but as the gift of oneself in one's physical and spiritual totality, a gift involving life.

Paul's choice of words in verse 2 is significant and deserves some consideration. The Greek word for "conform" comes from a root which signifies the changeable outward form of a thing. The meaning that Paul wants to convey is that Christians are not to pattern themselves after the changing patterns of the world (fashions not just in clothes, but in religion, politics, and all other areas of everyday living), but to pattern themselves on Christ.

"Conform" is sharply contrasted with "be transformed," which comes from a root meaning what is essential, or unchanging, about something. Thus, to be transformed involves an essential change in nature. One literally becomes a "new creation," as Paul says in his second letter to the Corinthians (II Cor 5:17).

Similarly, the word which he uses for "renew" means to make new, not in point of time (which is changeable), but in point of essence (which is eternal). Our transformation takes place by the renewal, the Spirit-enabled shift in orientation from "flesh" to "spirit," of our "mind." Paul means the word "mind" here to indicate the entire human person. In Romans 8 he has already given us a detailed account of the transformation process which every Christian experiences through the empowerment of the Holy Spirit, and he intends for his readers to recall that chapter here.

In this verse (v. 2), Paul is basically admonishing Christians to totally give themselves to the conversion process which they are undergoing. This commitment to conversion, in turn, enables us to "judge" what is God's will. "Judge" here means to discover or to discern. Thus, a thorough conversion is the surest road to concrete guidance.

Asserting his authority as an apostle ("in virtue of the favor given to me"), Paul counsels modesty in regard to one's place within the Christian community (12:3). It is helpful to recall in this context that Paul wrote his letter to the Romans from Corinth, where the church had had serious problems with infighting and factionalism. Probably assuming that every Christian community would be experiencing these problems to a certain extent, he takes the opportunity to write to the Romans about the meaning of community, much as he had instructed the Corinthians in his first letter to them (I Cor 12).

Using the analogy of the body, where the whole could not exist were it not for the cooperation of the individual parts (v. 4), Paul envisions the Church as one body composed of individual members (v. 5), each with a different calling. Verse 5 assumes the solidarity of Christians with one another through their solidarity with Christ.

In verses 6–8 Paul mentions seven God-given gifts of ministry. He lists these gifts at random: one gift is no "better" or more important than another; all are necessary for the well-being of the community as a whole. These gifts are:

1. *Prophecy*—not speculating on the future, but delivering God's challenging and healing Word for the present.

2. *Ministry*, or, more accurately, service—helping the Church in various practical ways, such as distributing food and alms to those in need.

3. *Teaching*—unfolding the content of the faith through systematic explanation. In the early Church the teaching ministry was especially important in the context of the catechumenate, the preparation of adults for entering the Christian community.

4. *Exhortation*—has the nuance of encouragement. The ministry of exhortation is the gift of building up the community through good will and good cheer.

5. *Almsgiving*—sharing not only the excess, but giving of the substance of one's material blessings so that the poor, in turn, might be blessed.

6. *Ruling*—refers specifically to the authority of those in leadership positions within the early Church.

7. *Works of mercy*—spontaneous acts of compassion reflecting Jesus' compassion.

The most striking thing about this list is that four out of the seven ministries mentioned—prophecy, service, almsgiving, and works of mercy—are not limited to the Christian community, but overflow from that community to those in need in the world-at-large. This mirrors Paul's conviction that the Church is not to be self-centered, but Christ-centered, which empowers it to reach out to others.

12:9-12 comprises a miscellancy of various guidelines for Christian living, both general and specific. Echoing his emphasis on love in his first letter to the Corinthians, Paul begins his guidelines with the injunction that love must be "sincere," literally, not-hypocritical, or two-faced (9a). Doing good and avoiding evil (9b) has served for centuries as the fundamental principle of Catholic moral philosophy.

Returning to his concern for the well-being of the Christian community in verses 10-13, Paul underscores the family relationship of Christians with one another (10a), admonishes each person to take the initiative in honoring the others in the community (10b), and calls for enthusiasm (a living, vital Lord deserves a living, vital faith—v. 11). Paul's counsel to "Rejoice in hope" (12a) is future-oriented: Christians are to be filled with joy at the promise of fullness of life in the Kingdom. Being patient under trial and persevering in prayer (12b) are guidelines for the present. The adjectives "patient" and "persevering" describe the Christian's attitude of joyful endurance. Verse 13 builds on the reality of Christian solidarity. The identification between one Christian and another should be so strong that it expresses itself concretely in acts of hospitality.

In verses 14-21 (with the exceptions of vv. 15 & 16, which are again addressed specifically to the Christian community) Paul lays down some guidelines for the interaction of Christians with nonChristians. He tackles the most difficult situation first, that of persecution. The natural human response to persecution would be hatred. Probably intentionally echoing a saying of Jesus (compare Romans 12:14 with Matthew 5:44 and Luke 6:28), Paul maintains that the Christian response to persecution is to bless. The Christian, like Christ (and, incidentally, like St. Stephen, whose death Paul—then Saul—personally witnessed; see Acts 7:60), is not to retaliate, but to ask God's mercy on his or her enemies.

When Paul advises Christians to "rejoice with those who rejoice" and to "weep with those who weep" (v. 15), he is concerned with the effectiveness of Christian witness. To be an effective witness to the Gospel, a Christian must be able to empathize with the person with whom he is sharing the Good News.

The opening words of verse 16, which the NAB translates as "Have the same attitude toward all" (making it seem contradictory with v. 15), are literally "Be of the same mind toward one another," or, as the RSV has it, "Live in harmony with one another." Paul directs these words to the Christian community. Again, probably remembering the magnitude of the problem of spiritual one-upmanship at Corinth, he demands real solidarity, or relationship, with Christians who are "lowly." In his day, as well as ours, to be "lowly" meant to be poor, of low social status, illiterate, elderly, sick, or all of the above.

Returning to the relation between Christians and the larger world in verse 17, Paul echoes his earlier "Bless your persecutors; bless and do not curse them" (v. 14) with "Never repay injury with injury" (17a). He is concerned that Christians do not take advantage of their pagan neighbors, but treat them with the same high level of morality which they show to one another (17b). The "If possible" in verse 18 hints at any important qualification to living "peaceably with everyone." A Christian, Paul seems to be implying, should never shortchange the truth for the sake of a sham peace.

Returning yet again to the theme of non-retaliation (to "get even" with their Jewish and Roman persecutors must have been one of the major temptations of Christians during these early years), Paul uses his most formidable resource, which for him is

a quotation from Scripture (v. 19). He cites Deuteronomy 32:35
to the effect that a Christian is not supposed to get even with
anyone, since this is only God's prerogative. Paul is quoting
Scripture to clinch his argument because, for him and for his
audience, Scripture is the final, authoritative word.

As with so many of his quotations from the Old Testament,
however, this one falls flat, and it does this because it reflects a
lower level of spiritual development than Jesus. Again, we are
unwittingly subjected to the picture of a God who is patiently
waiting to inflict His wrath on those who dare to oppose Him.
Again, we would say that it is truer to God's loving and long-suf-
fering nature to consider the "wrath" as something which a person
inflicts on him or herself.

Paul's quotation from Proverbs 25:21 & 22 in verse 20 is
more positive, in as much as the "burning coals" to be heaped
on the head of one's enemy are figurative of the shame which
he is supposed to experience because of his good treatment at the
hands of the person he is abusing, shame which will hopefully
lead to repentance and salvation.

Verse 21 summarizes the thrust of the entire miscellancy of
guidelines: the Christian should be a person who takes the initiative
and overcomes evil, not by doing more evil, but by persisting in
good.

Romans 13:1-7 is Paul's famous text on the relation of the
Christian and the state. It has been, and continues to be, one of
the most abused texts in the Bible. The deadly combination of
ignoring its background, taking it out of context, and reading too
much into it has led to a disastrous obsequiousness on the part
of many Christians toward the state, as in Nazi Germany, and in
the "Moral Majority" movement currently in vogue in the United
States.

We are so used to reading this text apart from its historical
background that it comes as something of a shock to realize that
its original intent was to counter within the Christian community

a growing sense of disrespect and disobedience in regard to the claims of the state. We need to remember that Jesus was crucified by the Romans for political reasons and that the Jews had a natural animosity toward Rome, an animosity which they would likely carry with them into the Church when they became Christians. Apparently it was all-too-tempting for the early Christians to disparage the very existence of the state. It is to check this temptation that Paul writes what he does.

It is fitting that the immediate context of these verses is Paul's discussion of the Christian's obligation to "live peaceable with everyone" (12:18), not to retaliate (12:19), and to "conquer evil with good" (12:21). The label "Chapter 13" tends to make us think that with a new chapter a new topic has been introduced. In reality, chapter and verse designations were not part of the biblical text. They were added many centuries later for ease of reference, and their character is often quite arbitrary. In context, Romans 13:1-7 is really a concrete illustration of the principles which Paul has introduced in chapter 12, and will continue to present in the rest of chapter 13. This text, then, is a picture of Christian love and non-retaliation in action.

The word which the NAB translates as "obey" in 13:1 is not literally obey, but "be subject to," a subtle, but important, difference. In New Testament usage, "obedience" springs from a personal choice to follow Christ. "Being subject to" carries the connotation of embracing a less-than-perfect situation as part of one's cross of being a Christian. The realities to which a Christian is subject are broken, but necessary, realities—realities resulting from the "fall" and now necessary to keep some kind of order in the world. Government is one such reality. Thus, for a Christian to "be subject to" the "authorities" means that he or she will, normally, comply with the laws of the land.

The word which the NAB translates as "authorities" is literally "power." While it undoubtedly refers to governmental power in the context of this chapter, it also refers to something more.

This is the word which Paul invariably uses to describe the behind-the-scene powers (both good and evil) which contemporary Judaism believed influenced the course of human events. In other words, Paul believed that government is more than a human institution; it is also a vehicle for the operation of higher—especially satanic—powers. Basically the same understanding is reflected in St. Matthew's Gospel, in the story of the temptation, when the devil offers Jesus the kingdoms of the world if He will worship him (see Matt 4:8-9). The fact that the devil can make this overture to Jesus indicates that the kingdoms of the world are indeed his to give.

Why, then, should the Christian, of all persons, be subject to a power which is less than God? Because, in a fallen world, subjection to this power is necessary for society to exist. The sense is that God, in what we might call his "passive providence," allows these powers to exist for the ordering of the world. The fact that the root of the word which the NAB translates as "established" is actually "to order" or "to organize" substantiates this interpretation.

The sense of Romans 13:1, then is much more passive than it is active. The text is not saying that God in His active will ordained government, but that God in His passive will allows the powers that be to provide some order in a broken world. Following Jesus' example, Christians are to be subject to the authorities. This subjection is part of the cross of following Christ.

Still combatting what must have been a radical disrespect for the government on the part of many Christians, Paul states flatly in verse 2 that "the man who opposes authority rebels against the ordinance (literally: ordering) of God," thus choosing a self-inflicted condemnation.

To understand verse 3 we need to bear in mind that Paul wrote this *before* the Empire had started persecuting Christians, when it was descriptively accurate to say that "Rulers cause no fear when a man does what is right but only when his conduct is evil." Here, as well as in verse 4, he probably also has in mind situations where Christians have disgraced the faith by breaking the law. Much of his argumentation in these verses is based on common sense.

Verse 4 is somewhat confusing because, true to form, Paul describes everything in terms of God's active will. Thus, he makes it sound like the ruler is an active instrument of God's will in inflicting wrath, with the implied (and devastating) corollary that rulers like Hitler are somehow a direct expression of God's punishment. Whereas we would say that the rulers of the world are within God's "passive providence" (things which He allows to happen out of respect for our free will), and that with someone like Hitler (who, after all, was put in power through human choice) God's "active providence" is to suffer with His suffering people.

Once again, we need to understand "wrath" not in terms of a personal lashing out on God's part, but as the impersonal and inevitable consequence of violating the moral order, or structure, of the world. Just as the law of gravity dictates that a person jumping from a high building will be broken, the natural consequence of violating the moral order (which Paul talks about in Romans 1) is to be subject to "wrath," or moral self-destruction.

Because God uses the authority of government as part of His moral ordering of the world, a Christian should comply with the laws of the state from a higher motive than that of fear. Compliance is not a matter of escaping punishment, but of conscience (v. 5). Paul cites paying taxes as an example of necessary Christian compliance (v. 6).

In verse 7, however, he brings another dimension—the dimension of discrimination, or evaluation—into his argument. He does this by referring to Jesus' saying (recorded in all three synoptic Gospels: Mark, Matthew, and Luke; see, for example, Mark 12:17), "Give to Caesar what is Caesar's, but give to God what is God's." We know that Paul is referring to Jesus here because the word "Pay" in "Pay each one his due" is the same word as "Give" in "Give to Caesar;" since there are a whole variety of words available to express this idea, the fact that Paul uses the same one as the synoptics is significant.

Paul, of course, is using "pay each one his due" in a positive sense in verse 7. He is emphasizing the fact that Caesar *is* entitled to certain dues. Jesus' initial statement, "Give to Caesar what is Caesar's," had an obverse, "but give to God what is God's." So, too, Paul's "Pay each one his due," carries within it the built-in corollary "but do not pay someone what is *not* his due (but God's)."

At this point in his life, the writing of the letter to the Romans, Paul was focusing, for reasons already discussed, on the "Pay each one his due" side of his position. Several years later, in the midst of the first great persecution of Christians by the Roman Empire, Paul was forced to act on the "do not pay someone what is *not* his due" side of his position by refusing to affirm that "Caesar is Lord" or to say "anathema Jesus." The witness of Paul's own life—that is, his martyrdom—is the strongest argument against those who argue that Paul taught an undiscriminating allegiance to the state.

Although Paul does not actually come out and say it in these verses (Romans 13:1-7), his whole argument—especially given the discussion of Christian non-retaliation immediately preceding in chapter 12—presupposes that violence against rulers or the state is *never* a viable alternative for a Christian. When government oversteps its bounds (what is "due" it), it is not only permissible, but imperative, that a Christian resist. But this resistence, like Jesus', must be non-violent in nature.

Again, with our chapter and verse distinctions, even paragraph headings, such as "Love Fulfills the Law" in the *New American Bible*, we tend to lose the continuity between much of Scripture. And translation often masks connections. The English hides the fact that, for example, the Greek root for "due" (v. 7) and "owe" (v. 8) is the same, thus making a stronger linkage, both linguistically and visually, than we find in our Bibles. The fact is that for Paul Romans 13:1-7 is of one fabric with what comes after as well as with what comes before.

The general theme of love is picked up again in verse 8; verse 7 was a particular application of this general rule. Paul, in a manner similar to Jesus' summation of the law in Mark 12:28-31, condenses the social aspects of the law into one great commandment, "You shall love your neighbor as yourself" (v. 9). Paul explains why this one commandment covers all in verse 10; it does so because "Love never wrongs the neighbor."

Referring back to the entire miscellany of moral guidelines which he has presented from the beginning of chapter 12, he underlines their urgency by using eschatological imagery—pictures of the end time—in verses 11 and 12. He lists several "deeds of darkness" in verse 13, sins which were quite popular in the church at Corinth and undoubtedly not unfamiliar to the church at Rome. To "put on the Lord Jesus Christ" (v. 14) is an injunction for Christians to take their solidarity with Christ so seriously that they will allow His Spirit to guide their actions.

14:1-15:13 consider another problem which was prevalent in the early Church: the tension between those with scruples concerning the eating of certain foods and the observance of certain days, and those without; in broader terms, the tension between a more conservative element and a more liberal element in regard to what was acceptable and what was not acceptable in particular areas of Christian behavior. Paul had already dealt with a similar issue at length in his first letter to the Corinthians. There a controversy had raged about whether it was all right for a Christian to eat meat which had been sacrificed to idols. The "knowledgeable" (those who supposedly "knew" better) had taken the pro position and the "weak" the con (see I Cor. 8-10).

Here, in Romans, Paul's discussion is more general. He is not speaking to a specific problem which he has heard about in the Roman Church, but to the tension between the "weak" and the "strong," "conservatives" and "liberals," which could be assumed to exist in every church. This would include the problem of idol-meat, but go beyond it to cover such items as asceticism and the observance of various kinds of special days as well.

Paul first addresses the "liberals," instructing them to graciously receive, or accept, those who are "weak in faith" (14:1). In this context "weak in faith" describes those who have not progressed very far in the Christian life, those who are still using various types of "crutches" (Paul will mention several in his discussion) to augment the stark reality of grace. Paul, speaking as a wise pastor, enjoins the liberals not to give in to the temptation to try and argue the overly scrupulous out of their concerns. He knows that disputes of this kind usually leave weak faith even weaker. Underlying Paul's advice is the realization that it is common for many Christians to be a little too works-oriented at the beginning of their faith. He seems to count on a gradual deepening process of growth in the Spirit to work the scruples out of their scrupulosity.

Giving a concrete example of the kind of opposition about which he is talking—the fact that some Christians will eat anything, while others are vegetarians (v. 2)—Paul goes on to demand, in verse 3, toleration on the part of both parties. Each side must renounce its own special temptation; for the liberals this was to ridicule the conservatives, and for the conservatives this was to judge the liberals.

In 3b-4 he defends the liberals and castigates the conservatives. There is no doubt in Paul's mind that the liberals are theologically justified on this issue; that is, they are right in not putting much stock in things like dietary laws. Paul was probably familiar with an early "sayings" source of Jesus (a collection of His teachings preceding the writing of the Gospels), and is probably thinking of one of Our Lord's sayings.akin to Mark 7:15a, "Nothing that enters a man from outside can make him impure," when he defends the liberals on the basis that "God himself has made him welcome" in 14:3b, and that "the Lord is able to make his stand" in 14:4b. The point that he wants to drive home to the conservatives is that they have no business in judging another man's (that is, God's) servant.

Introducing another example in verse 5—the observance or non-observance of special days of fast or festival—Paul maintains, simply, that it does not really matter what position one takes, so long as each is "certain of his own conscience"—acts out of the context of his or her own relationship with God, and not someone else's. Paul holds that there is no *essential* difference between observing special days or not, between eating or fasting, because in each case the person is acting from the same motivation; namely, to "honor the Lord" (v. 6).

Returning to his earlier master-servant image in verses 7-12, Paul now uses it to call *both* sides to their senses. No Christian lives or dies as his or her own master; in life and in death a Christian's first allegiance is to the Lord Jesus (vv. 7-8). Verse 9, with its reference to the Resurrection ("came to life again"), emphasizes Christ's total Lordship. Paul criticizes both the conservatives, who "sit in judgment," and the liberals, who "look down on your brother," in verse 10, and this on the ground that both parties are usurping a role that belongs only to God. He quotes from Isaiah in verse 11 and paraphrases the quotation in verse 12 to stress the inappropriateness of Christians judging one another when they themselves will be judged. They have no authority to be making the kinds of judgments that they are—only God does.

As we have seen, Paul has already singled out the scrupulous for reproach (14:3b-4), and pitted both sides against God's judgment to bring out the unreasonableness of each side (14:7-12). Up to this point the liberals may have had reason to think that they were getting off rather easily, presumably because they were, after all, correct theologically. Now, however, in 14:13-15:4,

Paul singles out the liberals for reproof, and this in much greater depth and extent than he had the conservatives. The technique of seeming to let something off the hook, then suddenly pouncing on it, is a favorite, and highly effective, rhetorical device of Paul's.

After summarizing his previous thought on judgment (13a), he abruptly turns on the liberals and asks them to quit being a "stumbling block" to their weaker brethren (13b). A charge of causing someone else to fall—to cause someone to lose their faith—was, of course, quite serious, much more serious than the petty judgments of the weak against the strong.

In the first part of verse 14, Paul solemnly affirms the validity of the liberal position theologically, and he does this on the authority of the Lord Himself. Again, he is probably recalling the above-mentioned saying of Jesus. Here he comes close to quoting it. In his explanation of this saying in the second part of the verse, however, he extrapolates an important moral principle, the fact that conscience decides what is "clean" or "unclean" for a particular individual. To incite someone to act against his conscience—Paul uses the example of convincing him to eat something which he really considers "unclean"—is no less an infraction than breaking the "rule of love" (15a). Even more seriously, it is to become responsible for bringing a fellow Christian to "ruin" (15b).

Verse 16 reads literally "Therefore do not let your good be blasphemed." In other words, the liberals need to be on guard against turning something which is good in itself (a Christian's freedom from dietary restrictions) into its opposite, an act which becomes a mockery of God.

Paul points out the silliness of this issue in verse 17 by contrasting "eating" and "drinking" with the "kingdom of God," which is comprised of "justice" (salvation), "peace," and "joy"— all gifts of the Spirit. In the context of God's Kingdom, eating and drinking are matters of no consequence—unless they become stumbling blocks for one's brother or sister, in which case they become occasions of serious sin.

The "way" of which Paul speaks in verse 18 is the sacrificial way of giving up some of one's freedom in order not to become a temptation to others. In verse 19 he recalls the liberals to the more important values (much more important than eating and drinking) of peace and "mutual upbuilding" (RSV).

Verse 20 summarizes what he has said to the liberals thus far. In verse 21 Paul becomes quite explicit and flatly asks for abstention in any problematic area. The verbs in this verse refer to particular occasions; in other words, a Christian ought never to use his or her freedom in situations where it might be detrimental to another.

The first part of verse 22 reads literally, as the RSV renders it, "The faith that you have, keep between yourself and God." Paul seems to be telling the liberals here that it is perfectly all right for them to exercise their freedom in private, and that they have just cause to celebrate their clean conscience in doing so (22b). He reminds them of the serious plight of the scrupulous in verse 23.

Identifying himself with the "strong" through his use of the personal pronoun "we" (15:1), Paul goes on to ask the liberals to give more of themselves to their "weak" brethren than just passive tolerance. The NAB's "patient" in this verse is too weak; the Greek word is the same that on several occasions is used for the attitude of Jesus in bearing his cross; the connotation, then, is one of active, even sacrificial love in helping the scrupulous bear their scruples. The goal for the strong should be to "build up" the weaker brother instead of tearing him down (v. 2). In doing this, the strong are following no less an example than Christ (3a), who did not "please himself" by remaining above and beyond the concerns of the world, but who completely gave Himself in the Incarnation. The intent of Paul's quotation in 3b (from Psalm 69:10) is to show the depth of love to which Jesus was willing to go: to take upon Himself the rejection directed at the Father.

Quoting from the Hebrew Scriptures reminds him of their unique place in the life of the Christian (15:4). They are intended for our instruction, or enlightenment, to provide us with hope through the "patience," or steadfastness, which their "words of encouragement" give us. God Himself is the Source of this patience and encouragement, and thus the ultimate Source of our hope (5a; see also 15:13).

Verses 5 and 6 are actually a prayer, or benediction, in which Paul asks the blessing of "perfect harmony" for the Church at Rome. This harmony reflects the "spirit of Christ Jesus," and empowers the Christian community—precisely as a community, or united body—to offer fitting worship to the Father.

"Accept" in 15:7 and "welcome" in 14:1 are the same Greek word, meaning, literally, "receive." Paul is in the process of summarizing the message of mutual affirmation which he introduced at the beginning of chapter 14. Once again, this "welcome" or "acceptance" is no passive reality, but means actively following in the footsteps of Christ, who has already received all of us, "weak" or "strong," Jew or Gentile, so that the Father may be praised.

Following Jesus' example means, among other things, to become a servant, just as Jesus "became the servant of the Jews" (8a). In this way God's "faithfulness" (actually "truthfulness" in the Greek) was revealed; the Father has, indeed, kept His promises to the fathers of the faith (8b), and through the fulfillment of His promises has also revealed His mercy, or compassion, to the Gentiles (v. 9).

Paul follows his reference to the Gentiles with a collage of Old Testament quotations (from the Psalms, Deuteronomy, and Isaiah) to prove that the Gentiles were, all along, included in God's promises (15:9b-12). He ends this section with another prayer, addressing God as the "God of hope," and asking Him to bless the Roman Christians with the joy and the peace of faith. This living faith will, in turn, empower them with the Holy Spirit, who will see to it that they have "hope in abundance" (v. 13).

*Questions for Personal Reflection/Group Discussion*

1. Paul regularly follows the pattern of drawing out the ethical implications from his theology. This process of coming to *live* the Good News as well as believing it is a crucial part of what it means to be a Christian. How do you make the transition from theology (belief) to ethics (action) in your own life?
2. Paraphrase—rewrite in words and concepts personally meaningful to you—Romans 12:1-2.
3. Which of the gifts of ministry which Paul mentions in 12:6-8 are yours and how do you exercise them? Remember, you cannot say that you do not have any, since *every* Christian has one or more.
4. Why do you think Paul makes such a big deal about non-retaliation in chapter 12?
5. Given the proper historical background and literary context of Paul's famous teaching on the Christian's duty toward the state, Romans 13:1-7, what is the real substance of what he is teaching?
6. How might what Paul teaches in 14:1-15:13 concerning the relationship between the "weak" and the "strong," or the "conservatives" and the "liberals" go far in reconciling some of the differences in the Church today? Try to apply what Paul has to say as specifically as you can to particular tensions between liberal and conservative elements in today's Church.

## Chapter 8:   Concluding Matters

*Please read Romans 15:14-16:27.*   Parts of the preceding moral section have been quite emphatic, not to mention the intensity of much of Paul's theology in this epistle. Now, as he begins to bring this letter to a close, he takes the opportunity to praise the Roman Christians (15:14), and accounts for his boldness. This boldness is, first of all, a statement of what they already know (15a) and, secondly, an expression of his authority as "Apostle to the Gentiles" (vv. 15b-16).

The word which Paul uses for "minister" in verse 16, *leitourgon* (from which we derive our English word "liturgy"), has priestly connotations. Paul sees himself as a mediator between God and the Gentiles, the vehicle through which the Gentiles are brought into contact with God. More important than his person, however, is the fact that he fulfills the "priestly duty of preaching the Gospel." Here the proclamation of the Good News is seen as a hallmark of the priestly ministry. It would not be long before the early Church would extrapolate from this insight the further understanding that proclaiming the Gospel was, in itself, a sacramental act; that is, an activity in which Christ becomes truly present to His people. This is why Catholics (and other liturgical traditions) stand when the Gospel is proclaimed.

Paul's liturgical image of presenting the Gentile to God as a "pleasing sacrifice" captures the essential meaning of sacrifice as "making holy." The Gentiles who have responded to the Gospel have been made holy by that very Gospel. They are now a *living* sacrifice (see Romans 12:1) to the Father.

Paul is proud of the effectiveness of his ministry, but gives the credit for his success specifically to Jesus and the Holy Spirit (vv. 17-19a). The words "through me" in verse 18 are significant and witness to Paul's understanding of himself as a vehicle, or vessel, of God's grace.

He comments on the extent to which he has been able to preach the Gospel—all the way from Israel to what is present-day Yugoslavia (19b). "Preaching the gospel" meant, for Paul, making a number of converts in key, strategically located cities; converts who, in turn, would take it upon themselves to further extend the preaching of the Good News.

Alluding to his frustrating experience with the "super-apostles" in Corinth (who "stole" his converts from him—see II Cor.

11:4-5), Paul boasts that it has been his way never to usurp another person's territory, but to always act as pathfinder, carrying the Gospel into regions where it had not previously been heard (v. 20). In verse 21 he cites a text from Isaiah (Is. 52:15) which he believes underscores the validity of his method.

His intense and extended missionary activity has made it impossible for him to visit the Romans in person (v. 22). This is a hope which he has entertained for several years, and now that his work in the eastern half of the Empire is completed, he looks forward to the fulfillment of his desire (v. 23). In verse 24 Paul mentions his intent to pioneer the Gospel in Spain. Rome would have been the ideal base of operations for a mission to Spain, and his statement "I trust that you will send me on my journey" probably contains within it a subtle appeal for material assistance (in a rather similar context, see I Cor. 16:6, where he is not so subtle in his request for help).

There is only one thing keeping him from proceeding to Rome, and this is his commitment to accompany a good-will collection to Jerusalem (v. 25). This is the same collection which Paul refers to in his letters to the Corinthians (see I Cor. 16:1-3; II Cor. 8 & 9). It has now been successfully completed (v. 26) and Paul is concerned to get it to Jerusalem. This collection has both theological and symbolic importance for Paul. Theologically, it is only fitting that the Gentile Christians should express their appreciation for the priceless spiritual gifts they have received from the Jewish Christians by responding to their poverty (v. 27). Symbolically, a sizeable free-will and good-will offering could go far in healing the tensions between Gentile and Jewish Christianity. It would demonstrate in a tangible way the real solidarity between these two groups. Paul's intent is to press on to Spain via Rome as soon as the collection has been delivered (v. 28).

Paul's statement in verse 29, "I shall come with Christ's full blessing," which literally reads "in the fullness of the blessing of Christ I will come," is touchingly ironic given the actual circumstances of his "visit" to Rome. It is obvious in verses 30 and 31 that Paul does not particularly *want* to go to Jerusalem. For him it is a "struggle," and he is aware of the danger that awaits him there from "unbelievers," his Jewish enemies who are determined to destroy him.

As we know from Acts 21:15-28, Paul's arrival in Jerusalem triggered a sequence of events that led to a riot (which was staged by his enemies), his arrest, and eventual extradition to Rome. He arrived in Rome not, as he was hoping when he wrote this letter—as a free man on his way to evangelize Spain—but as a prisoner in chains. Thus, the "fullness" of Christ with which he came to Rome was not the fulfillment of a successful journey to Jerusalem, but the fullness of being called upon to practice the very sacrificial love he talked about earlier in this letter.

From a literary point of view, chapter 16 is the only controversial section of this letter. Many scholars find it impossible to credit Paul with knowing so many people apparently so well (he mentions twenty-four individuals and two households by name in this chapter) in a church he had not even visited, much less founded. This, plus the facts that Paul spent a considerable amount of time in Ephesus, and that the last known location of Prisca and Aquila was Ephesus (see I Cor. 16:8, 19), has led to the hypothesis that Romans 16:1-16 (and perhaps verses 17-27 as well) was originally part of another letter that Paul wrote to the Ephesians.

Verses 17-20 pose another problem for many scholars. Why, they ask, should Paul dictate so calmly for fifteen chapters and then suddenly turn to admonishment? It is argued that "those who cause dissension and scandal" (v. 17) better fit the situation in Ephesus or, better yet, the situation in Rome in the early 100's, when the church there was fighting Gnosticism (a philosophical system which stressed the learning of various secret doctrines for the attainment of heaven). Thus, some scholars make verses 17-20 part of an additional (and hypothetical) letter of Paul to the Ephesians, while others speculate that they are not from Paul at all, but from a later author using Paul's authority to combat the Gnostic heresy.

Finally, the great doxology, or benediction, in verses 25-27 constitutes a problem. This doxology occurs in different places in different early manuscripts of Romans. Most often it occurs in its present location, at the end of chapter 16. But it is also found at the end of chapter 14 and at the end of chapter 15. What are we to make of this? Again, many scholars refuse to ascribe this benediction to Paul, claiming that, for reasons of content and style, it does not "fit" with the rest of this letter. They would either assign it to the "lost" letter to the Ephesians or attribute it to another author.

While there is something to be said in favor of all these hypotheses, this author perceives the evidence as pointing to our text (chapter 16) as that of being the original conclusion of Romans.

Concerning verses 1-16, a little history can be a big help. We know that the Emperor Claudius (probably between the years 49 and 52) expelled all Jews from Rome, and that Priscilla (an informal form of Prisca) and Aquila were among those expelled (see Acts 18:2). Christians would have been among those forced to leave, since at this time the Empire made no distinction between Christianity and Judaism. We also know that this decree was rescinded, and that many of those who had been evicted eventually returned. Given the great extent of his missionary journeys, it is likely that during the course of his travels Paul would have met and befriended quite a few Christians from Rome. These, this author believes, are precisely the people (now returned home after their expulsion) that Paul greets in verses 1-16.

It seems obvious that Paul, writing to a church he had neither founded nor previously visited, would want to remember by name as many persons as he possibly could. This would demonstrate that he was already known by a large number of people in the

Christian community at Rome and that, presumably, he could be trusted. It is interesting in this regard that his letters to the Romans and Colossians (another community with which Paul had no direct connection) are the only ones in which he uses this kind of personal address. In his letters to the churches which he founded and which are well-known to him, *Thessalonians, Galatians, Corinthians, Philippians,* and *Ephesians,* he does not mention people's names in this way, probably so that he could not be accused of favoritism. Thus, there seems to be adequate evidence in favor of acknowledging verses 1-16 as in their rightful place in Scripture.

Anyone who has read Paul's earlier letters knows that abrupt changes in style are almost more the rule than the exception with St. Paul. To be sure, *Romans* is remarkably consistent in tone up to this point (16:17-20). But it would have been quite natural for Paul, realizing that his letter was rapidly coming to a close, to take the last opportunity to admonish (vv. 17, 19-20) and to rebuke (v. 18).

A number of scholars argue that Paul's phraseology in verse 17, "contrary to the teaching you have received" is that of a former pastor to one of his congregations. This contends against the present place of this text because Paul was never a pastor of the Roman Church. On the contrary, it seems that this is precisely what Paul would say if he *had not* pastored the Church at Rome. If he had, it seems that he would have said something more personal, like "contrary to the teaching you have received *from me.*"

There is nothing impossible in the words "those who cause dissension and scandal" (v. 17) referring to certain of the liberals whom he had addressed in chapters 14 and 15. This seems especially so since we know that the controversy Paul spoke to in these chapters revolved around food, and he makes a disparaging reference to "bellies" in verse 18.

Regarding the great doxology, verses 25-27, the manuscript evidence (with this doxology being found, in various manuscripts, at the end of chapters 14, 15, and 16) seems to indicate that from an early date Paul's letter to the Romans—because of its doctrinal importance—circulated to other churches in different "editions." Since chapters 14 and 15 were considered to deal with specifically "Roman" problems, it would be natural to omit them in favor of the earlier, more general, doctrinal and ethical sections.

As to the supposition that the doxology reflects neither the content of the letter to the Romans nor the style of St. Paul, this author simply disagrees. The doxology effectively summarizes the content of the letter by reflecting a number of Paul's major insights concerning the Gospel—insights such as its hidden mystery, the fact that it is now manifest through Scripture, and available to the Gentiles. As for style, it is nothing less than the mystical style which he displays whenever his theology becomes caught up in worship (see, for example, Romans 11:33-36).

\*       \*       \*

The chapter begins with a brief letter of introduction and recommendation for a certain Phoebe (vv. 1-2). Apparently she was moving from Cenchreae, the port city of Corinth, to Rome. She may have acted as messenger for Paul's letter to the Romans. She is called a deaconess which, of course, is the female counterpart of deacon, a position of administering the material resources and ministering to the material needs of the early Church. This is pure speculation, but Paul's commendation may have served to authenticate her role in an established and transferable ministry, much as the pastor of a parish today will write a letter for a catechist moving from one parish to another.

Prisca and Aquila (vv. 3-5) are close friends of Paul's. They are mentioned in Acts 18:1-3, 18, 26. The phrase "risked their lives" in verse 4 might refer to a pivotal role which they may have played in the "riot of the silversmiths" (see Acts 19). They were with Paul in Ephesus at the time, and as his good friends

quite likely (perhaps by approaching the town clerk) helped him
out of a difficult situation. "All the churches of the Gentiles are
grateful to them" because, in saving Paul's life they made it
possible for his missionary activity to continue. Note Paul's greetings to the "congregation that meets in their house" (v. 5). The
early Church had no "church" buildings, but was simply a gather-
ing of people—a community—united in Christ. Probably a dozen
or so of these little house-churches made up the Church of Rome
at this time.

The usage of "apostles" in verse 7 underscores the double
meaning which this word came to have very early in the history
of the Church. On the one hand, "apostles" refers specifically to
the Twelve, plus Paul. Paul uses the word in this way when he
designates himself as an apostle in Galatians 1:1 and I Corinthians
9:1. On the other hand, "apostles" soon came to have a broader
sense, becoming a designation for any authorized missionary. It
is in this sense that Paul speaks of Andronicus and Junias. Some
early manuscripts omit the "s" at the end of "Junias," turning it
into a feminine name. Whether or not the original text read "Junia"
or "Junias," however, the number of women Paul cites in verses
6-16 witnesses to the very active role which women played in
the life of the early Church.

The only name in verses 6-16 which occurs elsewhere in
Scripture is that of "Rufus" in verse 13. As yet an identification
between this person and the Rufus mentioned in Mark 15:21
(where Rufus is a son of Simon of Cyrene, the man who helped
Jesus to carry his cross) is mostly conjecture. The odds in favor
of this identification would increase dramatically with definitive
proof that St. Mark wrote his Gospel specifically for the Church
at Rome.

The reasons for considering verses 17-20 an original part of
the letter to the Romans have already been given. Note Paul's
commendation of the Church at Rome in 19a. We know from
church history that the Roman Church was indeed considered to

be a "model" church in many respects. 19b probably reflects another saying of Jesus which eventaully found its way into two of the Gospels (see Matthew 10:16 and Luke 10:3). Verse 20 ("crush Satan under your feet") likely alludes to Genesis 3:15.

Of the names mentioned in verses 21-24, Timothy (v. 21) is the only one about whom we know anything. He is frequently mentioned by Paul in his correspondence and was his faithful co-worker. Tertius, who was secretary for this letter, adds his own salutation in verse 22.

Paul closes this letter with a soaring doxology (vv. 25-27). This magnificent benediction, like the grand finale of a complex symphony, weaves together the major themes of the whole work. It also, with reference to "the God alone who is *wise*" (v. 27), at the same time looks back to another mystical section of Romans (11:33-36), and looks forward to what will be a major theme in his letters to the Colossians and the Ephesians.

## Questions for Personal Reflection/Group Discussion

1. In what sense is proclaiming the Gospel a sacramental activity?
2. (a) What does it mean to be a mediator of God's grace to others?

   (b) In what ways are *you* this for others?
3. Paul must have been greatly disappointed that his plans to carry the Gospel to Spain did not work out. Yet he kept the faith in spite of his disappointment.

   (a) What have been your greatest disappointments in life?

   (b) How has God brought meaning out of these disappointments?

# *Philemon*

## Introduction

Because of a plot against his life (see Acts 20:2b-3), Paul chose a rather complicated itinerary from Corinth to Jerusalem. Arriving there around the Feast of Pentecost in the year 58, Paul's presence soon provoked certain Jews to violence. They incited a riot against him, and he would undoubtedly have been killed (in the same manner as Stephen), if the Roman tribune had not stepped in and arrested him for his own safety. The situation in Jerusalem was so inflammable that Paul was sent to Caesarea, to be tried before Felix, the Roman Governor of Judea. Felix, hoping to receive a bribe, stalled on Paul's case for two years.

In the year 60 a new governor, Festus, came to power. With the new regime came renewed plots against Paul's life. Festus planned on having Paul stand trial in Jerusalem. Rather than be ambushed and killed on the way, Paul, using one of his rights as a Roman citizen, appealed for judgment to the Emperor. This forced Festus' hand, and he was obliged to send Paul to Rome, where he spent another two years (61-62) awaiting his trial.

It was during his imprisonment at Rome that Paul wrote his letters to Philemon and to the Colossians, to the Ephesians, and to the Philippians. Philemon and Colossians must be considered as having been written practically simultaneously, Philemon being addressed primarily to an individual, and Colossians to the church as a whole. Onesimus, the subject of Paul's letter to Philemon, is mentioned in the letter to the Colossians (Col. 4:9), as well as

Epaphras, Mark, Aristarchus, Demas, and Luke (compare Phlm. 23-24 with Col. 4:10-14).

We can piece together the story behind Philemon as follows: Onesimus, Philemon's slave, has runaway from his owner, undoubtedly helping himself to some of his master's assets in the process (Phlm. 18). He flees to Rome where, providentially, he encounters St. Paul, who makes a Christian out of him (Phlm. 10). Onesimus stays on with Paul, helping him in his ministry, and becoming his close friend (Phlm. 11-13).

Onesimus probably did not level with Paul about his runaway slave status until he had been with him for some time. At any rate, Paul (doubtless in consultation with Onesimus) decides that the only honorable thing to do is to send Onesimus back. His letter to Philemon is a plea for clemency on Onesimus' behalf.

But it is also much more than this. It is also an indirect (and more persuasive precisely because of its indirection) appeal to Philemon not only to forgive Onesimus, but to send him back to Paul.

Because he preserved Paul's letter, it is quite probable that Philemon released Onesimus into Paul's service. A number of scholars find a moving sequel to this story in the fact that St. Ignatius, in a letter written in the early years of the second century, addresses a certain Onesimus as Bishop of Ephesus. Ignatius is requesting the good bishop to release one of his deacons into his service, and his letter contains several striking similarities to Paul's letter to Philemon. Given this evidence, plus the fact that the highest administrative positions in churches which had been founded by Paul tended to go to Paul's trusted companions, such as Timothy and Titus, it is not at all unlikely that Onesimus, Bishop of Ephesus, is the former runaway slave!

If this is true, it also explains why Philemon, the only "private" letter of Paul's to be included in the canon, was preserved. It was preserved because it was of intense personal interest to Onesimus, Bishop of Ephesus, who, incidentally, was probably the same Ephesian Bishop responsible for one of the earliest collections of Paul's letters.

The question is often raised in the context of Paul's letter to Philemon as to why he did not simply repudiate the institution of slavery. As we have already seen in the thirteenth chapter of his letter to the Romans, Paul was not interested in overthrowing the Roman government. According to Paul, for a Christian to advocate violent revolution was a contradiction of his or her relationship with Christ, a relationship which was supposed to champion non-violence and non-retaliation. Just as a Christian was expected to obey the government except in matters directly contrary to faith, a Christian slave was expected to obey his master. In this way he would overcome the evil of his situation through the good of his obedience for the sake of Christ (see Romans 12:21).

Although Christianity did not directly challenge slavery, it did provide the transformative element within Western society which eventually led to its abolition. Significantly, it was the teaching of St. Paul, in such statements as

> There does not exist among you Jew or Greek, slave
> or freeman, male or female. All are one in Christ
> Jesus.   (Galatians 3:28)

> There is no Greek or Jew here, circumcised or
> uncircumcised, foreigner, Scythian (meaning
> "barbarian"), slave or freeman. Rather, Christ
> is everything in all of you.   (Colossians 3:11)

that acted as a powerful catalyst in the maturation of human consciousness to the point where it could no longer countenance slavery.

## Chapter 9:   Paul's Plea for Compassion and Assistance

*Please read Paul's letter to Philemon.*    Unlike the initial greeting of all his other letters, in this one Paul does not refer to his standing as an apostle (v. 1). He is writing, for the most part, as friend to friend, not apostle to subordinate. We say "for the most part" because already in verse 2 Paul expands his greeting to include two other persons and the Christian community which gathers in Philemon's home. This letter is to be shared with them and if, as many scholars think, the letter "coming from Laodicea" (a sister city to Colossae) is really the letter to Philemon (see Col. 4:16), it is to be shared with the Church at Colossae as well.

Thus, although Philemon is a "private" letter, it is private in a rather public way. Paul is determined not to authoritatively command Philemon to a certain course of action. At the same time, he is equally determined that Philemon do what he wants him to, and brings to bear on him all the indirect resources at his disposal, including peer pressure.

"Grace" and "peace" (v. 3) is Paul's typical blessing. There is an organic connection between these two terms. "Grace," which is the gift of relationship with God, naturally overflows into "peace," which is the fullness of life resulting from this relationship.

Employing his usual epistolary style, Paul follows his blessing with thanksgiving. This thanksgiving (vv. 4-7) is addressed specifically to Philemon. In it he emphasizes the quality of Philemon's love and faith. This is no accident, for Paul intends to appeal to his love in the body of the letter. Neither is it accidental that he mentions "sharing" in verse 6, with the implication of a positive relationship between sharing and growth in Christ. So too, the word "refreshed" in verse 7, used in the context of thanksgiving for Philemon's being a source of refreshment to others, prepares the way for "Refresh this heart of mine" at the end of verse 20, where Paul is making a personal request of Philemon. As we can begin to see, there is a lot of forethought behind this seemingly informal letter.

Circling nearer to his point, Paul firmly states his authority to "command" (v. 8), yet immediately softens this to an "appeal in the name of love" (9a). Ancient manuscripts differ over the word which the *New American Bible* translates as "ambassador" in 9b. Many of them omit a letter, changing the word to "old man" instead of "ambassador." "Old man" would seem to fit the context better, Paul calculating that an appeal to his advancing age would help to capture Philemon's sympathy. If this is so the text of 9b would read "I, Paul, an old man, and now also a prisoner for Christ Jesus."

Still building up to his point (which by now Philemon must have guessed on his own), Paul indirectly refers to Onesimus as his "child." This refers to the fact of Onesimus' conversion; Paul is indeed his "spiritual father." Having used the point of Onesimus' conversion as his final cushion, Paul now ventures to use the name of the slave directly (11a). But he does so in a playful way, punning on Onesimus' name, which literally means "useful" in Greek. With his conversion, Onesimus has finally grown into the meaning of his name.

Notice how Paul affirms Onesimus' present usefulness not only to Philemon, but to himself as well (11b). Paul is returning Onesimus to Philemon (v. 12), and now it becomes apparent that this letter is, among other things, to be a vehicle of reconciliation between them. The word which Paul uses for "send" has legal connotations: Paul is returning Onesimus for judgment, and it is obvious that the judgment Paul expects from Philemon is one of mercy.

Paul has not hesitated to express the close relationship between himself and Onesimus, both in calling him his "child" (v. 10), and in describing his return as the sending of his heart (v. 12). Now he begins to approach the second purpose of this letter, which is to inspire Philemon, not only to forgive Onesimus, but to send him back to Paul.

In verse 13 Paul clearly acknowledges his desire, which was to have Onesimus remain in his service. He again asserts his authority, assuming as a matter of course that he is entitled to the service of his subordinates. Again, he instantly disarms his statement by insisting that he wants a free will offering on Philemon's part, not an offering based on coercion (v. 14).

Paul is well aware of the fact that in spite of his plea on Onesimus' behalf, Philemon was likely to have serious reservations about the justice of forgiving a runaway slave, much less freeing him and returning him to Paul, which would seem like rewarding felony. The standard punishment for a recaptured runaway slave was crucifixion—a warning to the rest of the slave population. In verses 15 and 16 Paul shrewdly suggests that Onesimus' escape was part of God's providence, and that the relationship of Christian to Christian takes precedence over societal expectations. Implied in all of this is that Onesimus, in becoming a Christian, has indeed become a "new creation" (see II Cor. 5:17), and that the old rules no longer apply. Verse 17 brings Onesimus' new nature into play. Paul assumes a basic equality (established in Christ) between himself and Philemon. If this is so, there is a basic, Christian to Christian, equality between Paul and Onesimus, and thus between Onesimus and Philemon.

In the ancient world, when one person bought a slave from another, or bought freedom for a slave, it was expected that the buyer cover any debts which the slave had accrued. This is what Paul offers to do in verse 18. Indeed, he turns this into a written contract in 19a. He is so eager that Philemon consent to this transaction that he cannot refrain from reminding him of his (Philemon's) immeasurable debt. Paul was instrumental in Philemon's salvation. He makes it clear in verse 20 that he would very much appreciate a favor in return, the favor being nothing less than Onesimus' return.

Verse 21 is another example of Paul's curious balancing act between authority and tact. "Confident of your compliance" stresses his rightful expectations; "knowing that you will do more than I say" gives Philemon room to freely respond to these expectations.

"Get a room ready for me" (22a), given the context of Paul's imprisonment, is a profound expression of encouragement to his friends. It not only witnesses to his unquenchable hope, but also to his dauntlessness in the face of adversity. As always, Paul credits petitionary prayer with a very real effectiveness (22b).

The persons sending greetings with Paul to Philemon (vv. 23-24) are the very same persons sending greetings with him to the Church at Colossae (see Col. 4:10-14). This argues for a close proximity in time between the two letters, as well as witnesses to the fact that Paul had some good company during his imprisonment in Rome. He concludes this letter with a benediction on the theme of grace (v. 25).

## *Questions for Personal Reflection/Group Discussion*

1. The story of Onesimus is a powerful Christian "success" story—from slave to bishop. How has your own experience of faith been a powerful success story?
2. (a) Can you think of any areas in addition to the eventual abolition of slavery where Christianity has transformed the "ways of the world?"
   (b) What are some areas that still stand in need of the transforming power of the Christian faith?
   (c) How can you personally help with this process of transformation?
3. Has anyone every made a request of you somewhat similar to Paul's request of Philemon? Please describe the situation.

# *Colossians*

## Introduction

Tychicus, who delivered Paul's "private" letter to Philemon and accompanied Onesimus back to Colossae (4:7-9), also served as messenger for Paul's general letter to the Colossians. The church located at Colossae, a small city about a hundred miles east of Ephesus, was not founded by Paul himself (2:1). His method was to establish a Christian community in the largest city of the area—in this case, Ephesus—and to have his own disciples—in this case, Epaphras (1:7)—develop mission churches in the secondary cities of the district. Certain details in the letter, such as his shift from "Gentiles" to "you" in 1:27, indicate that the Colossian Church was primarily Gentile.

Epaphras had journeyed to Rome seeking Paul's help. The Church at Colossae was in danger of capitulating to an "empty, seductive philosophy" (2:8). This "new" teaching was not so much a heresy (a distortion of the Christian faith) as it was a competing religious system, a religious system which claimed not only to incorporate the best of Christianity, but to go considerably beyond it.

While we do not know the composition and teachings of this competing "faith" with exactitude, Paul's letter to the Colossians provides enough evidence for us to be able to make a fairly accurate reconstruction of its doctrine. It is an incipient form of Gnosticism (from the Greek word *gnosis,* which means "knowledge"): an esoteric system of secret "learning" and ascetic practices by means of which one eventually worked one's way into a state of "salvation." While Epaphras and, consequently, St. Paul, were probably combatting several different schools of this philosophy, all forms would hold the following postulates in common:

1. The basic assumption—which was claimed as Revelation—that matter was evil and spirit (in the sense of incorporeity) was good. Applying this presupposition to God, it follows that God, who is immaterial and good, could *not* have created the world, which is material and bad. To account for the fact of creation, the Gnostics posited a series of astrological, angelic, and/or demonic emanations running, much like a ladder, from God to the world. In this way God would not be implicated in material creation.

2. Human beings, with their dual dimensions of spirit and body, were a complex mixture of good and evil. According to Gnosticism, a person's goal should be to work oneself up the ladder of emanations—to transcend his or her bodily limitations by progressing to higher and higher levels of spiritual attainment.

3. To climb the ladder it was necessary to have the right initiation, the right knowledge, and the right passwords for each of a multitude of levels. These were the carefully guarded secrets of Gnosticism.

Sharing the above assumptions, there were apparently two main schools of Gnostic practice:

(a) The ascetic wing maintained that in order to climb the spiritual ladder one had to free oneself from one's enslavement to the body. To do this a complicated pattern of ascetic practices was devised. Heterodox Jews who turned to Gnosticism advocated a return to the Jewish dietary regulations as part of the necessary asceticism. Special days were also observed.

(b) The libertine wing maintained that since the body was of no consequence anyway, it simply did not matter what one did with it. Taking its cue from the practices of certain of the mystery rites, especially the Dionysian, libertine Gnostics held that the best way to overcome the body was to transcend it through orgiastic drinking and sex.

It is easy to see why Gnosticism was so popular. At first glance it looked liked a formidable and respectable philosphy. Christianity, in comparison, appeared too simple and straightforward. On the surface the Gnostic approach could well seem more exciting: there was the attraction of being an initiate, one who was admitted to the inner circle of the hidden mysteries of the universe. There was much lore to master and many levels to climb. There was the challenge of a demanding asceticism or an equally demanding debauchery.

The Gnostic threat stimulated Paul to some of his most profound insights concerning the nature and role of Christ. The basic assumption of Gnosticism, applied to Christ, denied His humanity, His status as Creator, and posited many mediators (all the astrological and angelic intermediaries between God and the world) in addition to Him. Paul countered by stressing the Incarnation, Christ as Creator, and Christ as the sole mediator of redemption. In addition, to undercut the Gnostic pretension of secret knowledge, Paul introduced a specficially Christian *gnosis*, based on the fact that in Christ "every treasure of wisdom and knowledge is hidden" (2:3). This contemplative dimension laid the foundation for a specifically Christian philosophy.

Paul's authorship of Colossians has been questioned on the grounds that (a) the theology, especially the Christology, is too developed; (b) the vocabulary which he uses in this letter is quite different from his vocabulary in earlier letters; (c) Gnosticism per se is a second, not a first, century phenomenon.

These arguments can be effectively countered by noting that:

(a) It is only to be expected that Paul's understanding of Christ, as that of any other Christian, would deepen and develop over the years. His imprisonment (first in Caesarea, then in Rome) provided him with the quietness and the lack of activity conducive to the profound meditation which is indicated in this letter. His insights in Colossians are not qualitatively new, but rather build on earlier perceptions, such as I Corinthians 8:6b (". . . one Lord Jesus Christ through whom everything was made and through whom we live") and Romans 8:35-39 ("Who will separate us from the love of Christ? . . . ).

(b) Paul's "new" vocabulary in this letter is, for the most part, the philosophical vocabulary of the position he is refuting. He wants to meet the Gnostics on their own ground, and uses their own words and concepts against them.

(c) It is true that Gnosticism as a philosophic system did not reach its "classical" expression until the second century. Its greatest exponents, however, needed something to systematize, and the materials for this eventual systematization were already present in the first century (and even earlier). The basic assumptions of Gnosticism were by and large the standard assumptions of the ancient world.

We consider Paul to be the author of this letter, writing from Rome in the year 60 or 61.

## Chapter 10: Christ as Lord of Creation and Redemption

*Please read Colossians 1:1-2:3.* As usual, Paul begins his letter with a reference to his authority. He is an apostle—one who has been sent forth to proclaim the Good News of Jesus Christ—not on his own prerogative, but "by the will of God" (1:1). He calls Timothy not "his" brother, but "our" brother, emphasizing the new family relationships that apply to all Christians: all Christians are brothers and sisters to one another. "Holy ones" (1:2a) is literally "saints;" that is, those who have accepted the Gospel and are living it out in their lives. He calls God "our Father," again bringing out the new family relationships among Christians, where God is Father of us all. "Grace and peace" is Paul's habitual invocation, "grace" referring to God's favor, and "peace" to the concrete blessings which this favor carries with it.

As is customary with the typical Greek letter of the time, a thanksgiving follows the greeting. This was not only proper etiquette toward the Colossians, but also toward God; it is only fitting that we should thank Him for what He has already given us before petitioning Him for further blessings.

In the course of our study of Paul's preceding letters, we have already encountered the word "Lord" several times, and have noted what a packed term this is. In the context of this particular letter and its polemic against the Colossian "heresy," the exclusivity of this title stands out. If a person called Jesus "Lord" (1:3), he or she could not use the designation for anyone else, whether it be other gods, the Roman Emperor, or, as some of the Colossians were apparently doing, any of the angelic intermediaries between God and the world.

Paul celebrates the three great virtues of faith, love, and hope in verse 4. A Christian's faith is "in" Christ Jesus, meaning that there is a relational solidarity between Jesus and the believer, a relational solidarity which inspires faith, not as a blind leap, but as confident trust grounded in real experience. This kind of faith naturally overflows into love for one's neighbor. In this verse Paul sees hope as the motivating power behind both faith and love. The hope to which he refers is the Christian's assurance that the relationship he has begun with God in this life will indeed by fulfilled in the next. This hope is a constituent part of the Gospel (1:5).

Verse 6 brings out the power inherent in the Gospel. Paul was probably thinking of what we now know as Mark 4:8 (the Gospel had not yet achieved written form; Paul was likely using a "sayings source" of our Lord's teachings), the only other passage in the Bible which links the verbs "bearing fruit" and "growing," referring to the efficacy of God's Word.

Paul's mention of "everywhere in the world" (1:6b) is actu-

ally an appeal to the Gospel's authority on the basis of its catholic-
ity. The point is that the Gospel preached and accepted at Colossae
is the very same Gospel which is proclaimed and accepted throughout the rest of the world. There is probably a subtle slam intended
here on the Gnostics, whose teachings, chameleon-like, took on
strikingly different forms depending on the locality of the sect
and the personality of its leader.

Verses 6c-7 are Paul's personal endorsement of the ministry
of Epaphras, the founder, on Paul's instructions, of the Church
at Colossae, and still his official representative. He is the one
who has brought Paul news from the Colossian Church (1:8).

The word "this" which Paul uses at the beginning of verse
9 refers to Epaphras' entire report, including the sobering news
of their near apostasy. This is apparent from the content of his
prayer, which employs two major Gnostic catchwords, "fullness"
and "knowledge." Gnosticism bragged that it, and only it, offered
the fullness of a truly complete spiritual system. This "fullness"
consisted of the secret (and supposedly Revealed) "knowledge"
of various angelic intermediaries and the passwords needed to
get beyond them.

Paul detoxifies these words by using them in a Christian
sense. He informs the Colossians that he has indeed been praying
that they may grow into "full knowledge" (v. 9), but that this
"full knowledge" is knowledge of God's will, which—unlike the
Gnostic "knowledge" of angels and passwords—spills over into
the practicalities of daily living (1:10). He links the attainment
of such knowledge to the God-given gifts of "wisdom" and
"spiritual insight" (9b). "Wisdom" echoes the wisdom tradition
within the Hebrew Scriptures, which is a unique blending of
theological understanding and practical application. Similarly,
the Greek for "spiritual insight" carries with it the connotation
of being able to apply spiritual principles in a concrete way.
Taking verses 9 and 10 together, it is apparent that Paul sees a
reciprocal relationship between good theology and good works;
for a Christian, one leads to the other.

The word "theology" used above is actually somewhat mis-leading. St. Paul never employs this term; it is not used in the entire Bible. When Paul speaks about the "knowledge of God" he is talking about a personal knowledge derived from a personal relationship. This is undoubtedly the biggest difference between Christianity and Gnosticism: a Christian's knowledge is a living knowledge originating from a living God, while a Gnostic's knowledge goes no further and deeper than his or her own imag-ination. For a Christian, then, theology can be called "good" only if it flows from a living relationship with God in Christ; if it is not based on this, but on speculation, it is no better and not much different than Gnostic "knowledge."

Paul is confident that God will empower the Colossians to "stand fast" in their faith (1:11); this empowerment is nothing less than sharing in His "glory." In other words, a Christian's steadfastness reflects God's own nature. The phrase "even to endure joyfully whatever may come" (11b) hints at the likelihood of ridicule and/or persecution, and carries with it the nuance of non-retaliation.

The prayer concludes with thanksgiving (1:12-14). Again, it is noteworthy that Paul chooses to give thanks for precisely those elements of the Christian faith which the Gnostics were denying. Thus, it is the Father (not one's own superior "knowl-edge") which makes one "worthy" of heaven (v. 12). It is God (not the power of one's secret passwords) who delivers us from evil, just as He delivered the Israelites from the domination of the Egyptians. It is God (not angelic intermediaries) who saves us through forgiveness (v. 14).

Note Paul's use of the past and present tenses in these verses: "having made you worthy" (v. 12), "rescued us" (v. 13), and "have redemption" (v. 14) serve to underline the fact that it is God—not we in our own eagerness to learn the Gnostic secrets—who has taken the initiative in our salvation. The Christian life is basically one of responding to God's freely given grace. Our salvation has already been accomplished. We do not, like the

Gnostics, have to continually try to save ourselves through the attainment of ever higher, and supposedly deeper, "knowledge."

The next section of Paul's letter to the Colossians, 1:15-20, is one of the most exalted Christological passages in the New Testament. Most scholars agree that this text is a hymn, or poem. They disagree, however, about the origin of this hymn; some say that it is an adaptation of a Jewish hymn to Wisdom, others that it was part of the liturgy of the very early Church, some that Paul composed it specifically for this letter, yet others a combination of the above. At any rate, its content admirably fits the context of Colossians. We shall assume that it is the work of Paul, whose mystical heights we have already encountered in Romans 8:35-39 and 11:33-36.

It is a pity that the *New American Bible*, unlike the *Jerusalem Bible*, has not attempted to visually capture the poetic structure of this text. We offer the following format, using the NAB translation, but our own arrangement. The spacing is intended to convey the parallelisms—all phrases directly underneath one another are echoes of the same basic thought. (Incidentally, the arbitrary nature of the established verses becomes apparent through this layout.)

(15)  a  He is the image of the invisible God,

       b     the first-born of all creatures.

(16)  a       In him everything in heaven and on earth was created.

       b         things visible and invisible,

       c            whether thrones or dominations, principalities
                       or powers;

       d        all were created through him, and for him.

(17)  a      He is before all else that is.

       b        In him everything continues in being.

(18)  a    It is he who is head of the body, the church;

       b  He who is the beginning,

| | |
|---|---|
| c | the first-born of the dead, |
| d | so that primacy may be his in everything. |
| (19) | It pleased God to make absolute fullness reside in him |
| (20) a | and by means of him, |
| b | to reconcile everything in his person, |
| c | both on earth and in the heavens, |
| d | making peace through the blood of his cross. |

Paul composed this celebration of the nature and role of Christ to counter the diminution of Christ's status according to Gnostic doctrine. He does not, at this point, take on the Gnostics directly, but this supreme statement of the meaning of Christ—replete with transformed Gnostic vocabulary—is intended to bring back wavering Christians to orthodoxy.

He begins with a phrase that he knows will impact profoundly on the Colossians: "He is the image of the invisible God" (15a). The pivotal word in this phrase is "image," in Greek, *eikon*, the word from which we derive "icon." Its meaning is "representation;" not, however, in a static sense, but in the active sense of "to make present."

The word *eikon* would be a powerful trigger-word for all Christians in Colossae, whatever their ethnic or economic standing. It would remind Jews of Wisdom (which, in the Greek version of the Hebrew Scriptures was at times described as God's *eikon*); it would remind Greeks of the Logos, or ordering principle, of God (in the writings of some of the Greek philosophers, the Logos was commonly identified as God's *eikon*). Those who had had no contact with either scripture or philosophy would still be touched by this term, in as much as *eikon* was the common word for portrait.

To say that Jesus "is the image of the invisible God" is to communicate nothing less than the fact that Jesus is God's visible counterpart. Jesus represents God, not only as His representative, but in the deeper sense of actually making Him present. This phrase is the source of the currently popular slogan, "If you want to see God, look at Jesus."

Paul's second phrase, "the first-born of all creatures" (15b), sounds a bit suspect to us, because we read "first-born" as having to do with time; thus, Paul seems to be saying that Jesus was a created being, although the first of those created—this is the Gnostic position! Actually, "first-born" is commonly used in the Hebrew Scriptures as an honorific title. It is a title designating pre-eminence, and is one of the titles used in connection with the Messiah (see, for example, Psalm 89:28). In Hebrew, "first-born" was the practical equivalent of the Greek "Lord." To say that Jesus is "the first-born of all creatures" is the same as to say that He is "Lord of all creation."

The reason why Jesus is called "first-born" or "Lord" of creation is given in verse 16. The Greek text of this verse actually begins with the conjunction "because." A more literal translation of 15b and 16a would read: "the first-born of all creatures, *because* in him everything in heaven and on earth was created."

The Gnostics claimed that Christ himself was created. Here (v. 16) Paul is celebrating Jesus as the Creator. The Gnostics held that matter, or the "visible," was evil, and that spirit, or the "invisible" was good. Here Paul proclaims Christ's Lordship over all creation, both matter and spirit, visible and invisible.

The "everything" of 16a is broken down into the "things visible and invisible" of 16b. In 16c Paul subdivides the "invisible" of 16b into four ranks of angels which the Hellenistic (Greek-speaking) Jews believed guarded the seven levels of heaven. These are the "thrones or dominations, principalities or powers." Paul does not contest the existence of these angelic beings. What he does repudiate, however, is their validity as objects of worship (see Col. 2:18). By naming them here, as examples of beings which owe their existence to Christ, Paul is emphasizing their created status. They are dependent on Christ, and should not be worshipped in their own right.

Paul uses three important prepositions in reference to Christ in verse 16: "in him" (16a), and "through him" and "for him" (16d). "In him" refers to Christ as the centering point of all creation; He provides the context, or milieu, in which creation is both possible and actual. "Through him" is causal, and refers to Jesus' role as the agent of creation. "For him" views Christ as the goal, or endpoint of creation, the Person toward whom all goodness, beauty, and truth tend.

"He is before all else that is," 17a, parallels 15b, "the first-born of all creatures." The phrase "He is" is intended in an ontological sense; that is, Jesus contains, and has always contained, the fullness of Being in His own person. Paul's usage here prefigures that of St. John, who frequently describes Jesus in terms of absolute Being (see, for example, John 8:58, where Jesus says " . . . before Abraham came to be, I AM.") "Before" refers both to Jesus' being in point of time (what theologians call His "pre-existence") and in point of importance (no other being can begin to compare with Him).

"In him everything continues in being," 17b, complements 16a, "In him everything in heaven and on earth was created." It is an elaboration on the significance of the preposition "in" when used in connection with Christ's power to create and to sustain His creation.

It is impossible to capture the power of this thought in only one translation. The *New English Bible* renders this phrase " . . . all things are held together in him;" the *Jerusalem Bible* translates " . . . he holds all things in unity;" and the *Revised Standard Version* offers " . . . in him all things hold together." These three translations, plus the *New American Bible's* "In him everything continues in being," *taken together* begin to convey some of the depth of meaning embedded in this phrase. It is a powerfully beautiful statement of the entire universe receiving its cohesiveness as a gift from Christ.

Our layout of these verses as poetry indicates that the next

line, 18a, "It is he who is head of the body, the church," is
parallel to lines 15b, "the first-born of all creatures" and 17a,
"He is before all else that is." The poem has been arranged in
this way because in Paul's thought there is a very real connection
between Christ's pre-eminence and His role as "head" of the
Church. His leadership of the Church *makes* him pre-eminent in
the same way that his being Creator makes Him pre-eminent.

In this poem Paul not only reaches new heights in his understanding of Christ, but also in his conception of Church. For the
first time in any of his letters, he makes an identification between
Christ and the Church. The Church is nothing less than His body.
It is a living organism with Jesus Himself as its "head," "head"
signifying that Christ is its authority, its guiding spirit, and its
energizing force.

Line 18b, "He who is the beginning," marks the start of the
second stanza. The first has celebrated Jesus as Lord of Creation.
The second will celebrate Him as Lord of Redemption.

The word "beginning" which, incidently, the *Jerusalem Bible*
capitalizes in this context, refers to Jesus as the beginning—the
Source, the motivating power—of a new, redeemed humanity.
"He who is the beginning" proclaims the fact that Jesus is the
New Adam, and that in Him humankind is enabled to taste the
fullness of being, the fullness of life in relationship with God,
which the Old Adam had made impossible. The sense of this line
echoes II Corinthians 5:17, " . . . if anyone is in Christ, he is a
new creation. The old order has passed away; now all is new."

"The first-born of the dead," line 18c, refers, of course, to
Jesus' Resurrection. It parallels line 15b, "the first-born of all
creatures," by proclaiming Jesus' pre-eminence in the order of
Redemption. The reality of the Resurrection is absolutely essential
to Jesus' pre-eminence, as is indicated by the strong connection
between line 18c and 18d: "*so that* primacy may be his in everything."

As the layout in poetic form makes clear, 18c is a further

complement to 18a, "It is he who is head of the body, the church." Indeed, it is the reality of the Resurrection which makes Jesus head of the Church.

Verse 19, "It pleased God to make absolute fullness reside in him," repudiates the Gnostic notion that spiritual fullness can only be found in the whole host of angelic mediators and the initiate's progression through their various spheres of influence. Paul claims Christ as the only mediator between us and the Father. And Jesus' mediation is not, like the negative "mediation" of the Gnostic's angels, designed to protect God by keeping us away from Him; Jesus' mediation is the positive mediation which brings us directly to the Father.

Some versions translate verse 19 is such a way as to bring out the identity between Jesus and the Father. Thus, the *Revised Standard Version* has "For in him the fulness of God was pleased to dwell" and the *New English Bible*, even more forcefully, states "For in him the complete being of God, by God's own choice, came to dwell."

Again, there is a parallel between Christ's headship of the Church (18a) and the "fullness" which resides in Him (19). His being head of the Church, the person who empowers a new, redeemed humanity, is an important expression of our Lord's perfection of being.

Verse 20 completes Paul's description of the redemptive work of Christ and concludes the poem as a whole. "By means of him" (20a) stresses Jesus' instrumentality in effecting reconciliation.

This reconciliation is not merely personal, but cosmic in scope (20b, c). Just as all creation was implicated in the fall, all creation shares in the Redemption. Implied here is the basic Christian understanding that creation is basically good (not, as the Gnostics would have it, fundamentally evil). The Lord Jesus is not satisfied with a partial redemption, excluding matter and exalting the spirit. No, He is busy effecting a total Redemption, which is, among other things, a real reconciliation between matter and spirit through the inSpiriting of matter. The healing, reconciling power of the sacraments stands as a reminder that the Redemption of ourselves and of our world is right now taking place.

Line 20d, "making peace through the blood of his cross," reminds us of the *how* of Redemption. Christ did not redeem us and our world through teaching or example, important as these may be, but through the transforming power of His sacrificial love.

Paul's hymn, or poem, 1:15-20, has been universal in scope; it is nothing less than a celebration of the cosmic Christ. At this point Paul applies the exalted theology of the hymn directly to the Colossians. The concept of alienation (1:21) implies freedom of choice. A person chooses to become alienated, and the apostle implies that the former distance between God and the Colossians was the direct result of their "evil deeds." Again, we see a correlation in Paul's thought of good deeds leading one to God, and evil deeds leading one away from Him. In the specifically ethical section of this letter, Paul will mention these evil deeds in detail (3:5-9).

Alienation, however, is a thing of the past for those who have accepted Christ and are living according to His way. Jesus' sacrificial death has achieved reconciliation—the exact opposite of alienation—for those who believe. Paul uses the carefully wrought phrase "in his mortal body by dying" (1:22) to underline the importance of Jesus' humanity in the process of salvation.

As we have seen, the Gnostics, because of their belief that matter was evil, simply could not accept the fact that Jesus had a real body, that he was a real person. Paul counters by stressing the Incarnation ("in his mortal body") and the Crucifixion ("by dying") as pivotal facts for our redemption. It is precisely Jesus' sacrifice of Himself as a flesh-and-blood human being that establishes His solidarity with us, and enables us to become acceptable sacrifices to the Father (see Romans 12:1).

The Colossians were apparently not doing a very good job

of holding fast to their faith, so this is the virtue to which Paul admonishes them in verse 23. He challenges them to be "firmly grounded;" in other words, to be solid, not to alter their faith to accommodate Gnostic teachings. He calls them back to the simple hope of the true Gospel; probably many were beginning to despair of this hope because the Gnostic way of salvation was so strenuous and so lengthy. He reminds them that his Gospel, unlike the "gospel" according to Gnosticism, is an expression of the one, true Gospel, which is the same throughout the world.

Since it was not himself but one of his disciples who had founded the Church at Colossae, Paul takes the opportunity to further introduce himself to the recipients of this letter (1:24-2:3). His vision of the Church as the body of Christ (24b) includes *all* Christians, not just those in the communities which he has personally established.

The "suffering" of which Paul speaks (24a) is his suffering in prison on account of the Gospel, for the sake of the whole Church. He finds meaning in this suffering—indeed, he can call it his "joy"—because he knows that his suffering is an expression of his solidarity with Christ. Speaking figuratively, he states that he is filling up what is "lacking in the sufferings of Christ." This phrase is not to be understood literally, as if Christ were really lacking in anything, but as a metaphorical expression of Paul's incredible closeness to Christ, a closeness which enables him to make Jesus' suffering his own. This intimate connection with Christ through the cross of vicarious suffering is not just Paul's prerogative, but the privilege of every Christian. As part of His body, the Church, our sufferings are really Jesus' own. Through Him, our sufferings become not only meaningful, but are transformed into vehicles of redemption for ourselves and for others.

Paul refers to his "commission" in verse 25, meaning his official authorization by no one less than God to proclaim the Good News. Notice how he claims that his commission empowers him to herald the Gospel "in its fullness." "Fullness" was one of the favorite words of the Gnostics, who held that they, and they alone, held the keys to the fullness of enlightenment. Paul, in effect, is turning this word against them, counterclaiming that it is the Gospel, not the Gnostic teachings, which contains everything needed for enlightenment—and salvation.

In verses 26 and 27 Paul considers one particular aspect of the fullness of the Gospel, a decisive aspect for people like the Colossians. This is the "mystery" of the Good News being extended to the Gentiles, an event which most of the Jews of Paul's day looked upon with astonishment and revulsion. The word "mystery" in this context refers to something previously hidden which has now been revealed. The phrase "the mystery of Christ *in* you, your hope of glory" emphasizes the believer's relational solidarity with Christ, a solidarity which is the foundation of a Christian's hope.

One of the most striking features of Gnosticism was that it prided itself on being the religion of the intellectual elite (the only persons who could possibly grasp its esoteric doctrine). "Common" people, according to the Gnostics, were hopeless and were best left alone to languish in their ignorance. Paul takes on this element of Gnostic teaching in verse 28, where in the original Greek he repeats three times the fact that the Gospel is for *everyone.*

Paul sees his great task in life ("For this I work and struggle"—v. 29) as being able to offer the Good News of salvation to everyone, Gentile or Jew, slave or free, intelligent or otherwise. The "energy" he cites as his motivating force is an oblique reference to his empowerment by the Holy Spirit.

Continuing his personal introduction (2:1), Paul mentions the struggle (given the context of his imprisonment, this struggle is probably the struggle of intense petitionary prayer) he has been experiencing on behalf of the Christians in Colossae and in the neighboring city of Laodicea (where this letter will also be read; see Col. 4:16). Thinking particularly of the Christians in Laodicea (2:2a), he expresses the same concern for the strength of their faith and the quality of their love that he has already expressed to the Colossians (see 1:9-14). He also asks (in effect, prays) that they may receive the blessing of knowledge, "knowledge" here meaning a practical understanding of the mystery of God as revealed in Christ.

He concludes what has become a prayer for the Laodiceans by adding a liturgical, and anti-Gnostic flourish (2:3). Christ—not a host of angelic intermediaries—is the locus of all wisdom and knowledge. These treasures are "hidden" in Christ in the sense that He, and only He, contains the fullness of salvation.

*Questions for Personal Reflection/Group Discussion*

1. Gnosticism, in the sense of a complex system of self-salvation, is very much alive and well in our modern world. The "old" Gnosticism of angelic intermediaries may have died out, but it has been replaced by many other ladders of achievement which supposedly lead to salvation. What are some contemporary forms of Gnosticism that you have noticed and what are their distinguishing characteristics?
2. How did ancient forms of Gnosticism distort orthodox teaching about Christ?
3. How do modern forms of Gnosticism deny Christ?
4. Why do you think that varieties of Gnostic belief and practice have been so popular throughout the ages?
5. In what sense does hope empower faith and love?
6. Throughout his letter to the Colossians, St. Paul cleverly picks up the major terms of the Gnostics, then turns these terms against them by using them in a specifically Christian way. Define the following terms as Paul uses them to stand for uniquely Christian realities:
   (a) "fullness"
   (b) "knowledge"
   (c) "mystery"
7. Paraphrase Paul's great hymn to Christ in Colossians 1:15-

20. In other words, transpose his thoughts and images into thoughts and images of your own.

8. What does it mean to say that Jesus is the *image* of God the Father?

9. What does Paul mean when he uses the following prepositions in connection with Christ?
   (a) "in"
   (b) "through"
   (c) "for"

10. What are some of the implications behind the revealed reality that "the Church is the body of Christ?"

11. How are the sacraments signs that the total Redemption of ourselves and of our world that Jesus promised has already begun?

12. How can suffering be meaningful for a Christian?

## Chapter 11:    Through, With and In Christ

*Please read Colossians 2:4-4:18.* At this point Paul becomes more direct, both in his advice, and in his criticism of Gnosticism. The "all this" to which he refers in 2:4 looks back to everything which Paul has already said about Christ in this letter, and also looks forward to all that he has yet to say. The verb for "delude" literally means to defraud one through faulty reasoning. "Specious arguments" is a colloquial expression equivalent to our "smooth line" or "fast talk." Apparently one of the things which made Gnosticism so dangerous was that, on the surface, it sounded so impressive. It was easy for the credulous to get caught up in its high-sounding rhetoric. In this sense, Gnosticism was very much like today's cults, which employ the same type of superficially imposing, but specious argumentation to lure the unwary into their ranks.

Paul reminds the Colossians that although it is not possible for him to be with them physically, as a fellow Christian—part of the same body of Christ of which they are a part—he is present to them in spirit (2:5a). He overstates his happiness in 2b in order to keep his letter positive; he is really admonishing them to follow the military virtues of "order" and "firmness" (5b). The Colossian Church is a church under siege. In order to survive it will have to adopt the kind of discipline that is customary in the military.

Verse 6 is literally "As therefore you received Christ Jesus the Lord, so walk in him." The sense, which the *NAB* captures with its use of the word "Continue," is one of remaining faithful (in terms of morality as well as theology) to one's previous commitment.

Paul mixes two of his favorite metaphors in 7a, one from farming, "rooted in him," and one from construction, "built up in him." In this case they mix rather well, giving us a picture of a mature Christian, who is not only grounded in Christ, but continues to grow in Him. "As you were taught" is another reference to the validity of Epaphras' ministry. Again in this epistle, Paul cites "gratitude," or thanksgiving, as one of the hallmarks of Christian faith.

In verse 8 Paul becomes quite blunt, both in his warning ("See to it") and in his description of the Gnostic threat. Picking up another of their pet terms, he calls it a "philosophy," but qualifies this philosophy as "empty" and "seductive." Gnosticism made much of its ancient roots; Paul calls these "mere human traditions;" in other words, teachings not based on Revelation but speculation.

In the last phrase of this verse, "a philosophy based on cosmic powers rather than on Christ," Paul is attacking the Gnostic doctrine of angelic intermediaries. He is also punning on the Greek word for "cosmic powers," which is literally "elements," and can mean elements in the sense of the most elementary parts or principles of something, as well as elements in the sense of crucial life substances (such as earth, air, fire, and water), each of which was believed to have its angelic and astrological manifestation. Paul is saying, in effect, that the "high" Gnostic doctrine of angelic intermediaries is, in reality, so elementary as to be simple-minded.

Colossians 2:9-15 echoes Paul's magnificent poem in 1:15-20. It especially develops the redemptive role of Christ (the theme of the second stanza of the poem). This whole section is a profound reminder, or review, of basic Christianity.

Paul begins by making a shocking and repulsive statement from the point of view of Gnosticism, that "In Christ the fullness of deity resides *in bodily form*" (v. 9). This affirmation was not only impossible but blasphemous to the Gnostics, who considered all matter in general, the human body in particular, as a manifestation of evil. To say as Paul does that "the fullness of deity resides in bodily form" was to make a radical pronouncement concerning the basic goodness of the material world.

Paul was also underlining the reality of the true humanity of Christ, or Incarnation. Christ, for those Gnostics who allowed Him into their systems, was a bodiless spirit. Paul is implying that Jesus' Incarnation is a constitutive element of Redemption; in other words, if the fullness of reality had not resided in Christ in bodily form, there would be no Redemption.

Because Jesus was fully human, one of us in everything but sin, the believer experiences a real, not merely symbolic, solidarity with Him. It is this solidarity which enables the Christian to share in "this fullness" (9b), the very fullness of God.

Verse 10 restates the pre-eminence of Christ. All the ranks of angels (which Paul sums up in his reference to the "principalities" and "powers") are subject to Him.

Throughout the rest of his reflection on the meaning of Redemption (vv. 11-15), Paul alludes to Baptism and the radical transformation which it effects in the life of the adult convert. This transformation has been made possible by the believer's fundamental solidarity with Christ.

The ascetic wing of Gnosticism—those who insisted on all sorts of rules and regulations to "tame" the body—had adopted the Jewish rite of circumcision and adapted it to serve its own ends; namely, mortification of the body. In verse 11, Paul contrasts Christian "circumcision" (that is, Baptism) with Gnostic circumcision and, as usual, finds the Christian practice far superior to the Gnostic. Christian Baptism—unlike Gnostic circumcision, which is "administered by hand" and is, by implication, worthless because it is merely a human tradition (see 2:8)—"strips off the carnal body completely." "Carnal body" is literally "body of flesh." Paul consistently uses this phrase to designate humankind's propensity to sin. Thus, when Paul speaks about Baptism stripping off the fleshly body completely, he is talking about the total reorientation of personality, involving both body (material) and soul (immaterial), which Christian Baptism effects.

He alludes to the baptismal ritual of the early Church in verse 12, a ritual which prescribed total immersion. The descent of the adult convert into the water was symbolic of the actual death which his or her "old" self was undergoing; ascending from the water signified the real reorientation of the "new" person, a reorientation made possible through solidarity with Jesus' Resurrection.

The Greek of this verse is fascinating. The verbs for "buried" and "raised" are both preceded by the prefix *syn* which states *total identification between the actions of two or more people*: the action of one becomes the action of the other(s); in this case, Christ's action becomes that of the believer. Literally the verbs read "co-buried" and "co-raised." The Greek is able to capture, much more than the English, the real and really transforming solidarity of the Christian with Christ.

Verse 13 emphasizes God's initiative in the redemptive process. Again the momentous prefix *syn* occurs, this time before the verb for "gave new life." The sense is that God gave us new life in Jesus by forgiving all our sins. The past tense indicates that this is an accomplished fact.

The term that Paul uses for "bond" in verse 14 is the legal

term referring to a promissory note. The "bond" is our own sinfulness, which stands against us like an outstanding note. In a daring image, Paul portrays Jesus' sacrificial death (and our acceptance of and participation in His death through Baptism) as revoking the bond of our sinfulness. Because of Jesus' sacrifice, our sinfulness no longer stands as a barrier between us and God.

Paul views the "principalities and powers"—the angelic intermediaries of Gnosticism—as hostile to God in verse 15. Angels, of course, are not God's enemies in and of themselves. In a Gnostic context, however, where they are held to be essential mediators between God and humankind, they become such. From this perspective Jesus' life, death, and Resurrection—where He is revealed to be the only mediator between God and people—is a total debacle for the Gnostic "principalities and powers." God, like a victorious Roman general leading his captives in a victory procession, exposes these hostile angelic powers to ridicule.

Having completed his review of the meaning of Redemption, Paul proceeds to tackle many of the specific religious practices of the Gnostics in the next section of his letter, (2:16-23). The observance of certain dietary regulations (such as not eating meat and not drinking wine) was intended to serve as a put-down of the body (16a). The celebration of certain special days was supposed to put one in the good graces of the angelic intermediaries (16b).

It is noteworthy that Paul does grant these practices a certain validity, they are at least "a shadow of things to come." But the duration of their legitimacy is now over, because that which was to come has come. He whom they served as shadow—namely, Christ—has come in bodily form (v. 17). There is a pun here on the word "body," which means (a) the physical reality, or Incarnation, of Christ; (b) the substance behind the shadow, and (c) the extended body of Christ, the Church.

The verb which the NAB translates as "to rob of one's prize" in 18a comes from the athletic arena and means to disqualify.

"Servility" should not modify "the worship of angels," but should stand in its own right as self-mortification. Paul is attacking two things here, self-righteous asceticism and angel worship. He sees these as the two deadly sins of Gnosticism.

Describing the typical Gnostic guru of the time, Paul claims that the revelation such a person has to offer is no real Revelation, but the deification of his or her "visionary" experience. As such it is the revelation, not of God, but of the seer's own pretentiousness (18b). Such a person is misguided and misguides others because he or she is not united with the "head," which, of course, is Christ (v. 19).

Again reminding the Colossians of their Baptism (compare with 2:12 above), through which they presumably died to the temptation to worship anyone besides Christ, Paul simply cannot understand how they can follow rules and regulations derived from other mediators (2:20). He cites some of these rules in verse 21, and goes on to ridicule them in verse 22; "things that perish in their use" are, literally feces. Such utterly worthless rules and regulations are man-made, not God-given. They seek to impress by giving the person who practices them a feeling of holiness, humbleness, and abstemiousness, but in reality they are willful expressions of pride (v. 23).

Paul returns to the theme of Baptism in 3:1-4, this time using it to introduce his ethical teachings. Colossians follows the pattern of most of his letters, which is that of doctrine followed by morality. This pattern reflects the important theological truth that Christian morality flows out of a Christian's relationship with Christ.

"Raised" in 3:1 is literally co-raised, again pointing to the Christian's solidarity, or identification, with Christ. Because of this solidarity, initiated through the contiguous realities of conversion and Baptism, the believer is expected to identify with Jesus' values. The phrase "seated at God's right hand" refers to the Resurrected Christ's position of power, or Lordship. Between the lines of this verse is the message that because of our identification with Him, Christ is empowering the Christian to live a life worthy of His calling.

In verse 2, Paul admonishes the Colossians to identify with the values and teachings of Jesus, not those of the world.

Verses 3 and 4 consider the Christian life from the perspective of past, present, and future. "You have died" (3a) states the qualitative change that the Christian *has already* undergone in his or her conversion/Baptism. Because of this qualitative change, which included the "death" of one's "old" self, and the birth of one's "new" self through a personal relationship with Christ, the believer *is now* "hidden," or contained, in Jesus' relationship with the Father (3b). The word "hidden" was another favorite Gnostic term. For them life was hidden in their secret teachings. For the Christian, life is hidden in a personal relationship with the Father through, with, and in Christ. This relationship *will come* to its complete fulfillment at the Second Coming ("When Christ our life appears") when we too will receive our resurrected bodies ("in glory")—verse 4.

Paul continues to use baptism imagery in the next main section of his letter, 3:5-17. The allusions to Baptism are so many that some scholars think that Paul has taken this portion of his letter from the baptismal catechesis of the early Church; it reads like a kind of moral catechism. At any rate, Paul is definitely reminding the Colossian Christians of some of the promises that they made when they became part of the Body of Christ through Baptism.

The baptismal instruction and imagery involved "putting to death" (3:5) or "putting aside" (3:7, 9) one's self, and "putting on a new person" (3:10), one which is "clothed with" (3:12) the Christian virtues. This transformation was actually acted out in the celebration of Baptism, where the person to be baptised stripped off his old clothes (removed the "old" self), descended naked into the baptismal water (allowed the old self to be killed), ascended from the water (became a "new" self through identification with Christ and His Resurrection), and was clothed with a white robe (accepted a new set of values, those of Christ).

The vices which Paul lists in 3:5 are peculiarly pagan vices (Jews, because of their different background, would tend to be tempted by different things), indicating that the Church at Colossae was largely Gentile. "Fornication" and "uncleanness" largely overlap, as do "passion," "evil desires," and "that lust which is idolatry." The latter three vices form a progressive triad: allowing oneself to be ruled by one's passions leads to a dwelling on evil which, in turn, eventually becomes a complete sell-out to the pleasure principle.

The concept of "God's wrath" (3:6) has been discussed at length in our commentary on Paul's letter to the Romans. Suffice it to say that these sins are obviously self-destructive, and that their very destructiveness can be seen as their self-contained "punishment." There is no need to posit God as stepping in and inflicting punishment.

The second listing of vices (v. 8) concerns those which have to do with the tongue, which Paul, following Jesus, considered to be particularly susceptible to evil. "Anger" refers to something which is steady, almost an habitual hatred. "Insults" is really blasphemy against another person, or slander.

Lying (9a) is singled out, probably because Paul has heard that it is rather widespread among the Colossians. Again Paul emphasizes the fact that a Christian has already "put aside," or stripped off, the old self (9a), and is now a new person (10a). Paul acknowledges the developmental, or deepening, character of the Christian life in 10b. The "knowledge" in which one grows has a practical aspect; it is not abstract knowledge, but relational knowledge, which manifests itself in action as well as thought. The "Creator" is Christ; it is He who, through our personal relationship with Him, forms us anew in His image. Our solidarity with Christ enables us to become the persons that we are intended to be.

In Christ all divisive human distinctions collapse because in

Him we are all part of the same Body, which makes us brothers and sisters to one another (v. 11).

At this point (3:12-17) Paul considers the virtues which are to replace the vices which he has just examined. The interesting thing about these virtues is that they are all conducive—indeed, essential—for life in community. The vices which he mentions lead to estrangement and isolation, whereas the virtues lead to reconciliation and community.

He begins by applying to the Christians at Colossae, the majority of whom were Gentiles, three special words which, until his apostolate to the Gentiles, had been reserved exclusively for the Jews. Paul acknowledges them as God's "chosen," "holy," and "beloved" (3:12). The very words which God has called His people, Israel, are now extended to all Christians, whatever their nationality, previous religion, race, level of culture, or social class. The virtues themselves, "heartfelt mercy," "kindness," "humility," "meekness," and "patience" stand in need of no explanation. Their challenge lies not in the realm of understanding, but in that of internalization and practice.

To "bear with one another" (13a) simply means that Christians must not give up on each other. Paul's emphasis on forgivensss (13b) probably reflects Jesus' petition in the Our Father, "and forgive us the wrong we have done as we forgive those who wrong us" (Matthew 6:12). As in I Corinthians 13, love—specifically in the sense of *agape*, which is Christ-centered, other-directed and, if need be, sacrificial—is the cohesive force behind the integration of the Christian as an individual and the harmony of Christians in community. Peace (not just the absence of conflict, but the fullness of life in relationship with God) is a primary expression of love, and another first order virtue (15a). Peace, both within the individual and within the Church, should be a natural expression of a Christian's solidarity with Christ.

Three times between verses 15b and 17 he admonishes the Colossians to be thankful. For Paul, thankfulness is not an optional or recommended part of the Christian life, but an essential expression of the Christian's transforming and empowering relationship with God.

Paul moves on to counsel the Colossians in terms of specific relationships (3:18-25). This particular form of exhortation, the "compendium of household duties," was a well-known feature of much Greek moral philosophy, from which Paul took it, Christianizing it in the process.

The very fact that Paul adopts such a form shows that he has become much more comfortable (although *resigned*, in fact, might be more accurate) with the idea of an indefinite period of time before the Second Coming. His advice to the married and to the unmarried in I Corinthians 7 was largely based on his expectation of the Lord's imminent Return: "In the present time of stress it seems good to me for a person to continue as he is . . . I tell you, brothers, the time is short . . . the world as we know it is passing away" (I Cor. 7:26, 29, 31).

Approximately seven years later, in his letter to the Colossians, this reason is not even mentioned. Instead, he counsels specific roles in relationships as an outward expression, or reflection, of a Christian's all-important interior relationship with Christ. The phrase "in the Lord" or "for the Lord" occurs like a refrain throughout this section. It points to the fact that for the Christian, Christ Himself is present in all of his or her relationships. Paul goes into much more depth and detail concerning these relationships in his letters to the Ephesians, where we, in turn, will study his thought at greater length.

At first glance, it appears that Paul's charge to wives to be "submissive" to their husbands (3:18) is simply an echo of the male chauvinistic society of his day, where women were treated mainly as property by the Jews and largely as playthings by the Greeks. In neither case did they enjoy rights of any significance. Given this negative context, it seems particularly unfortunate that he enjoins submission as a "duty to the Lord."

On the other hand, in the next verse (19), he does something which no Jewish theologian or Greek philosopher up to this time had ever done. He demands of husbands that they *love* their wives. And the word that he uses for love is the self-sacrificing *agape*.

Men have been inclined to emphasize the submissiveness of the wife rather than the sacrificial love of the husband. Both injunctions taken *together*, however, enable the most Christ-revealing of all human relationships, a true Christian marriage, about which we will have more to say when the subject comes up in Ephesians 5.

Paul's instruction to children, that they "obey their parents in everything" is likewise balanced by his command to fathers that they "not nag their children" (3:20-21). In a similar way, he counterpoints his charge to slaves to be obedient to their masters (3:22-25) with the admonishment to masters to deal justly and fairly with their slaves (4:1).

In each of these cases, wives to husbands, children to parents, and slaves to masters, Paul affirms the normative position of the society of his day, but by adding an equally authoritative qualification to the stronger party, manages to transform this normative position, at least for Christians. Submissiveness plus sacrificial love is not just plain submissiveness, but a new reality, in the same way that obedience plus justice and fairness is no longer simple obedience. In speaking to *both* parties in the relationship, Paul is affirming—in a way which no one before him except Jesus had done quite so profoundly—the dialogical (two-way) nature of relationship. Affirming the *dialogical* nature of relationship is probably the most important catalyst for the *transformation* of relationships.

Having completed his brief "compendium of household duties," Paul returns to admonitions of a more general nature in 4:2-6. Verse 2 is literally "Persevere in prayer, watching in it with thanksgiving." The participle "watching," when linked with prayer, suggests that prayer is a strong antidote to temptation, a powerful support of morality. Again, Paul incorporates the theme of thanksgiving—even in the face of temptation.

Paul asks for their petitions on his behalf (4:3-4), especially in regard to continuing and effective evangelization. This request is followed by a few last exhortations to the Colossians, centering on the theme of tactfulness to those outside the faith (vv. 5-6). Particularly in the area of "witnessing," or attempting to share the faith with others, the Christian needs to be a model of diplomacy.

The letter concludes with assorted greetings and messages (4:7-18). Tychicus, who had accompanied Paul to Jerusalem with the collection (see Acts 20:4), serves as messenger for this letter and the letter to Philemon. He will relate to them Paul's personal news (v. 7). Paul concentrated on faith and morals in his letters, leaving most news about himself to his personal messenger. Tychicus also accompanies Onesimus on his return to Philemon. It is significant that in his letter to the Colossians Paul makes no reference to Onesimus' slave status, but simply calls him his "dear and faithful brother" (v. 9).

Aristarchus (4:10a), whom Paul probably met on his mission to Thessalonica, aided him during the crisis of the riot at Ephesus (see Acts 20:4), and went with him to Rome (Acts 27:2). Paul pays him a great compliment, calling him a fellow prisoner for Christ. Mark (10b) is the same John Mark mentioned in Acts 13:13 and 15:38. Apparently he has won back Paul's trust since he instructs the Colossians to welcome him. Tradition credits him with the authorship of the second Gospel. Nothing is known of Jesus Justus (11a). Paul's reference to circumcision in 11b indicates that these three men were converts from Judaism.

In verses 12-13 Paul gives Epaphras, his disciple and the founder of the Church at Colossae, the highest possible recommendation. Somewhat humorously, he cannot resist sermonizing, even as he commends Epaphras: "stand firm," "be perfect," "have full conviction about . . . God's will" (v. 12). Laodicea and Hierapolis are neighboring cities of Colossae (v. 13). Luke (4:14a), the "beloved physician," was probably serving Paul in this capacity during his imprisonment in Rome. Tradition holds him as author of the third Gospel and its sequel, the Acts of the Apostles. Demas (14b) is mentioned in Paul's letter to Philemon as a "fellow worker" (Phlm. 24).

Paul sends greetings to the Christians in the nearby city of Laodicea (4:15). He instructs the Colossians to share their letter with the Church at Laodicea (which was probably undergoing Gnostic temptations similar to those at Colossae), and notifies them of a circular which will be coming to them from there (v. 16).

Verse 16 is fascinating because it gives us a glimpse into how the canon of the New Testament was formed. Already at this early date (60 or 61) Christian writings were circulating and, presumably, collected. This same process of being shared from church to church would happen to the Gospels as they were written throughout the remainder of the first century. It would only be a matter of time before the Church was called upon to make a decision as to which of these writings to consider authoritative.

Verse 17 is a gentle, but public, reminder to Archippus (who is also mentioned in Philemon 2) to complete a certain commission. Paul ends the letter with his usual signature and benedicition (v. 18). "Remember my chains" is a last appeal to the Colossians to take the message of this letter to heart.

## Questions for Personal Reflection/Group Discussion

1. Most "modern" falsehoods are variations of ancient ones. Can you think of any correlations between the teachings of today's cults and yesterday's Gnosticism?

2. The Christian Church of today could also be described as a "church under siege." What do you consider to be some of the forces besieging the contemporary Church?

3. Why is the Incarnation one of the crucial doctrines of Christianity?
4. Paraphrase and personalize (using the first person "me" whenever possible) Colossians 2:9-15.
5. In what sense were pagan beliefs and practices a "shadow" of Christianity?
6. In what sense are current secular beliefs a "shadow" of Christianity?
7. What are the two deadly sins of Gnosticism and why are they deadly?
8. As Christians, how is our faith simultaneously past, present, and future?
9. Why do you think Paul considers thanksgiving as one of the most important Christian virtues?
10. How has Paul's inspired juxtaposition of submissiveness with love, and obedience with justice and fairness, led, over the centuries, to a major societal shift in the understanding of marriage and slavery?

# *Ephesians*

## Introduction

Next to the "Pastoral Epistles" (Titus, I & II Timothy), Ephesians is the most contested of Paul's letters in terms of authorship. Mainstream Christian scholars are about equally divided on the issue, roughly half maintaining Paul's authorship, the other half denying it and positing one of his disciples in his place. This balance of differing opinion should caution us against taking a rigid position on the issue. There are good reasons to go either way.

This author takes the position that Ephesians is one of Paul's authentic letters because all the arguments against his authorship can be effectively countered. These arguments focus on the areas of vocabulary, style, and content. We will consider each of these in turn.

1. *Vocabulary*. The fact that some 80 different words occur in Ephesians but in none of his other letters gives one reason to pause. On closer examination, however, we find that these "new" words largely correspond to some of the "new" areas of his thought; namely, the section on the Church as Christ's bride (5:25-33), and the metaphor of Christian armor (6:13-17). Also, when one compares the number of so-called new words in this letter with the number of "new" words in his other letters, Ephesians does not appear to be that outrageous; the number of so-called new words in Philippians and Colossians, for example, is in the same neighborhood.

2. *Style.* The way in which Paul expresses himself in this letter *is* markedly different. Instead of his usual terse, staccato sentences born in the heat of argument, we find in Ephesians writing which is much closer to contemplation than it is to controversy. In fact, in the original Greek, 1:13-14, 15-23; 2:1-7, 11-13, 14-18, 19-22; 3:1-19; 4:1-6, 11-16, 17-19, 20-24; 6:14-20 is each one long, run-on sentence!

Ephesians claims to be a prison letter (3:1; 4:1; 6:20) and, granting the truth of this, helps to explain Paul's change in style. Most of his other letters were dashed off in response to specific crises in particular churches. Romans was not "dashed off," but is still polemic in nature. Colossians, another prison letter and, if our chronology is correct, written immediately before Ephesians, has already begun to exhibit some of the same stylistic characteristics as Ephesians.

Our hunch (in concord with that of many other scholars) is that, given the powerful catalyst of prison for inspiration, Paul was able to make a major Christological breakthrough in his letter to the Colossians, a breakthrough which he relentlessly pursued into the higher reaches of contemplation in Ephesians. Ephesians has the same relationship to Colossians as Romans does to Galatians: the later letter is more general and considerably more developed than the earlier.

And it is not as if we meet Paul's soaring prose for the first time in Ephesians. To be sure, his amazing long sentences are unique to Ephesians, a uniqueness, it might be said, fashioned in the ecstasy of contemplation. But we have already witnessed similarly transcendent visions in earlier letters, even if these did follow the rules of grammar a bit more closely. To cite just a few of many possible examples: I Corinthians 13 (his famous chapter on love), II Corinthians 3:18 ("All of us, gazing on the Lord's glory with unveiled faces, are being transformed from glory to glory into his very image by the Lord who is the Spirit), Romans 8:35-39 (nothing can separate us from the love of Christ),

Romans 11:33-36 (the mystical conclusion to his discussion of the relationship between Christians and Jews), Colossians 1:15-20 (his hymn to Christ as Creator and Redeemer). The biggest difference between Ephesians and these other letters is that in the other letters the visions occur more or less as intermissions, while in Ephesians the vision is sustained throughout the entire letter, with the exception of some of the sections on ethics.

3. *Content.* The quasi-institutional nature of the Church described in Ephesians is held to be incompatible with Paul's earlier, supposedly more charismatic, understanding of the Church. It is possible to counter this argument by pointing to prison as the "perfect" environment for coming to realize the importance of a continuing institution. What would be more "natural" than for Paul, realizing the likelihood of his death, to see the question of authority, even institutionalization, in a new, more serious light?

The problem with denying Paul's authorship of this letter, as this author sees it, goes beyond the limited categories of vocabulary, style, and content. As we have seen, the evidence in these areas against Paul's authorship is certainly not conclusive. The bigger problem is that to argue against someone's authorship on the basis of differences in vocabulary, style, and content from earlier works is, from a literary point of view, questionable. It is questionable because it, in effect, denies the very development in vocabulary, style, and content that is not only natural, but is to be *expected* in any artist worthy of the name. With a genius like Paul we would be surprised *not* to find a significant development—even qualitative changes—from his earlier to his later works.

Jumping to the conclusion of alternative authorship is a penchant of a good deal of modern biblical scholarship. It is an inclination which tends to shortchange an author's artisitic creativity, not to mention divine inspiration (which, after all, is a subtle blend of nature and *grace* and not just nature).

Let us consider the writings of another famous prisoner,

Dietrich Bonhoeffer, as a parallel. His last book, *Letters and Papers from Prison*, is qualitatively different in vocabulary, style, and content from his earlier writings, much more different than Ephesians is from Paul's previous letters. If the biblical scholars who deny Paul's authorship of Ephesians were to apply the same principles in the same way to Bonhoeffer, they would also have to deny his authorship of *Letters and Papers from Prison*, on the basis that it was "impossible." And they would be quite wrong.

What really happened was that Bonhoeffer's prison experience enabled and inspired him to come up with some radically new directions in his theology. Like Paul's new insights in Ephesians, one can see hints of these new directions in his earlier writings. It was the crucible of prison, however, which served as catalyst in both cases.

We must be careful not to sell St. Paul short. The evidence against his authorship of Ephesians can all be controverted, and given the lack of incontrovertible evidence it seems wiser to follow the unanimous tradition of the early Church in claiming Paul as the author of this letter.

A surprising fact, one for which there *is* adequate evidence, is the fact that Ephesians, while probably written by St. Paul, was *not* a letter to the Ephesians. We know from the book of Acts that Paul spent at least three years ministering in Ephesus and that he was on very close terms with the Ephesians (see Acts 20:17-38). Given this information, it is difficult to account for the extremely general nature of this letter.

In addition to this, Paul writes as if the recipients of this letter were not familiar with him personally (see 1:5; 3:2), and as if they were mostly Gentiles (see 2:11; 4:17), when we know that the Ephesian Church was composed mostly of Jewish Christians.

Finally, the words "at Ephesus" do not occur in the earliest manuscript of the Greek New Testament, and have been added to the text (in a different hand) in the two best manuscripts. The designation "at Ephesus" was apparently added later because this letter had come to be associated with this name.

On the basis of this textual evidence, a number of scholars have inferred that Paul's letter "to the Ephesians" was really a general, circulating letter (somewhat similar to what Catholics know today as an "encyclical") which Paul wrote for the edification of the churches (such as those in Colossae and Laodicea) in Asia Minor which had been founded by his disciples. This author concurs with this inference.

The biggest argument against this is that there is no known parallel to a circulating letter in the secular literature of the time. Using the principle that "Necessity is the mother of invention," one could reasonably posit that Paul was certainly capable of inventing a new literary form to meet his needs. After all, Plato did as much in his Socratic dialogues.

Taking into account all of the above, the following appears to be a likely approximation of the events leading up to and surrounding this letter:

Epaphras' news of the Gnostic temptations besetting the Church at Colossae prompted Paul to write his letter to the Colossians. In the process of doing so he received some major new insights into the nature of Christ, insights which he wanted to share, in a more general way, with all the churches in Asia Minor.

Thus, shortly after completing his letter to the Colossians, he began work on what came to be known as his letter "to the Ephesians." "Work" is actually a misnomer for this profound and lyrical epistle, written during just a few sittings of prayerful, contemplative ecstasy.

Paul entrusted both letters to Tychicus for delivery (see Col. 4:7 and Eph. 6:21), who was also to accompany Onesimus back to Philemon (see Col. 4:9). The weeks he had in company with these close friends (not to mention Luke and Mark, who we know were also with him in Rome at this time) and during which he

wrote letters to Philemon, to the Colossians, and his great encyclical letter "to the Ephesians" must have been among the most
intense, and most intensely fulfilling, weeks of his entire ministry.

## Chapter 12:   The Father's Redemptive Plan in the
##                       Cosmic Christ

*Please read Ephesians 1.*   Here, in 1:1, and in four other places
throughout this letter (3:1-4, 7-13; 4:1; 6:19-22) Paul speaks in
the first person. Those who claim that the letter was not written
by Paul maintain that these sections are clever feints on the part
of the forger who, they allege, was mimicking parts of Paul's
real letters, especially Colossians. On the other hand, even by
the rather "loose" (from a modern point of view) standards of
ancient authorship, a hypothetical forger would be going a bit far
in insinuating himself into the letter in this way. And, if the close
proximity of Ephesians and Colossians is, in fact, true, the echoes
of Colossians in this letter are just what one would expect.

Paul's greeting (1:1-2) is interesting because it introduces in
a very short space the main themes of this letter. Christ is mentioned three times, prefiguring His central and exalted position
in the letter as a whole. The "will of God," in the sense that God
has a definite plan which He is unfolding; the "holy ones," in
the sense of the Christian community, which is nothing less than
the Body of Christ; and "peace," in terms of the definitive reconciliation which Jesus has effected through His death and Resurrection—all are leitmotifs in this letter, and will come up again and
again.

1:3-14, which the *New American Bible* breaks down into
three separate sections (making good sense according to content),
is actually one long sentence in the original Greek, the first of
several contemplative visions that form the backbone of this letter.
These are not poems, or hymns, like Colossians 1:15-20, with

complex and intentional parallelisms. They are more like free verse, piling thought upon thought in contemplative ecstasy. The spirit of this passage is better captured in a more poetic format, so we will rearrange the *NAB* translation into free verse:

(3)   a  Praised be the God and Father of our Lord Jesus Christ,
      b  who has bestowed on us in Christ
      c    every spiritual blessing in the heavens!

(4)   a  God chose us in him before the world began,
      b  to be holy and blameless in his sight,
      c  to be full of love,

(5)   a  he likewise predestined us through Christ Jesus
      b    to be his adopted sons
      c  —such was his will and pleasure—

(6)   a  that all might praise the glorious favor
      b  he has bestowed on us in his beloved.

(7)   a  It is in Christ and through his blood
      b    that we have been redeemed and our sins forgiven,

(8)   a  so immeasurably generous is God's favor to us.

(9)   a  God has given us the wisdom to understand fully the mystery,
      b  the plan that he was pleased to decree in Christ,

(10)  a  to be carried out in the fullness of time:
      b  namely, to bring all things in the heavens and on earth
      c    into one under Christ's headship.

(11)  a  In him we were chosen;
      b  for the decree of God,
      c  who administers everything according to his will and counsel,

(12)  a  we were predestined to praise his glory
      b    by being the first to hope in Christ.

(13)  a  In him you too were chosen;
      b  when you heard the glad tidings of salvation,
      c  the word of truth,

     d  and believed in it,

     e  you were sealed with the Holy Spirit who had been
        promised.

(14)  a  He is the pledge of our inheritance,

     b  the first payment against the full redemption

     c   of a people God has made his own,

     d  to praise his glory.

While not a baptismal hymn as such, with its elements of adoption, solidarity with Christ, forgiveness, and the seal of the Holy Spirit, this text could be called a baptismal meditation. It and, indeed, most of the first three chapters of this letter, could also be called one long *berakah*, a Jewish thanksgiving prayer form which is used during Passover, which Jesus used in the context of the Last Supper, and which the Mass includes in its eucharistic prayers.

The salient point of any *berakah* is praise of God the Father, and this is precisely what we find in 1:3a. The phrase "God and Father of our Lord Jesus Christ" gives us an interesting insight into the relationship between the Father and Son. Although they are equal from an ontological point of view, relationally speaking, the Father is Jesus' Father in the same way that He is our Father. The Gospels substantiate this by revealing Jesus' whole ministry as centering in his close personal relationship with the Father, a relationship in which He invites us to share.

Thus, even though Jesus is God "just as much" as the Father, from a relational point of view He reverences the Father as His God. One of Jesus' unique "roles" (quotation marks are in order because words crack under the weight of these realities) in the Trinity is to praise and honor the Father, and to draw us into His worship.

In the second part of this verse (3b) Paul shifts his focus from the Father to the Son, concentrating on the blessings (which he will proceed to enumerate and describe throughout the rest of this meditation) which the Father has made available to us in Jesus.

The whole of verse 3 and, in fact, the entirety of this text (1:3-14), and the totality of this letter presupposes an amazing solidarity between Jesus and the Father, a solidarity in which we are enabled to share through our access to the Father in Jesus.

The phrase "in the heavens" is probably a tacit criticism of the Gnostic emphasis on heavenly intermediaries. "Every spiritual blessing" Paul is saying, resides in Christ, and not "in the heavens" (the various spheres of being on the way to God) themselves.

Again, in verse 4, the initiative lies with God the Father, who "chose us in him," that is, chose us in Jesus, even before the creation of the world. God, in other words, had a plan for the salvation of his creation from the very beginning, and in Christ we are part of His plan. "Holy" and "blameless" become our attributes through our solidarity with Jesus. "Blameless" is literally "without blemish" and refers to the Jewish requirement that sacrificial offerings be "without blemish." Through our relationship with Christ, we are able to offer ourselves in an unblemished, or blameless way to the Father. Finally, our identification with Christ empowers us to "be full of love," the most important Christian virtue.

Continuing to underline the element of divine forethought throughout the whole process of salvation, Paul speaks of Christians being "predestined" in verse 5. He is using this term as a parallel to "chose us in him" in verse 4.

Extreme Calvinists would say that the concept of predestination means that from all eternity God chose some and rejected others. Roman Catholics and other mainstream Christians would say that God chose *everyone* to be with Him, but that some people reject God's choice of them. It would seem that the Catholic position is more in line with Jesus' saving death and Resurrection being for everyone and not just for those previously predestined. Predestination, to make any sense at all, must be universal. God chooses us all. But we, for our part, have to accept His choice of us. God will not force Himself on anyone.

God's choice of us, through the saving ministry of Jesus,

enables us to become his adopted children (1:5). With Jesus, we are able to address God as "Our Father . . ." Our new status as adopted members of God's family should inspire us to praise God for His grace and goodness (v. 6). And this is exactly what Paul (and hopefully we ourselves, as we make his words our own) is doing.

Verse 7 reads literally "in whom we have redemption through his blood, the forgiveness of sins," a reading which brings out the parallelism between "redemption," and "the forgiveness of sins," both of which are effected "through his blood." The forgiveness of sins is tantamount to redemption, because it is sin which holds people in the bondage from which they need to be freed.

As is consistently the case with Paul, there is an irreducible link between Jesus' sacrifice and our salvation. It is important, however, that we understand the nuance of Paul's thought concerning redemption and sacrifice. He sees redemption not in the primitive sense of ransom, but the Old Testament sense of *power*. When God redeems His people Israel from their slavery in Egypt, He does not pay for their release, but leads them forth with His power.

Thus, for Paul the real significance of Jesus' sacrifice is not in any sense that it is a "payment" to God for our sins, but that the Father was totally present in this sacrifice, using it and the connected event of the Resurrection as the vehicles for the greatest manifestation of His transforming, redeeming power that the world has ever known. It is no wonder that Paul breaks into ecstatic praise of the overwhelming generosity of God's grace (v. 8).

"The wisdom to understand" in 9a is a combination of two concepts, "wisdom," which is knowledge of eternal truth, and "intelligence," which in this context means the ability to apply one's wisdom to practical, everyday concerns, to live it out in one's life.

The "mystery" referred to in 9a is the mystery of God's

"plan," His design for salvation. Again, the notion of "mystery" signifies something previously unknown which has not been revealed. A significant expansion of the content of the "mystery" has taken place from Colossians, where it was the fact that Gentiles were included in God's plan for salvation, to Ephesians, where the content of the "mystery" includes "all things in the heavens and on earth" (v. 10). Contemplation has led Paul to a substantive development in his theology.

The phrase the "fullness of time" (10a) considers time from a qualitative, not quantitative, viewpoint. In other words, the "fullness of time" refers to the redemptive transformation of time (and therefore history) which has already taken place, continues to take place, and will eventually bring "all things" to fulfillment through the saving Lordship of Jesus. "All things" reaches beyond the human race to include the entirety of material and spiritual creation in solidarity with humankind through Christ.

Verses 11-14 are an echo and an expansion of verses 3-6. The effect of this section is to underline the purposiveness of God's plan for salvation.

The pronoun "we" in 11a refers specifically to Jewish believers, with whom Paul identifies himself. The Jewish people had the distinction of being "the first to hope in Christ" (12b)—they were the first (and only) nation to look for the coming of the Messiah.

In verse 13 Paul counterbalances the "we" of the Jews with the "you" of the Gentiles who, by accepting the Good News of the Gospel, have also been "sealed with the Holy Spirit." In the ancient world, to be stamped with a seal signified that one belonged to a particular person (as in the case of a slave) or to a particular god (as in the case of devotees of a mystery cult). The Christian's seal was the sacrament of Baptism, which signified that the Christian belonged to Christ. The actual seal of this belonging was no mere tattoo, but an interior relationship and empowering by the Holy Spirit. The gift of the Holy Spirit had been promised by the prophets in such passages as Ezekiel 36:26:

> I will give you a new heart and place a new spirit
> within you, taking from your bodies your stony
> hearts and giving you natural hearts.

The "we" of verse 11 and the "you" of verse 13 expand to become the "our" of verse 14. Salvation, in other words, is extended equally to Gentiles as well as Jews, who share the same seal from the same Spirit. The Holy Spirit is the "pledge of our inheritance," which means that His presence in our lives is the down payment, or guarantee, that the total redemption (our personal resurrection as a part of His resurrected people) will, indeed, finally be ours. This united people is now and will be an instrument of His praise. Thus ends the first of Paul's contemplative excursions.

Immediately he embarks on another, 1:15-23, like 1:3-14, being one continuous, ecstatic sentence in the original Greek:

(15) a  For my part,
     b  from the time I first heard of your faith in the Lord Jesus
     c  and your love for all the members of the church,
(16) a  I have never stopped thanking God for you
     b    and recommending you in my prayers.
(17) a  May the God of our Lord Jesus Christ,
     b  the Father of glory,
     c  grant you a spirit of wisdom and insight to know him
        clearly.
(18) a  May he enlighten your innermost vision
     b    that you may know the great hope to which he has called
        you,
     c  the wealth of his glorious heritage
     d    to be distributed among the members of the church,
(19) a  and the immeasurable scope of his power in us who believe.

(20) a  It is like the strength he showed in raising Christ from the dead

     b  and seating him at his right hand in heaven,

(21) a  high above every principality, power, virtue, and domination,

     b  and every name that can be given in this age

     c  or in the age to come.

(22) a  He has put all things under Christ's feet

     b  and has made him, thus exalted,

     c  head of the church,

(23) a  which is his body:

     b  the fullness of him

     c  who fills the universe in all its parts.

As he reflects on the spread of the Gospel throughout Asia Minor, Paul's praise becomes more personal. 1:15-23 is a powerful fusion of thanksgiving and intercession.

The natural and expected progression of the Christian life is reflected in verse 15. Authentic "faith in the Lord Jesus" should spill over into "love for all the members of the church." For the Christian, faith and love are inseparable virtues.

Paul refers to the constancy of his prayer on their behalf in verse 16. The substance of his petitionary recommendations is the soaring meditation in verses 17-23.

He begins by requesting for them a "spirit of wisdom and insight" (v. 17). Again, wisdom is *sophia*, the knowledge of eternal realities. This time, however, it is coupled with "insight" (literally "revelation"), his prayer being that God will grant them (through the Holy Spirit) a knowledge which is truly revelatory. The purpose of this revelatory knowledge is not to grow wiser, but to "know him clearly." Christian knowledge, then, is *revealed* (as opposed to humanly concocted) and *relational* (as opposed to general, or abstract). Put another way, we could say that Christians know God in order to love Him.

Continuing his prayer for their increase in knowledge and love, Paul complements "revelation" (v. 17) with "enlightenment" (v. 18). The phrase "your innermost vision" (18a) is literally "the eyes of your hearts," and reflects the Jewish understanding that the center of discernment and commitment was the heart, and not (as with the Greeks) the head.

Again, the purpose of having the eyes of one's heart enlightened is not self-centered but God-directed: it is to "know" (to personally experience) "the great hope to which he has called you" (18b). The actual content of this "great hope" is enveloped in the clouds of contemplation (and expressed in Greek which is so compressed that it refuses to be successfully unpacked), but we know that it has to do with God's promises ("the wealth of his glorious heritage," 18c) and the celebration of these promises *in community* ("to be distributed among the members of the church," 18d). The fulfillment of God's promises which each Christian will personally experience is not for his or her own self-gratification, but for the celebration of the community as a whole.

The "immeasurable scope of his power in us who believe" (v. 19) is nothing less than the power that God demonstrated in the Resurrection and exaltation of Jesus, the Messiah (v. 20). This is an amazing claim and again presupposes the relational solidarity, or identification of the Christian with Christ and through Christ of Christians with one another and with the Father.

Verse 21 stresses the superiority of Jesus over all angelic intermediaries (a topic of much concern to Paul due to the negative influence of an incipient Gnosticism throughout much of Asia Minor), and over all time. His superiority, in other words, is incontestable and eternal.

Negatively speaking (given the Gnostic dependence on angels and the enslavement to time which is characteristic of the human condition), angels and time compose part of the "all things" which the Father has set under Jesus' authority (22a). Positively speaking, the glorified Christ has been made authoritative head of the Church (22b), which Paul identifies with "his body" in verse 23, saying that it (that is, the Church) is nothing less than "the fullness of him who fills the universe in all its parts."

This (and other similar statements in this letter) constitutes one of the high points of New Testament ecclesiology. The Church is described as forming a living unity with its Lord. It is the supreme expression of the completeness of the exalted Christ, and as such has a crucial role to play in the cosmic drama of salvation.

*Questions for Personal Reflection/Group Discussion*

1. According to Ephesians 1:5-14, what are the blessings which the Father has made available to us in Christ?
2. Compose your own free verse poem of praise to God the Father for the blessings He has given you in Jesus.
3. Explain the Catholic approach to predestination.
4. Describe the viewpoint from which Paul considers redemption, and the efficacy of Jesus' sacrificial death.
5. We are beginning to see some of the ways in which Paul's prayer life led him to deeper insights in his theology. How has your prayer life led you to a deeper understanding of some of the Christian mysteries?
6. How does your "faith in the Lord Jesus" spill over into "love for all the members of the Church?"
7. (a) What is the real point of growing in knowledge of God?
   (b) Has your reading of this book helped you to *love* God more deeply? If so, in what way(s)?
8. Why do you think the communal dimension of Christianity is so terribly important?

## Chapter 13:    The Fulfillment of the Promise in Christ

*Please read Ephesians 2-3*.    Chapter two contrasts humankind's
prior state of alienation with its present state of reconciliation in
Christ. Paul begins by addressing the Gentiles—the word "You"
in 2:1 (and 2:2) refers to them. He describes them as "dead"
because of their "sins" and "offenses." A "sin" is literally a
"missing of the mark," and an "offense" a "false step." Thus,
their death is seen as the living death of not measuring up to their
true humanity, of getting sidetracked off the true path of life.

In verse 2 Paul links the "sins" and "offenses" and the "death"
which they entail to the "present age," which stands for the fallen
and ultimately self-destructive ways of the world. According to
ancient astrology, both Gentile and Jewish, the air was believed
to be inhabited by various angelic and demonic beings. The
"prince of the air" refers to one of these, in this case a personified
force of evil. "Rebellious" in this context is a synonym for "dead,"
rebelliousness being a hallmark of those who are stepping wide
of the mark.

Paul's perspective expands in verse 3; now it is "All of us,"
that is, the Jews as well as the Gentiles, who "were once of their
company"—who were once "rebellious" (v. 2) or "dead" (v. 1).
Notice the past tense. This condition of lostness is a past reality
because Paul is addressing Christians, those who are now alive
and whose lives are now "on target" in Christ.

Still expanding on his description of humankind's deadness
until the coming of Christ, Paul characterizes it as a life "lived
at the level of the flesh" (3b). Here, as elsewhere in his writings,
"flesh" is not a specific reference to the body, but a general
referent to humanity's fallen state, with its proclivity toward sin
in all its forms.

The *New American Bible* telescopes the literal Greek of the
next phrase, which reads "doing the desires of the flesh and of
the understandings," into "following every whim and fancy." The
literal sense, while admittedly awkward, better conveys the sense

of the basic dividedness of the human person which Paul wants to communicate. "Understandings," especially, though not correct English, captures the lack of single-mindedness which is so characteristic of the person without Christ.

Again, the reference to "God's wrath" (3c) is, in the opinion of this author, an unnecessary personification of sin's inherent self-destructiveness as punishment from God.

In verse 4 Paul goes on to affirm the Father's essentially compassionate and loving nature. It was through the Father's initiative in Christ that we have been "brought to life" (v. 5), "raised up" and "given a place in the heavens" (v. 6). Each of these verbs is preceded by the prefix *syn*, indicating our essential union, or solidarity, with Christ in these actions. In other words, the Father has already included us along with Christ in His Resurrection and exaltation, which infuse us with new life.

Paul's consistent use of the past and perfect tenses in this letter is indicative of two things. On the one hand, it points to a lessening of Paul's eschatological fervor. In earlier letters such as those to the Thessalonians and Corinthians, Paul consistently referred to salvation as a future event, an event in which the Christian was already participating to a certain degree, but nevertheless predominately future.

On the other hand, in his letter to the Colossians, and here in Ephesians, Paul speaks of salvation as an already accomplished reality in which we are presently participating and which will continue into the future. The future is not totally excluded (as verse 7 indicates), but his emphasis is definitely on the present.

This rather subtle change in his use of tenses witnesses to a significant development in Paul's faith and theology. As his expectation of Jesus' imminent return weakened over the years, it was replaced by a deeper realization of the saving reality of his *present* life with God. This present redemptive relationship with the Father through Christ becomes the foundation of Paul's mature theology.

Verses 8 and 9 are a splendid summary of the "Gospel

According to Paul:" salvation is a matter of "favor" (literally "grace") and faith; it is totally gift, in no way dependent on our good works. In other words, there exists no program of righteousness by means of which we can earn our way into heaven. Salvation is God's free gift, a gift which can be received only through faith in the Giver.

This, of course, does not obviate "good deeds" (v. 10) as a necessary expression of the Christian life. It simply puts them in their proper place as an *ex*pression (a reaching outward) of our faith *in God*. If salvation is dependent on good works (as it has become in much of the Judaism of Paul's day), the works, even though "good," become self-destructive declarations of faith in oneself. On the other hand, if one simply accepts God's loving compassion in Christ, and lives out of the context of one's personal relationship with the Father through Christ, good works will flow from this relationship as naturally as water spills over a waterfall.

The phrase "which God prepared for us in advance" (10b) is another echo of the loving choice and the redemptive plan which God had in mind for His people from the very beginning.

The next section (2:11-22) celebrates the bringing together of the two broken parts of the human race (Jews and Gentiles) and the making of a qualitatively new human community through Christ. This new community, the Church, is God's down payment, so to speak, on His promise "to bring all things in the heavens and on earth into one under Christ's headship" (Ephesians 1:10).

Paul is going to consider the ways in which the Gentiles were at a loss because they did not share the faith of Israel (v. 12). First, however, he casts a disparaging glance at circumcision, calling it a "hand-executed rite," meaning that it is no more than skin deep. He does not see circumcision as a decisive element of Jewish *faith*.

On the other hand, Judaism did enjoy certain crucial benefits, blessings which the Gentiles were emphatically without. These deficiencies Paul proceeds to mention in verse 12. The first is that they "had no part in Christ." "Christ" is the Greek for the

Hebrew "Messiah," meaning "Anointed One," the one chosen to inaugurate God's Kingdom. The Greeks had no real parallel to the Jewish expectation of Messiah; thus, the word "Christ," lacking a referent, soon became part of Jesus' proper name. This very lack is part of the spiritual inadequacy of the Gentile world. Since they did not look forward to the coming of the Messiah, they could have no real hope for salvation.

Secondly, the Gentiles were "excluded from the community of Israel." They were not a part of God's redemptive plan in the same way that Israel was (although, in the bigger prophetic picture, Israel was being prepared precisely to minister to the Gentiles). At this point Paul is looking at the narrower picture, and this excludes the Gentiles from "the covenant and its promise," leaving them "without hope and without God in the world."

"Covenant" is plural in the Greek text, and refers to all God's solemn promises to Israel, the decisive part of each being the promise of continuing relationship. The Gentiles lacked this sense of God's presence in their lives and in their history. True, there were a number of mystery cults through which one could supposedly attain union with God, but this "union" was usually chemically induced, and was not seen, as in Judaism, as a consistent part of one's *everyday* life.

The ancient world was overwhelmingly a world which was "without hope." If our modern world idealizes its carefree sex and its fixation on other bodily pleasures, it is because, having rejected the possibility of real relationship with God, it is caught in the same despair as the ancients. This despair inevitably leads to the same meaningless acts in the same futile attempt to find meaning. The Gentiles, in short, were "without hope" because they were "without God;" they were not connected with life at its Source.

This was how things used to be. They are no longer this way because Jesus' sacrificial death has definitely broken down all barriers to God, enabling the Gentiles to enjoy the same spiritual blessings as the Jews (v. 13). The reference to Christ at the end of this verse is actually a reference to "*the* Christ," underlining Jesus' role as Messiah. It is because He is Messiah, the bringer of God's Kingdom, that His sacrifice was and is efficacious.

The "peace" to which Paul refers in verse 14 and onwards is the new reality of reconciliation between Gentile and Jew. Because of Christ, Jew and Gentile are caught up together into a new act of creation. Together they form the Church, which is the embodiment (eventually to be called the sacrament) of this new act of creation.

Peace is not something which Gentile and Jew would have been able to accomplish on their own. Peace, for the Christian, does not center in any human achievements, but in the person of Christ.

The "barrier of hostility" (14b) is an allusion to the Temple, which was divided into various, increasingly restricted, sections. The outer court, or Court of the Gentiles, was separated from the Temple proper by a wall. Gentiles were not allowed beyond the wall. "No Trespassing" signs were prominently posted along this barrier. The penalty for trespassing was death.

Paul goes on to describe the way in which Jesus is peace. "In his own flesh" (v. 15) is a reference to the Incarnation, the fact that the fullness of God has been embodied in a human person. "He abolished the law with its commands and precepts" by offering Himself in its place. "Through his cross" (v. 16) is a direct reference to Jesus' sacrificial death, the specific means through which peace has come about.

We see in verses 15 and 16 the closest possible connection between the Incarnation, Crucifixion (and though not actually stated, the Resurrection—the reality of which underlies the entirety of Paul's thought). Through the saving event of His Incarnation-Crucifixion-Resurrection, Jesus has brought together the two alienated halves of humankind—the Gentiles, those "who were far off" and the Jews, those "who were near" (v.17)—and established in Himself (and in His extended Body, the Church) a qualitatively new humanity.

Verse 18 is a profound indication of how the early Church eventually instituted the doctrine of the Trinity. The word Trinity does not occur in the New Testament. It had to be coined around the year 200 to describe the experiential reality already mentioned in the New Testament in such texts as Ephesians 2:18. The experience of Paul and the early Church was that *through* the saving ministry of Jesus and *in* His continuing presence in the Holy Spirit, the Christian is empowered to stand in the presence of the Father. The word for gaining "access" is used in connection with one person introducing another at a royal court, and this is precisely what Jesus does for us, with the addition that He introduces us as members of the royal family.

Paul, in fact, uses family imagery when he tells the Gentiles that they are in no way second class citizens, but "members of the household of God" (v. 19). Plunging into one of his favorite analogies, that of a "living" building, he sees the Gentiles as comprising a significant part of a building whose foundation is the "apostles and prophets" (v. 20).

Some scholars see this solemn reference to the apostles and prophets (itinerant preachers) as an indication that Paul himself did not write this letter. They claim that this must be the work of someone later than Paul looking back to the "golden age" of the Church. On the other hand, nothing seems more natural than that Paul, reflecting in prison, and combatting heretical teachings which threatened the life of the Church, should not have emphasized the crucial role of "apostles and prophets."

Again, it is not through human effort per se that the "temple" takes shape, but "Through him" (v. 21) and "in him" (v. 22). The image of fitting together alludes to the honing process by which the stones of an ancient building were fitted (literally: interlocked) together.

The *New American Bible* has transposed verses 1 and 2 of

chapter 3 in an attempt to clarify Paul's meaning. 3:1-19 is actually one long sentence, and 2-13 is a lengthy parenthesis within this long sentence! What has happened is that his opening statement about being "a prisoner for Christ" triggers him to reflect on the meaning of his ministry, his ministry being the cause of his being a prisoner.

The phrase "This is why" of 3:1 will link up with the phrase "That is why" of 3:14 after the long parenthesis. This whole passage, 3:1-13, is rather reminiscent of some of Paul's self-recommending, boastful passages in II Corinthians. Here, however, Paul boasts without the bitterness and defensiveness which characterizes his second letter to the Corinthians. As in II Corinthians, Paul considers being a prisoner for Christ to be a great honor:

> Are they ministers of Christ? Now I am really
> talking like a fool—I am more: with my many
> more labors and imprisonments, with far worse
> beatings and frequent brushes with death.
> (II Corinthians 11:23)

In the Greek, Christ is prefaced by the article "the" (3:1). This construction, "*the* Christ Jesus," or "*the* Christ," or "Jesus *the* Christ" is quite frequent in this letter, and alludes to the fact of Jesus' Messiahship. Paul, then, is stating that he is a prisoner not only on behalf of the Gentiles, but on behalf of the Messiah as well.

The churches to whom his traveling letter was sent had not been founded by Paul himself, but by his disciples. This explains the phrase "you have heard" in verse 2. "Secret" (v. 3), is really "mystery," again referring to something previously hidden which has now been revealed. "As I have briefly described it" is a rather humorous reference to his previous descriptions of the mystery in this letter, which, given several of the longest sentences in the New Testament, have been anything but brief.

Paul knows that what he has said thus far in this letter has been magnificent and profound, and he does not hesitate to say so (v. 4), at the same time giving full credit to the Holy Spirit for revealing the content of the mystery (v. 5). Again we find mention of the "apostles and prophets," a citation which witnesses to Paul's growing realization of the importance of these ministries for the transmission of Revelation.

Verse 6 describes the content of the mystery: the fact that "in Christ Jesus"—in solidarity with Christ—the Gentiles are now on an equal footing with the Jews in terms of salvation. It is difficult for us, living nearly two thousand years after the revelation of this mystery, to grasp the truly radical nature of this teaching. The ancient world clung to the correctness of its divisions with a vengeance. The Jews considered themselves to be the Chosen; everyone else, the "Greeks," were deemed the "unchosen" and untouchable. The Greeks considered themselves to be the sole possessors of civilization; everyone else was a "barbarian." Similarly, there were rigid distinctions of privilege between master and slave, male and female. "In Christ Jesus" none of these distinctions held; in Him the world is destined to become one common human family.

The words which the *NAB* renders as "co-heirs," "members," and "sharers" in the Greek all begin with variations of the prefix *syn*, the prefix which signifies solidarity. Literally speaking, the Gentiles are called "joint-heirs," "joint-body," and "joint-sharers" (of the promise of salvation), a powerful expression of the new-found solidarity, oneness, and community of all Christians with one another in Christ.

His reference to the Gospel at the end of verse 6 causes him to reflect on the event which empowered him to become "a minister of the gospel" (v. 7); namely, his conversion experience on the road to Damascus (see Acts 9:1-6). Remembering his former persecution of the very Church he is now convinced is the pinnacle of creation, Paul, in a way reminiscent of I Corinthians 15:9 ("I am the least of the apostles; in fact, because I persecuted the church of God, I do not even deserve the name."), Paul calls himself "the least of all believers" (v. 8).

Again, at the end of verse 8, Christ is preceded by "the." The "unfathomable riches of Christ" are the limitless riches of the Messiah. Verse 9 is another reference to the mystery, in this case in the context of God's "design," or plan.

Verse 10 again celebrates the crucial role of the Church, not just in our world, but in the entire universe (the "principalities and powers" being the angelic intermediaries who controlled the various heavenly spheres). The cosmogony of Paul's day may be outdated, but his theology—being the expression, not of observation, but of Revelation—is not. According to St. Paul, the Church is nothing less than the locus of the New Creation; as the Body of Christ it contains His fullness, a fullness which is in the process of transforming creation as a whole (see Colossians 1:15-20).

The purposiveness of God is again underlined in verse 11. Jesus Christ, and His extension in the Church, brings to its fulfillment God's age-old plan of salvation history. A Christian can approach the Father as his or her own loving Father "In Christ and through faith in him" (v. 12). This phrase is literally "In whom, through the faith of him," and suggests the faithfulness of Jesus to His own ministry as the basis of our access to the Father.

Returning to the thought of his imprisonment in verse 13, Paul asks his readers to regard it as part of Christ's gift to him. Because of his identification with Christ, Christ is with him in his imprisonment, transforming it into an act of redemptive, sacrificial love on behalf of His Church. The sufferings which we latter-day disciples endure for the sake of our Lord are likewise redeemed and made redemptive by Him.

His digression having run its full course, Paul resumes his original thought, which is actually an ecstatic prayer (3:14). Since the usual Jewish and early Christian prayer position was standing, kneeling would indicate that the person praying is approaching prayer with uncommon intensity, which is indeed the case here.

Paul uses the definite article before Father in much the same way that he uses it before Christ. Just as *the* Christ signifies the one and only Messiah, *the* Father emphasizes the aspect of the loving Fatherhood of God. He brings this out explicitly in verse 15 with a play on words (in Greek the words for father and family are exceptionally close) which highlights God as the great exemplar of all fatherhood.

Verses 16 and 17 contain another implicitly Trinitarian understanding of God. The phrases in these two verses all complement one another. "Gifts in keeping with the riches of his glory" (16a) really means limitless gifts, which it is the Father's loving nature to give. Paul mentions one of these gifts in 16b, the strengthening, or empowerment, of the inner person (the seat of intelligence, conscience, and volition) through the power of the Holy Spirit.

He immediately asks for his readers another of the Father's priceless gifts, the indwelling presence of Christ in their hearts (17a; "hearts" is parallel to the "inwardly" of v. 16). There are several verbs for "to dwell" in Greek, and the one which Paul chooses is the one with the denotation of permanency and the connotation of comfort (as in "being at home"). Faith—the personal acceptance of God's promises in Christ—is our personal invitation for Christ to enter our lives.

Paul concludes his Trinitarian petitions with an intercession that "charity," or love (*agapē*: the sacrificial love which is the subject of I Corinthians 13) serve as both "root" and "foundation" in the lives of his readers. Again, he mixes agricultural and building metaphors; perhaps it would be better to say that he simply combines them in the contemplative thought of a life which is like a "living" building.

All these petitions—the riches of His glory (16a), the inner strengthening through the Spirit (16b), Christ's indwelling presence (17a), and a life nourished and grounded on love (17b)—add up to the contemplative finale of verses 18 and 19. "To grasp fully" (18a) does not mean merely to comprehend, but to make one's comprehension an integral part of oneself. This process is

not done in isolation, but in company "with all the holy ones."
Because of a Christian's identification with Christ, he or she is
intimately related to all other Christians through Christ. The
Church as a whole grows in "the breadth and length and height
and depth of Christ's love" (18b), which is another way of saying
that the Church, and the individual Christian in union with the
Church, grows more and more fully into Christ's love, which is
infinite and limitless.

This love is not a "head trip," but an actual experience,
something so personal and so transcendent that it "surpasses all
knowledge" (19a). That is, Christ's love, in which the Christian
and the Church participate, both goes beyond and is better than any
conceivable knowledge. This love empowers us to participate
(again, through our mystical solidarity with Christ) in "the fullness
of God himself" (19b)—a reality which defies description.

At this point Paul's prayer overflows into doxology: intense
praise. Paul addresses his praise specifically to the Father, and
the form of this praise is the formidable affirmation that His
"power now at work in us can do immeasurably more than we
ask or imagine" (v. 20). Thus does Paul at the same time (1)
acknowledge our smallness, (2) exalt God's greatness, and (3)
celebrate the fact that our smallness is being transformed through
His greatness.

This is the only one of Paul's doxologies which presents the
Church as a parallel to Christ (v. 21). It is quite fitting that he
do this in this particular letter, since this is the letter which, more
than any other, proclaims the Church as the Body of Christ; in
other words, as an *essential* part of His being.

*Questions for Personal Reflection/Group Discussion*

1. How might a change in emphasis from an understanding of
   salvation largely in terms of the future, to a celebration of
   salvation largely in terms of the present, indicate a significant
   development, or maturation, in one's faith?

2. According to Paul, what is the proper relationship between faith and works?
3. (a) Think of as many similarities as you can between our modern world and the ancient hellenistic world.
   (b) What do you think accounts for these similarities?
4. (a) How has Jesus brought about a definitive reconciliation between Jews and Gentiles?
   (b) How is Jesus *our* peace?
5. Summarize Paul's teaching on the nature of the Church in Ephesians 2-3.
6. Someone has said that one simply cannot be a Christian in isolation. Why is the community of the Church a necessary complement to one's personal faith?
7. Why does Paul tell us that love surpasses knowledge?
8. Paraphrase Paul's prayer in 3:14-19. Offer your paraphrase as a prayer for your local parish.

## Chapter 14:   The Church's Call to Unity in the Lord

*Please read Ephesians 4.*   Following the pattern of most of his letters, Paul has first concentrated on doctrine (chapters 1-3). Now he focuses on the practical application of this doctrine (chapters 4-6). As we have seen, the major thrust of the letter has been on humankind's new unity in Christ. The practical part of the letter continues in this vein, with unity being the focal point of its exhortations.

Paul has just completed a breathtakingly eloquent description of the Christian vision of reality; he now makes a personal appeal to the readers of this letter, that they embody the beauty of the Christian vision in their own lives (4:1). The concept of "calling" contains within itself the notion of God's plan, and the Christian's part within that plan. The Christian, in other words, has been summoned to play a part in a drama of cosmic significance. But in this case the drama is real life, and the part one has been called to play is one's truest, deepest self.

He immediately mentions four virtues which are crucial for the victorious living of the Christian life: humility, meekness, patience, and love (4:2). The ancient world did not consider humility to be a virtue, but a vice; it stood for servility and was to be avoided at all costs. This was because the lack of a real understanding of sin and forgiveness left one stranded with self-sufficiency and self-righteousness. The Christian, on the other hand, could afford to be humble because he knew not only the reality of sin, but the even greater reality of forgiveness.

"Meekness" is rather a synonym of humility and has the connotation of gentleness; gentleness with oneself as well as with others. "Patience" refers specifically to the quality of being longsuffering and non-retaliatory toward other people. "Bearing with one another lovingly" is literally "forbearing one another in love." The word used for love, as might be expected, is *agapē*, the sacrificial love of Christ. The Christian is called upon to reflect the sacrificial love of Jesus toward others. These four virtues are precisely the ones which are crucial for the cohesiveness of the Christian community.

The unity which Paul refers to in verse 3 is the unity, or oneness, of the Church. The word for "preserve" has the sense of "maintaining something by keeping a close watch over it." Thus, for Christians to "preserve the unity" of the Church, they must guard this unity, being ready to intercept any threats against it. The unity of the Church is founded on the presence of the Holy Spirit and maintained by Christ, who is Himself peace (see Eph. 2:14).

In verses 4-6, Paul celebrates the unity of the Church within the context of the unity of the Trinity. He mentions seven expressions of unity:

1. One body—this body is the Church, which embodies the continuing presence of Christ in the world.

2. One Spirit—the Holy Spirit, whose presence within the Church keeps it united.

3. One hope—the anticipation of future blessedness, when the Church experiences its perfection as part of God's Kingdom.

4. One Lord—Jesus Christ, who has inaugurated the salvation which the Church now extends in His name.

5. One faith—the Church's experience of its Risen Lord, and the content of this experience.

6. One baptism—through this rite, all Christians share in the death and Resurrection of Jesus the Christ. Baptism establishes the fundamental solidarity between Christians and their Lord, and thus their solidarity with one another.

7. One God and Father—who, through His love, has initiated and continues to sustain the entire process of salvation.

What began as exhortation in verse 3 has turned into praise by verse 6. Paul rejoices in the Father, whom he describes as being "over all," "through all," and "in all." "Over all" brings out the aspect of God's authority; "through all" the aspect of God's providence; and "in all" the aspect of God's continuing presence. The "all" used here refers not just to the Church, but to the entire universe.

The "Each of us" which begins 4:7 is inclusive; it includes all Christians, without exception. "Favor," or "grace," adverts to the special gift(s) which each Christian has been given for the well-being of the Body of Christ. "Measure" suggests a differentiation among these gifts. Thus, the total sense of this verse is that Christ has blessed each Christian with a distinct gift for the upbuilding of His Body, the Church.

The thought of gifts reminds Paul of a passage from one of the psalms (68:19), which he quotes rather freely, changing the context to suit his purpose of having Christ's Ascension occasion the giving of various ministerial gifts (v. 8).

"Ascended," in turn, prompts a brief digression on the meaning of the ascent/descent of Christ (vv. 9-10). According to Paul's typically Jewish logic at this point, ascent (Jesus' return to the Father) implies a prior descent. In this case the descent is into the underworld, and demonstrates Christ's victory over death (through His Resurrection) and thus His solidarity with *all* of creation; nothing is excluded from His Lordship. Again, our understanding of the structure of the universe may have changed (we no longer think of the "underworld" as existing in the same dimension as this world), but this does not affect the theological truth of Paul's statement, which is that Christ is Lord of all creation.

Similarly, "high above the heavens" in verse 10 refers to an outdated cosmogony: God was believed to dwell beyond the last of several heavenly "spheres," or regions. Theologically speaking, this is a reference to God's transcendence. Jesus' Ascension is understood in terms of His transcending all earthly limitations and now (through the Holy Spirit) being immanent in all things (the "all men" at the end of v. 10 is literally "all things," and echoes Paul's cosmic perspective in this letter).

Returning to the theme of gifts in verse 11, he cites four ministerial roles as examples of God's gifts to the Church: apostle, prophet, evangelist, pastor-teacher. These positions are admittedly much more "clerical" than those mentioned in I Corinthians 12 or Romans 12:3-8. In these two earlier discussions, Paul is addressing himself to a specific community, and his vision of the Church emphasizes unity through the cooperation of various individuals, each of whom contributes his gift for the good of the body as a whole.

In Ephesians, Paul is addressing himself to the universal Church, and his vision highlights four key roles which were already well on the way to becoming "offices;" that is, positions which were believed to carry with them a "special" grace. (It is, of course, problematic to speak of a certain grace being "special"—all grace is special! The thought we are trying to convey is that the early Church soon realized that some positions were more important than others in terms of leadership; a person entering one of these positions was believed to receive a special charism.) This is a significant step on the road to the sacrament of "Holy Orders," or ordination.

Paul's understanding of the Church in his earlier letters was less hierarchial than it is in his later ones. We have already been introduced to the inspired insight that Christ is the "head" of the Church in Colossians. Now Ephesians presents certain ministries as "heading" the Church; in other words, as being so crucial to the well-being of the Christian community that they are endowed with grace which corresponds to the uniqueness of the position. Like all grace, however, this special charism for leadership is not received in a mechanical way, but is dependent on the depth of faith of the person receiving it.

Some scholars insist that the same Paul could not have authored his "horizontal" vision of the Church in I Corinthians and Romans, and his "vertical" understanding of the Church in Colossians and Ephesians. Indeed, it is *not* the same Paul; it is a growing, developing Paul who took years to mature from one stage to the other. His "two" visions of Church are not contradictory, but complimentary. Nothing could be more "natural" than that, during his imprisonment, with reports of doctrinal and moral defection reaching him, Paul realized the necessity of emphasizing the leadership roles within the Church. These roles included:

1. Apostles—the great "patriarchs" of the faith who had known the Lord personally or, like Paul, had received a direct revelation from him.

2. Prophets—charismatic itinerant preachers of God's Word. This "office" was soon abandoned because it was so often misused.

3. Evangelists—commissioned missionaries who brought the Good News of the Gospel into new areas.

4. Pastors/teachers—the "shepherds" of a local church, who were responsible for its total well-being, including the fact that faith and morals were taught in their integrity.

Paul envisions these leadership positions not in terms of

prestige or power, but in terms of *service* (v. 12). A more literal translation of "in roles of service for the faithful" would be "for the perfecting of the saints in ministry." Thus, *the* crucial function of the Church leader, as Paul sees it, is calling forth and enabling the various ministries (ministries in addition to leadership) which are necessary for the Church to really be the Body of Christ.

The overall goal of all this ministry—the ministry of leadership and the ministries of those who are led—is the process of the entire Church becoming more and more Christlike, and eventually experiencing the fullness of salvation as a new corporate person (v. 13). Paul's image of a "perfect man" does not destroy personality or individuality, but presupposes a new dimension of creation, in which the solidarity of Christians with their Lord and with one another is fully realized. The concept of solidarity involves two or more essentially different beings who are, nevertheless, united in an essential way. It brings to completion the notion of "unity within diversity."

Given this magnificent goal, Paul exhorts his readers to grow up in verse 14. He uses the word "children" in the disparaging sense of being flighty. He is probably thinking of the reports he has heard concerning the inroads of Gnosticism, and is calling for mature Christians who know what they believe and why they believe it.

To "profess the truth" (v. 15) means to "embody the truth," and this can only be done "in love," the sacrificial love of putting others before oneself. Without the empowering force of sacrificial love, the truth will remain an unredemptive abstraction, an abstraction with no more holding power than Gnostic "knowledge." "Professing the truth in love" is the only way to grow into the "full maturity of Christ." Christian faith, in other words, is a developmental process empowered by love.

Paul continues to emphasize the motivating power of Christ's love in verse 16. "Through him" (the first phrase) and "in love" (the last phrase) are, in this case, synonymous. This whole verse, with its interconnections between Christ, the various members of the Church, and love, reveals a profound solidarity between Christ and His Church, sacrificial love being the medium in which this solidarity is realized.

Having presented an inspired and inspiring vision of the essential unity of the Church, Paul goes on to combat the vices which are destroying this unity. He knows that not a few who claim to be Christians are still the prisoners of immorality. Thus he uses his apostolic authority to make an official pronouncement that real Christians "must no longer live as the pagans do" (v. 17). He now proceeds to describe the self-destructiveness of the pagan world, much as he had done in Romans 1:18-32.

He mentions the "emptiness," or futility, of their thinking in 17b (this futility being the result of reflecting on things empty in themselves), and their consequent "darkness" of understanding—their unenlightenment (18a). Their "ignorance" (literally: false knowledge) and "resistance" (literally: hardness of heart) have separated them from God (18b). This implies that they—not God—are responsible for this state of separation. Paul states this explicitly in the next verse (19) when he says that "Without remorse" (literally: with callousness) they have "abandoned themselves," or gave themselves over to, insatiable lust.

Paul does not emphasize the concept of the "wrath of God" in this letter as he did in the letter to the Romans. There, however, we saw that the "wrath of God" is not something that God inflicts on people, but something which one abandons oneself to; namely, the self-destructive consequences of one's sin.

Allowing oneself to be possessed by lust is incompatible with real Christianity (v. 20). Assuming the acceptibility of the instruction they have received (v. 21), Paul proceeds to remind them of their baptismal promise, which was to "lay aside" (v. 22) their old selves (to put off as one casts off a stinking garment), and to "put on that new man created in God's image" (v. 24). This "new man" is Christ; through solidarity with Him they will discover their lost humanity.

Having described pagan immorality in general, Paul moves

on to tackle some of its particular manifestations in the largely
Gentile churches he is addressing in this letter. His injunctions
are probably based on a combination of his own experience with
Gentile churches that he himself founded, and reports on these
churches that had come to him in Rome. Consonant with his
stress on the unity of the Church throughout this letter, these
exhortations are directed to interactions among Christians. Paul's
purpose in giving them is to build up the Church. He simply
assumes that Christians will demonstrate the same high standard
of morality to non-Christians.

The first vice which he mentions is lying (4:25). Christians
are "members of one another" through their solidarity with Christ.
Thus, the destructive repercussions of a lie affect not only the
person lied to, but the entire community, including the liar, whose
action is self-destructive.

Next, Paul refers to anger (v. 26). Anger itself (Paul was
probably thinking of righteous anger here, such as Jesus' righteous
anger at the moneychangers in the Temple) is not blameworthy,
but must not be prolonged. To prolong it would be to give the
devil an inroad into one's life (v. 27).

Christianity accepted converts from all classes of society. A
person's past did not matter. The present and future, however,
did matter, and a former criminal or prostitute was expected to
renounce his or her former way of life upon conversion. In actual
practice this was not always the case. Paul very matter-of-factly
reminds the Christian thief to give up his stealing (28a)—it contradicts the "new man" which he put on at his Baptism (see 4:24).
Like lying, stealing is a sin against the Body of Christ. Rather
than tear down this Body, Paul admonishes the thief to find a
job so that he can help build it up through his ability to give to
the poor (28b).

"Evil talk" (v. 29) is a general term, and includes everything
from gossip to swearing. In its place Paul enjoins words of encouragement.

Verse 30 brings out the truly intimate nature of our relationship with God, in this case the Holy Spirit, who personally indwells every Christian, and whose presence is the pledge of our salvation. When we sin the Holy Spirit is not so much offended as "saddened," or grieved; in other words, personally (and emotionally) disappointed at our faithlessness. It is as if we had rejected Him for another lover.

"Bitterness," in verse 31, refers to resentment of long duration; "passion" to quick-tempered anger of short duration; and "anger" to long-standing hostility.

Paul exhorts his readers to replace the vices listed in verse 31 with the virtues cited in verse 32. "Kindness" has the connotation of placing others' needs on a par with one's own; "compassionate" is literally "tenderhearted." Mutual forgiveness is absolutely essential, being a direct reflection of a gift the Christian has already received in Christ. Like all the blessings which a Christian has received, forgiveness must be shared (extended to others) before it can become effective in one's own life.

*Questions for Personal Reflection/Group Discussion*

1. Humility was not considered to be a virtue in the Western world until Christianity made it one.
   (a) In your own words, describe the meaning of humility for a Christian.
   (b) Humility is definitely on the way out in modern, secular society. Why do you think this is so?
2. On a scale of 1 to 10 (1 being low, 10 being high), where would you rate your parish church in terms of the total unity of its members? Give reasons for your rating.
3. (a) Which of the seven expressions of unity—one body, one Spirit, one hope, one Lord, one faith, one baptism, one God and Father—would you say is the strong point of your parish church?

(b) Which of the seven would you say is its weak point?
Please give reasons.

(c) Suggest several ways by means of which this weakness
might be able to be strengthened.

4. Describe the gift(s) that God has given *you* for the upbuilding
of His Church.

5. (a) How is Paul's understanding of Church different in Ephesians from his understanding in I Corinthians and Romans?

(b) Account for these differences.

## Chapter 15:    Some Controversial Guidelines

*Please read Ephesians 5-6.*    Expanding on the meaning of discipleship, Paul urges the Christian to imitate God in the same
way that children imitate their fathers (5:1). The "way of love"
which he enjoins in 2a is the way of *agapē*, or sacrificial love,
a meaning which he makes explicit in 2b by referring to Jesus'
sacrificial death.

Given the depth of Jesus' love and the Christian imperative
to embody this love, unChristian conduct becomes unthinkable.
Paul focuses on sexual sins in the next five verses (3-7), not
because these sins were worse than any others, but because these
sins were so common among the Gentiles. Sexual immorality
was almost expected in the exceptionally permissive society from
which they came. Apparently some pagan converts did not leave
this kind of behavior behind with their Baptism.

When Paul insists that they not even talk about these things
(v. 3), he is well aware that such talk often leads to action; both
the talk and the action are incompatible with Christianity. He
makes essentially the same point in verse 4, this time criticizing,
among other things, dirty jokes, which cheapen sexuality.

The proper Christian attitude toward sex is simply one of
thanksgiving (5a). He becomes extremely blunt in 5b, equating

sexual immorality with idolatry—making sexual gratification one's ultimate concern—and unequivocally stating that an idolater (by his or her own choice) has forfeited heaven.

Paul is cognizant that a certain element (probably a Gnostic element, which maintained that the body did not matter, and therefore that it did not matter what one did with one's body) within the Church was teaching that promiscuity and Christianity were compatible. Therefore he warns his readers against "worthless arguments" or, literally, "empty words" (6a). Again he emphasizes the seriousness of such disobedience (6b), using the concept of "God's wrath," and says that the best way to deal with such false guides is to avoid them (v. 7).

In a daring metaphor, he pictures his readers as "darkness" before they became Christians; now, through their identification with Christ, they are "light" (5:8a). As in most cultures, the realities of darkness and light had metaphysical and moral connotations for both the Greeks and the Jews. Darkness not only symbolized, but was believed to share in the properties of death and evil.

In a similar way, light participated in life and goodness. As befits their new nature in Christ, Paul admonishses his readers to live as "children of light" (8b). Operating on the principle that like produces like, he links light with "goodness" (a goodness which is overflowing due to its generosity), "justice" (moral uprightness), and "truth" (a relational truth which spills over into one's life).

Verse 10, "Be correct in your judgment of what pleases the Lord," reads literally, "proving what is acceptable to the Lord." To prove means to test (as in testing a metal for hardness or purity). "Acceptable," or "well-pleasing" is a term used to describe a suitable sacrifice. The sense of this phrase is thus a call to distinguish between true and false values using the criterion of what Christ would find commendable.

The phrase "Take no part in" (v. 11) is literally "Have no

fellowship with," and implies a personal identification with the "vain deeds done in darkness." The word which the *NAB* translates as "condemn" can also mean "expose." In verses 11-13 Paul is calling Christians to expose the works of darkness so that the light of Christ can shine on them, show them for what they are, and heal them. Verse 14, quite likely a verse from an early Christian baptismal hymn, celebrates the possibility of repentance and the availability of redemption in Christ.

The maintenance of authentic Christian morality requires both watchfulness and thoughtfulness (5:15). The false values of the present generation provide the Christian with plenty of opportunities for witnessing to the light of Christ (v. 16). Ignorance is no excuse for a Christian, inasmuch as he or she is challenged to "discern the will of the Lord" (v. 17), which requires an ongoing growth in understanding.

Paul's injunction to Christians to avoid drunkenness (18a), is in marked contrast to the practices of many of the mystery cults, which utilized drunken ecstasy, often followed by ritual fornication, as a means of communion with their patron deity. His enjoinder against drunkenness, however, was not aimed only at the cultic variety; it also included drunkenness of the simple, everyday kind.

Being filled with the Spirit is the antithesis of being filled with alcohol (18b). The Christian's infilling with the Holy Spirit leads, not to debauchery, as with alcohol, but to inspired worship (v. 19) which overflows into thanksgiving (v. 20).

Verse 21, "Defer to one another out of reverence for Christ," does not conclude, or summarize, the above-mentioned injunctions (4:25-5:20). Rather, it introduces the "household code" which follows (5:22-6:9). This is obvious in the Greek, where verse 22 had no object of its own; it uses the object in verse 21. In this household code Paul speaks specifically to Christians, enjoining on them a much higher and deeper understanding of marriage and family life than was the rule in either Jewish or Greek culture at the time.

Verse 21, which reads literally, "Be subject to one another out of fear of Christ," instructs Christians to be mutually submissive to one another. In using the phrase "fear of Christ" in this way, Paul is both asserting this authority to speak for Jesus on this matter and claiming that his teaching reflects the Spirit of Jesus' teaching. The directive "Be subject to one another" is, for Christians, a moral absolute, a universal moral principle. As we shall see, Paul himself is not entirely consistent in his application of this principle; he allows the culture of his day to color his interpretation.

He begins by stating bluntly that "Wives should be submissive to their husbands" (v. 22). This was already a cliche in Paul's time; he reasserts it because he is not interested in overturning the traditional morality. His method, that of transformation, is much more subtle than this.

The phrase "as if to the Lord" (22b; the word "if" does not appear in the Greek) is based on the solidarity of Christians and the Church with Christ. This fundamental solidarity provides the context for Paul to form the analogy which he does in verses 23 and 24; just as Christ is head of his body the Church, the husband is head of his wife. "As the Church submits to Christ, so wives should submit to their husbands."

In reaching such a conclusion, Paul is not being consistent with the principle of *mutual* submission which he previously stated in verse 21. His analogy is based on the hierarchial thinking of his day, thinking which simply assumed that "the husband is head of the wife." If the mutual submissiveness of verse 21 is the pivotal point theologically, then the analogy which follows would actually be along the lines of wives and husbands submitting to *one another* because this is Jesus' intent, and Jesus is head of the Church.

Paul, possibly anticipating that in their marriage relationships most husbands could easily tend to exaggerate the element of authority and downplay the element of love, states in verse 25: "Husbands, love your wives, as Christ loved the Church. He gave himself up for her." The word which he uses for love in this context is *agapē*. Taken all the way, it describes the self-sacrifice that Christ underwent on behalf of the Church. *Agapē* also has an intermediate meaning, however, and this is to put someone else's good, the fulfillment of someone else's needs, ahead of one's own.

Although his sentiments are noble, Paul loses some of the transformative power of his vision by limiting the call to *agapē* to the "higher" member of the marital union, the male. His hierarchical thinking gets him in trouble here. The mutual submissiveness enjoined in verse 21 is virtually synonymous with *agapē*, and thus should be the centering point in the spirituality of *both* parties.

Verses 26 and 27 are parenthetical, Paul's mention of Christ's relationship to the Church in verse 25 having sparked in him a vision of the Church as His bride.

Returning to the subject of Christian husbands in verse 28, Paul admonishes them to "love their wives as they do their own bodies." This translation sounds a little self-seeking. The literal Greek reads "love their wives as *being* their own bodies," and attempts to communicate the consummate solidarity between husband and wife. Thus, "He who loves his wife loves himself" (28b). It is unfortunate that Paul did not add, for the sake of mutuality, something to the effect that "She who loves her husband loves herself." Verses 29 and 30 repeat (for a third time) his injunction of sacrificial love to Christian husbands.

Next, in verse 31, he quotes the classic Old Testament text establishing the sanctity of marriage, Genesis 2:24, a text which was dear to Jesus (see Matthew 19:4-6 and Mark 10:6-8). Paul considers this text to refer to a great "foreshadowing" (literally: "mystery"); namely, that the intimate relationship between husband and wife hints at the radical solidarity between Christ and his Church (v. 32). He concludes his thoughts on Christian marriage with a final reminder to both husbands and wives of their "proper" roles in the marital relationship (v. 33). Again, Paul would have been more consistent if he had described these "proper," hierarchical roles in terms of mutuality and complimentarity.

Although Paul adopts the traditional idea of submissiveness on the part of the wife, he does not stop here. To this basic, culturally given, idea he at least states the principle of mutual submissiveness and adds the requirement of sacrificial love on the part of the husband. These divinely inspired additions, in spite of Paul's own inconsistencies, accomplish nothing less than the total transformation of the original idea. No longer can marriage be characterized (as the typical Greek and Jewish marriages of the time could be) as the embodiment of male chauvinism which exploits women. Rather, it has become the qualitatively new institution of *Christian* marriage, a new kind of relationship in which the organic oneness of the couple is achieved through mutual submissiveness and sacrificial love.

Theologically speaking, a profound development has taken place in Paul's thought in the nine or so years between his treatment of marriage in I Corinthians 7 and his discussion of marriage in Ephesians 5. In Corinthians, Paul treats marriage in terms of an interim ethic—something to do (if one is not able to choose the higher calling of celibacy) until the Lord returns. In Ephesians Paul considers Christian marriage as nothing less than a reflection of the illimitable extent to which Christ loves the Church.

Paul's instruction to children and parents, slaves and masters (6:1-9) is quite similar to his teaching in Colossians 3:20-4:1. Again, what is most significant concerning these admonitions is that—like his injunctions to wives and husbands—for the first time in the history of the ancient world they summon *both* parties to responsibility. No longer are wives, children, and slaves regarded primarily as property, to be used and abused according to the whims of husband, father, and master. For Christians, these relationships are no longer one-sided, but mutual, carrying responsibilites for both sides. It would not be going too far to say that Paul did more to redefine the nature of relationship in terms of mutuality than any other person in the history of Western civilization with the single exception of Jesus.

Christian children are expected to obey their parents (6:1). Obedience implies the acquiescence of children to the leadership of their parents. Paul assumes that the persons being obeyed truly have the good of the child at heart. He quotes the appropriate injunction from the Ten Commandments to underline his point (6:2-3).

Having considered the proper role of Christian children, Paul goes on to consider the responsibilites of Christian fathers (mothers would be included in his reference to "fathers" because of Christian solidarity). Not angering one's children (4a) means to avoid the arbitrariness and inconsistency which so often characterize the parent-child relationship. Parents, in other words, should treat their children as persons, not things. Furthermore, parents have the obligation of providing their children "with the training and instruction befitting the Lord" (4b). "Training" includes the notion of "discipline" which, in turn, implies a consistent pattern of coaching in terms of values and behavior. "Instruction" refers to the truths of the Christian faith, which it is the responsibility of all Christian parents to see that their children not only learn, but live.

Turning to the slave-master relationship, Paul first admonishes slaves to serve their masters as they would serve the Lord himself (6:5-7). The relationship with his or her master was the slaves's primary relationship, and it was this relationship that Paul seeks to transform through Christian love. The inner transformation which slaves have already experienced through their solidarity with Christ should overflow into their relationships with their masters. This should be the slaves' primary motivation for cheerful, dedicated service. Only secondarily does Paul introduce the motive of future judgment (v. 8).

"Masters, act in a similar way toward your slaves" (9a)

implies that their own transforming relationship with Christ will spill over into their relationships with their slaves. Just as the master is a manifestation of Christ for the slave, the slave is a manifestation of Christ for the master. This is an incredibly radical teaching for a society which considered slaves as things to be disposed of at will. More than anything else in the history of Western civilization, this teaching set the stage for the eventual dissolution of slavery. Again, Paul introduces the reality of future judgment as a secondary motive for taking his teaching seriously (9b).

Paul moves into the conclusion of this letter with a forceful and sustained metaphor in which he compares the various attributes of the Christian life to the various pieces of armor worn by the typical Roman soldier. Considering that he was chained to a soldier for the duration of his imprisonment in Rome, it is easy to see how he gained familiarity with the various armaments and their uses.

Here, as in other places, Paul shows a penchant for military imagery; he likes the picture of a well-disciplined and well-equipped infantryman. It is fascinating how, on the one hand, he has a definite attraction for the well-turned military image while, on the other hand, he never employs this imagery to describe any kind of violence between Christians and other people.

According to Paul, Christians are, indeed, involved in a battle, but this battle is not against other people, but against hostile spiritual forces. The "weapons" with which a Christian fights are the non-violent weapons of truth, justice, missionary zeal, faith, salvation, the Spirit, and prayer.

He begins this, the greatest of his military metaphors, by stating unequivocally that a Christian's strength (in this context the power, not only to endure, but to endure victoriously) comes "from the Lord and his mighty power" (6:10). In other words, Christian "weapons" are not simply natural gifts of personality, but supernatural gifts of grace. God has endowed every Christian with these gifts. The only requirement for keeping them is to *use* them.

Paul clearly identifies the Christian's opponent as the "devil" in verse 11. The devil, for Paul, is a personal, supernatural force of evil intent upon the total destruction of God's creation. This force of evil was believed to express itself in various forms. Paul mentions some of these forms in verse 12. The "principalities and powers" are connected with the then fashionable belief in astrology; they were evil spirits who controlled access to the various heavenly spheres. The "rulers of this world of darkness" probably refers to the Roman pantheon, which Paul considers to be demonic, opposed to the worship of the true God.

These various expressions of evil are obviously culturally and historically determined; that is, they are the manifestations of a particular culture at a particular time in history. But they are also *more* than this, and this is the important point. These specific expressions of evil may be time-bound, but the essence of the personal, supernatural force of evil, that which Paul calls the devil, or Satan, transcends all limitations of time and space.

The Evil One uses different (dis)guises at different times; apparently one of his favorite tactics in modern times is to convince most people that he is a "medieval" superstition—that is, that he does not exist. If Paul were here today, he, like Pope Paul VI, would caution us that the devil is as alive and well as ever, and that we twentieth century Christians need the full complement of God's armor (v. 13) just as much as our first century counterparts.

This armor consist of the following:

1. The belt of truth (14a). Truth in this context means that Christianity is the only approach to reality which fully corresponds to reality. The belt was the device from which the solider hung his sword. In this case the sword is the inspired "word of God" (v. 17), which is only as true and, consequently as effective, as the truth on which it hangs.

2. The breastplate of justice or righteousness (14b). The breastplate covered the vital area of the heart and lungs. The

"righteousness," or total quality of a Christian's life, is his or her final line of defense.

3. The footgear of missionary zeal (15). Footgear suggests mobility; a Christian must be on the move proclaiming the "gospel of peace." The word peace recalls Paul's earlier emphasis in this letter (2:11-22) on Christ Himself being our peace, our ultimate reconciliation between the warring parts of ourselves, our conflicts with other people, our estrangement from nature, and our alienation from God.

4. The shield of faith (16). Faith—an inner trust in God no matter what the outward circumstances—is, like a shield, a Christian's front line of defense.

5. The helmet of salvation (17a). Salvation describes the Christian's new status before God as a redeemed son or daughter. This qualitatively new state of being enables a Christian to look forward, to meet whatever may come, in safety.

6. The sword of God's inspired Word (17b). God's Word—the truth and the transforming power which it contains—is the Christian's great offensive weapon.

All this armor is empowered, that is, made effective, through prayer (18). Prayer might be described in this context as the vital force behind all this equipment. Without a living relationship with God, a relationship expressed most concretely through prayer, this Christian armor would be like a suit of armor in a museum; interesting, perhaps, but hardly fit for battle without a person inside.

God's armor may seem highly individual, being shaped, as it is, slightly differently for each person. Yet the necessary communal dimension of this armor is at least implied with the mention of prayer. Prayer, for Christians, is nothing less than mutual empowerment through solidarity with God through Christ in the power of the Spirit. Paul knows this and counts on this by asking for the prayers of his readers (vv. 19-20).

Having presented that which many commentators consider to be in many ways his most profound and contemplative letter,

Paul brings it to a close with a commendation of Tychicus (v. 21). Tychicus, if our hunch is right, carried with him the letter to Philemon, to the Colossians, and this circular letter, which he was to deliver first to Laodicea (see Colossians 4:16b), a town close to Colossae. Apparently Tychicus was to accompany this letter to its various destinations, bringing with it news of a more personal nature concerning Paul's imprisonment in Rome (v. 22). In accord with the expansive style of the entire letter, Paul expands his customary benediction of "grace and peace" to include "love" and "faith." These four key words sum up the essence of this epistle.

## Questions for Personal Reflection/Group Discussion

1. The ancient world rationalized a lot of sexual immorality on the ground that the body and its activities were of no consequence.
    (a) How does modern, secular society justify its return to sexual immorality?
    (b) Why should sexual immorality be unthinkable for a Christian?
2. Summarize Paul's teaching on the husband-wife relationship in Ephesians 5.
3. In what ways would you say that a truly Christian marriage reflects the mystery of Christ's relationship with his Church?
4. *How* did Paul do so much to redefine the nature of the husband-wife, parent-child, and master-slave relationships?
5. (a) In what sense is Paul's understanding of some of the manifestations of the devil culturally and historically determined?
    (b) In what sense is Paul's understanding of the devil valid for all time?
6. Summarize the significance of the various elements in the Christian panoply: truth, justice, missionary zeal,faith, salvation, Word, prayer.

# *Philippians*

## Introduction

The Church at Philippi was the first Christian community that Paul established in Europe. The dramatic story of its founding is detailed in Acts 16:7-40. As with his other missionary outposts, Paul, under the guidance of the Holy Spirit, chose to base a church at Philippi largely for strategic reasons. The city straddled the pass which, practically speaking, separated Europe from "Asia" (what we would call the Near East today). It was located on the Egnatian Way, the major thoroughfare between Rome and the East. From Philippi as beachhead it would be possible to carry the Christian message into the rest of Greece, which is just what happened.

Scholars, as they so often do concerning matters of this debatable nature, hotly contest the dating of this letter. Traditionally, Philippians was considered to be the last letter which Paul wrote during his "First Imprisonment in Rome." This would date it sometime during 62-63.

However, with the discovery that there was a "praetorium" (1:13) in every major Roman city, and that "those in Caesar's service" (4:22) referred to all civil servants throughout the Empire, many scholars started searching for another time and place, a time and place which they believed would better account for the following:

1. The style and content of Philippians seem to have more in common with the style and content of Paul's early and middle letters (particularly Galatians, I Corinthians, and Romans) than

with the late Colossians and Ephesians, written from Rome. Most
noticeably, Philippians contains frequent references to the Second
Coming (1:6b, 10b; 2:16; 4:5), while Colossians and Ephesians
minimize Jesus' Return and maximize the transformative role of
the Church within history.

2. This letter presupposes a rather large number of visits
between Paul and its recipients. The distance from Rome to
Philippi was some 800 miles, and would have taken some four
or five weeks to traverse. An origin for this letter closer than
Rome is therefore argued as likely.

3. Paul mentions in this letter that if he is released the first
thing he will do is to visit his beloved friends in Philippi. This
fact seems inconsistent if this letter was written from Rome (where
one would have expected his next destination to be Spain), but
not inconsistent if this letter had been written from one of the
"Eastern" cities where Philippi would have been more or less on
the way to Rome and the West.

Given these problems with the traditional thesis, a small
number of scholars argue that Paul wrote his letter to the Philippians from Caesarea (sometime during the years 58-59). A large
number of scholars maintain that this letter was written during
Paul's ministry in Ephesus, and date it around the years 54 or
55. Caesarea seems unlikely because the somber tone of Philippians (based on the finality of the upcoming trial with its possible
martyrdom) does not square with the trump card—appeal to
Caesar—that Paul held and finally used during his imprisonment
at Caesarea. In addition, Caesarea is even further from Philippi
than Rome.

Ephesus, on the other hand, was a journey of a mere week
from Philippi by sea. Although the book of Acts fails to mention
a specific imprisonment there, it can be argued that Luke was
not intent on providing a complete account of Paul's life. Besides,
we know from Paul's own letters (I Corinthians 15:32; II Corinthians 1:8-9) that his life was endangered probably not once but

several times in Ephesus, and that imprisonment may well have been part of the danger to his person. Finally, if his letter to the Philippians was written from Ephesus, a visit of Philippi would not be contradicting his stated intention to return to Spain. These relatively minor reasons, plus the major evidence of style and content, have convinced many scholars that Paul wrote Philippians from Ephesus.

It seems to this author, however, that the total weight of the evidence still favors a Roman origin, and thus a late rather than early date, for this letter. The evidence in favor of Rome consists of (a) the fact that all objections to it can be met, (b) additional considerations that scholars in favor of Ephesus tend to ignore, and (c) an overwhelming amount of internal evidence.

First, in answer to objections:

1. The style and content is only *superficially* similar to that of the earlier letters. Paul summarizes in one verse, 3:9, the essence of his argument against the law, an argument that took up the larger part of his letters to the Galatians and Romans. A summary of this magnitude implies a later date than the material which it summarizes. Actually, the style and content of Philippians are unique in the Pauline corpus. With the single exception of II Timothy, this is by far the most intimate of Paul's letters. As such it bears little resemblance to either the early theological letters or the later contemplative ones.

2. In this letter Paul hopes for release, yet rather expects his death. This is not unusual in a capital case. His return to the hope and the imagery of the Second Coming seems quite natural given the constant presence of the likelihood of death.

3. We know from the extent of Paul's various missionary journeys that he would not have been intimidated by a mere 800 miles, and this 800 miles on a safe, well-constructed road, the ancient equivalent of today's freeway.

4. Any *major* imprisonment in Ephesus would surely have been recorded by Luke in Acts. Philippians 1:12-13 certainly

makes it sound like a significant amount of time has been involved, not just a week or so.

5. Surely Paul could have changed his mind about going to Spain. If he did write this letter from Rome in 62, his plans to visit Spain, expressed in his letter to the Romans, had been formulated at least five years earlier.

The following are added facts often overlooked by those who favor Ephesus:

6. In 2:21 Paul states that everyone around him is "busy seeking his own interests rather than those of Christ Jesus." We know from the book of Acts that Paul spent three years in Ephesus and that there he enjoyed his most successful ministry, at least in terms of numbers. The above reference to the meager amount of support he is receiving would make a lot more sense coming from Rome, where he had not founded the Christian community, and where he quite likely was considered by many to be something of a nuisance, than from Ephesus, where he was revered as a patriarch.

7. Paul has already received and is expecting a great deal more publicity from his imprisonment (see 1:12-14). This kind of publicity for the Christian faith better fits the context of Rome than Ephesus.

The most weighty evidence in favor of a Roman origin for this letter, however, are the following internal considerations:

8. Throughout this letter Paul converses with the Philippians as old and comfortable friends. The kind of relational intimacy apparent in this letter takes a long time to develop.

9. Much of the letter reads like a last will and testament. There is a definite preoccupation with death and resurrection. This is precisely what one would expect during a prolonged imprisonment before a trial involving a capital offense.

We conclude, then, that St. Paul wrote to his beloved friends at Philippi from prison in Rome sometime during the year 62. Epaphroditus, a leader in the Philippian Church, had been sent to him some months before with a gift of money. He had reported to Paul a growing lack of unity within that church, and Paul takes this opportunity to counsel them in this regard.

## Chapter 16:    Jesus Christ is Lord!

*Please read Philippians 1-2.*    Paul includes Timothy in his salutation (1:1) because Timothy was with him when he founded the Church at Philippi (see Acts 16:1-5), and was now with him in Rome, sharing both his joy and his concern for the Philippian Church. Unlike the greeting of most of his letters, Paul simply refers to Timothy and himself as "servants" (literally: "slaves") of Christ Jesus. He is able to dispense with the formality of referring to himself as an apostle because of his exceptionally close relationship with the Philippians.

His mention of "bishops and deacons" is significant, not because it proves the existence of an ecclesiastical hierarchy at this relatively early date, but because it evidences an intermediate stage in the evolution of that hierarchy. At this point "bishops and deacons" means simply "overseers and (their) assistants." The existence of these positions, however, does indicate that the leadership of the early Church was not merely spontaneous but organized, with several people in the community exercising real authority. Authority continued to be understood as added power for added service.

Paul gives his by now traditional blessing in verse 2, which joins the customary Greek greeting of "grace" (an expression of goodwill) with the customary Jewish greeting of "peace" (an expression of the hope that the person greeted will receive all the good things of life through God's bountiful goodness).

The prayer with which Paul follows his greeting (1:3-11) is one of the most personally moving prayers in any of his correspondence. The prayer opens with thanksgiving (v. 3), a motif which, together with its corollary, joy (v. 4), serves as a major theme of this letter. The word "Think" in verse 3 is actually "remembrance," which in Greek has the connotation of making present (re-membering). It is clear from these verses that Paul's petitions for his friends sparks in him a joyful remembrance of them, a remembrance which enables them to become present to him across the miles. One of the things about which he is most joyful is their fellowship, or partnership with him in the cause of the Gospel (v. 5). This fellowship is especially dear to him since its quality has been so consistent and so long-standing.

Verse 6 is filled with pathos, a pathos which is unfortunately lost in any English translation because our phrases "has begun" and "will carry it through to completion" do not have the liturgical connotations which they do in Greek, where they are the technical terms for the beginning and end of a sacrifice.

Although Paul is thinking of the entire Christian life as a progressive sacrifice—a process through which the Christian deepens in holiness—one cannot help but think (especially given the content of the following verse) that he is also reflecting on his own lot in prison. In other words, his prayer that God will sustain the Philippians through their sacrifice is at the same time a prayer that God will uphold him through his.

The "day of Christ Jesus" is a reference to the Parousia, or Second Coming, a reality which must have been continually on Paul's mind, given the likelihood that only death would end his imprisonment. Paul, then, is thinking of the "last things," not as an imminent reality for *all* Christians, like in his earlier letters, but as an imminent *personal* reality for himself.

Verse 7 is a poignant expression of Paul's solidarity (a solidarity in Christ Jesus which effectively bridges the 800 miles between Rome and Philippi) with the Philippians, and of theirs with him. Notice the way in which he is careful to include *all* his friends ("to a man;" in the Greek "all of you") in this solidarity. This phrase is repeated at intervals throughout the letter—an indication of Paul's concern for the unity and community of the Philippian Church.

The phrase "summoned to defend the solid grounds on which the gospel rests" (7b) adverts to his upcoming trial. It might seem strange that he does not mention the actual charge on which he is to be tried (starting a riot in Jerusalem), but this is quite in character, considering his passionate defense of the Christian faith in his "trial" before Felix (see Acts 24:1-21) and his audience with King Agrippa (see Acts 26:1-32).

His reference to his imprisonment and impending trial as "gracious" reveals the fact that he considers suffering for the faith to be a vehicle of God's grace. Suffering for the cause of Christ becomes redemptive suffering, the benefits of which are shared by the entire Church.

Paul was not the founder of the Church in Rome, and was probably looked upon by the Roman Christians with suspicion. Quite naturally, he feels lonely, and expresses his loneliness in terms of longing in verse 8. The phrase "with the affection of Christ Jesus" is literally "in the bowels of Christ Jesus." This is a common Hebrew idiom for exceptionally intense feeling.

He prays for a continuing increase in their love, the foremost Christian virtue (v. 9). Specifically, he asks that their love may overflow into "understanding" and "wealth of experience." "Understanding" is practical knowledge, especially in matters of morality. "Wealth of experience" actually refers to the mature discernment which a plentitude of experience can produce.

The "clear conscience" mentioned in verse 10 is the conscience which is pure, unalloyed with conflicting motives. "To value the things that really matter" means to be able to weigh different alternatives and choose the best one. The "harvest of justice" referred to in verse 11 consists of all the various acts of righteousness—we might say all the good works and positive attitudes—which typify the life of a Christian.

Thus, in verses 9-11 Paul is asking God to inspire and empower—to bless—his friends in Philippi with an even greater measure of Christian fulfillment than the high measure they are already experiencing. Even his beloved Philippians are not yet "perfect," and Paul hopes that they will never cease striving after Christian perfection.

Knowing that his imprisonment is causing them a great deal of anxiety, he presents his situation as positively as he can (vv. 12-26). Rather than stifling his ministry, his incarceration has actually augmented it (v. 12). Paul's imprisonment was a "house arrest" (see Acts 28:30-31), an arrest, however, which included the Roman custom of being chained to a guard at all times. We can imagine him making the most of this opportunity and sharing the Gospel with the various soldiers who took turns being chained to him. In this way the Gospel, which would otherwise have hardly made it into such a place, penetrated into the "praetorium," the royal garrison (v. 13).

In addition, Paul's imprisonment has inspirited many of his fellow Christians to a new level of evangelistic fervor (v. 14). This is something of a mixed blessing for Paul personally because some of those preaching the Gospel are doing so out of competition with him (vv. 15-17). In spite of their mixed motives Paul finds joy in the fact that the Gospel is being proclaimed (v. 18).

His lifework of proclaiming the Good News of salvation is the basis for Paul's own hope for salvation (v. 19). Significantly, he does not consider salvation—even his own—to be an individual affair. He thanks his friends in Philippi for their prayers on his behalf, prayers which he considers essential for his continuing empowerment to preach the Gospel fearlessly. Likewise, he mentions the strength he has received from the Holy Spirit. Paul's theological understanding of solidarity is present in a very personal way in this verse. It is his solidarity with Jesus through His Spirit and through His people that inspires Paul's joyfulness in the present situation.

Verse 20 expresses his eager expectation that he will, indeed, be able to meet the test of imprisonment. Paul must have been tempted more than once to become discouraged and resentful at the extent to which he was called upon to suffer for the sake of the Gospel. Part of the beauty of his acknowledgment of the prayers in verse 19 is that he recognizes his dependence on the ministry of his friends. This ministry gives Paul "full confidence" that he will be able to continue to glorify Christ, whether it be through continuing ministry (if the outcome of his trial is the verdict "Not Guilty") or through martyrdom (if the verdict is "Guilty").

He has become so centered on Christ that he is able to make the powerful statement in verse 21 that "To me, 'life' means Christ; hence dying is so much gain." He can consider death in this positive light because it stands as the doorway to an even closer relationship with Christ than is possible in this life.

Paul finds himself in a dilemma: on the one hand, "dying is so much gain;" on the other, his ministry is still needed. He describes the two horns of this dilemma in verses 21-24, coming to the conclusion (based on his internalization of *agapē* as self-giving love) that his ministry should take precedence over his personal desire to "break camp" (a more literal translation of the phrase "to be freed from this life" of v. 23) and be with Christ.

This process of reflection gives him a presentiment that he will be released and be able to rejoin his beloved Philippians (vv. 25-26). Biblical scholars are divided concerning the actual outcome of this imprisonment for Paul. Those (a slight majority of mainstream commentators today) who consider the Pastoral Epistles (Titus, I & II Timothy) to be written by a different author (or authors) than Paul believe that this imprisonment ended with his death.

Those (the minority, including myself) who consider Paul the author of the pastorals argue for his release, a few more years of ministry, and a second (and fatal) Roman imprisonment. We will consider this issue in more depth in our introduction to the

Pastoral Epistles. Suffice it to say at this point that Paul's faith did not tend to be delusional, and that his inspired intuition of continuing ministry needs to be taken seriously, and is, in itself, a strong argument in favor of his authorship of the pastorals.

Having shared his own need to stand firm in his faith, he goes on to admonish the Philippians to stand firm in theirs (vv. 27-30). The verb for "to conduct yourselves" (27a) denotes behavior characteristic of citizenship in a Greek city; thus, Paul is calling for public behavior which is compatible with that of being a citizen of "Christ's country." The fact that he has to mention some kind of "inspection" concerning their unity (either a personal visit or, if this is impossible, a report on their behavior) underscores the fact that there is a problem regarding unity in the Philippian Church (27b).

Paul's first visit to Philippi was a tumultuous one because of fierce opposition on the part of the local populace. Paul knows that this opposition to the faith did not cease with his departure, and entreats his friends not to be daunted (28a). Their steadfastness is a sign of their salvation, while the rejection of the Gospel on the part of their enemies points to their self-destructive end (28b).

The suffering they are called to undergo, as well as the suffering they have already undergone on behalf of Christ, Paul considers to be a "special privilege," nothing less than a personal participation in Jesus' redemptive sacrifice (v. 29). Their solidarity with Christ enables the Philippians and Paul to share a special closeness through their mutual suffering for the cause of the Gospel (v. 30).

At this point Paul solemnly pleads with the Philippians to embody the unity which is their calling in Christ (2:1-4). The actual Greek of verse 1 contains a fourfold "If . . . ": "If there is any encouragement in Christ," etc. Paul, in other words, uses everything he can think of—including their sympathy at his imprisonment—to arouse his friends to a new level of oneness among themselves. His petition "make my joy complete" (2:2) implies, of course, that his joy is currently incomplete, and incomplete precisely because of their lack of unanimity. The "one love" which he mentions is the same sacrificial love which he so eloquently wrote about in I Corinthians 13.

He focuses now on one particular aspect of *agapē*, that of its humbleness and other-centeredness (vv. 3-4). Apparently the Christian community at Philippi was experiencing no significant doctrinal difficulties. Its very existence as a community, however, was being threatened by internal conflicts, and these, like the disciples' conflicts with one another, converged on the issue of individual greatness. Powers and prestige in terms of position were becoming matters of real concern for some of Paul's friends in Philippi, and it is to them that he addresses this passionate plea for unity.

He has been carefully building up to his trump card, which is an appeal to the attitude of Jesus (v. 5). To hammer home his point he incorporates what is most likely a hymn (notice its careful construction and balance) originating from the Christian community in Jerusalem. This hymn (vv. 6-11) is one of the most important Christological statements in the entire New Testament. Since we shall study it in some detail, we reproduce the text here:

6 (a)  Though he was in the form of God,
  (b)      he did not deem equality with God
  (c)      something to be grasped at.
7 (a)  Rather, he emptied himself
  (b)      and took the form of a slave,
  (c)      being born in the likeness of men.

  (d)  He was known to be of human estate,
8 (a)      and it was thus that he humbled himself,
  (b)      obediently accepting even death,
  (c)      death on a cross!

9 (a)  Because of this,
  (b)      God highly exalted him

(c)        and bestowed on him the name
(d)        above every other name,

10(a)   So that at Jesus' name
   (b)        every knee must bend
   (c)        in the heavens, on the earth,
   (d)        and under the earth,
11(a)        and every tongue proclaim
   (b)        to the glory of God the Father:
   (c)        JESUS CHRIST IS LORD!

The word used for "was" in 6a is not the past tense of the verb "to be," but a technical philosophical word denoting the essence, or identity, of something. The meaning of this verb, plus the fact that it is used as a participle (in the continuing sense) manifests a very early belief in the pre-existence of Christ (his reality *before* the Incarnation), and this in such a way as to affirm His essential identity with God.

This affirmation is repeated in the word for "form." There are two words for "form" in Greek: *schēma*, which refers to the external appearance of a thing or person, an external appearance which is subject to change; and *morphē*, which refers to the unchanging essence of something. The word used for "form" in this first line is *morphē*, again emphasizing the fact that in His essence Christ shared the same nature as the Father.

This thought is further developed in 6b with the phrase "equality with God," a powerful affirmation of Christ's absolutely unique position in regard to the Father.

His unique status was not something which Christ misused in an attempt to glorify himself (6c). The word for "grasp" contains the connotation of "to seize by violence." There is an implicit contrast here between Christ's refusal to glorify himself and the attempts at self-glorification by both Adam (see Genesis 3) and Lucifer (see Isaiah 14:12-15).

Instead of presuming on his very real power and position, Christ did exactly the opposite: "he emptied himself" (7a). The reflexive (done by the self) nature of the verb highlights the fact that Christ freely chose to surrender his heavenly glory. Literally, he "poured out" his glory as one pours out the contents of a container. We should note, however, that the container still retains its essential nature, if not its changeable contents; to complete our analogy: Christ's giving up of power and prestige does not alter His nature as essentially divine.

The choice which Christ made was not merely one of giving up something (namely, his glory), but of taking on something else (namely, the "form of a slave"—7b). The word used for "form" is again *morphē* (inward essence as opposed to outward appearance), and underlines the fact that Christ's self-chosen slave-status was not merely an external appearance, but something which was real.

The word for "slave" can also be translated "servant." This line and, indeed, the hymn taken as a whole, looks back to the fourth of the Suffering Servant songs contained in the writings of the Second, or Deutero, Isaiah (a disciple of the original Isaiah who lived several hundred years after his master and celebrated the end of the Exile in Babylon. The song in its entirety can be found in Isaiah 52:13-53:12). The relationship of the early Christian hymn found in Philippians 2:6-11 to this fourth Suffering Servant song is one of fulfillment to promise. That is, our present text makes an identification between Christ and the Suffering Servant mentioned in Isaiah.

"Being born in the likeness of man" (7c) is, of course, a reference to the Incarnation. The word for "likeness," as is true for all the rather specialized words in this hymn, has been carefully chosen. "Likeness" might be said to stand midway between the absolute nature of essential form (*morphē*) and the changing nature of outward appearance (*schēma*).

The author of the hymn could not describe Christ's human

nature in terms of *morphē*, because this would limit Christ's nature to the human. Neither could he describe Christ's human nature in terms of *schēma*, because this would make His humanity seem superficial. As a compromise, then, Christ's human nature is described in terms of "likeness." By choosing this particular word the author is attempting to communicate the reality that Christ is *fully* human, yet at the same time *more* than human (that is, that He still maintains His essential nature as God).

These distinctions may seem difficult, which they are. Yet they are crucial if we are to continue, as did the early Church, to safeguard the integrity of an authentic orthodoxy, an orthodoxy which refuses to slide into the relatively easy alternatives of downplaying Christ's divinity in favor of his humanity, or vice versa. Incidentally, the sophisticated theology of this hymn points to the depth and complexity of Christology which the early Church had already achieved at a very early date.

The word which is translated as "estate" in 7d is *schēma*, outward appearance. The hymn is telling us that externally (in terms of human development, dress, speech, etc.) as well as inwardly (in terms of real identification) Christ chose to become a human being.

"And it was thus that he humbled himself," (8a): in other words, it was precisely as a human being that Christ chose to exercise His humility to its greatest extent. The Incarnation was already a significant humiliation; Christ's greatest act of humility, however, was His unswerving obedience to His Father's salvific will, which led to His death on Calvary (lines 8b & c). Both His obedience and His death on the cross are emphasized; obedience because, in a sense, it is so surprising given His prerogatives; the cross because it was the most servile form of death in the ancient world, serving as capital punishment for criminals and slaves.

Thus, in these verses an incredibly powerful contrast is made between Christ's rightful privileges (considering that He is God's "equal") and His self-chosen abasement (including not only His humanity but the sacrifice of even this for the sake of others). It is not difficult to see why Paul chose this particular hymn in his attempt to inspire the Philippians to humility: there is no more profound statement of the redemptive nature of humility in the entire Bible. Christian humility is redemptive because it participates in Christ's humility, which is the very basis of redemption.

At this point (exactly the midpoint of the hymn) there is an abrupt reversal, a reversal which is reminiscent of Jesus' own words in the Gospel:

> For everyone who exalts himself shall be humbled
> and he who humbles himself shall be exalted.
> (Luke 14:11; see also Matthew 23:12)

The words "Because of this" (9a, which reads "Therefore" in the original Greek) indicate a connection between what has happened (Christ's self-chosen humiliation) and the reality which is now celebrated in this hymn (His exaltation by the Father). This connection transcends causality; it is what we would call a *relational* connection, a connection which is founded on personal rather than mechanical interaction.

Christ has freely given (vv. 6-8); now the Father freely gives in response (vv. 9-11). Most significantly He gives to Christ "the name above every other name" (9c & d). Because of His willing sacrifice, the Father gives Him this name in *power*. Jesus' name now has the power to effect salvation in this world.

What is this name, the most powerful name that can be uttered on this planet, the name whose utterance contains within itself an act of allegiance? This name is LORD, which is English for *kurios*, which is Greek for *adōnai*, which is the Hebrew gloss for the divine name YHWH, considered to be so holy and so powerful that it was not allowed to be said or read directly.

In verse 10 the hymn goes on to make another radical equation (an equation so radical that Jews considered it to be blasphemy, while Christians affirmed it to be of the essence of the Gospel) between Christ and God. The hymn takes Isaiah 45:23d (in which *God* is reported as saying "To me every knee shall bend") and applies it to *Jesus*. Jesus, in other words, is God incarnate, and to Him "every knee must bend" (10b). This submission to Christ is all-inclusive (10c & d); it includes all beings (both angelic and human and, by extension, the entirety of creation) in all dimensions of being.

Verse 11 is a triumphant continuation of the equation being made between Isaiah 45:23e (the last line of this verse, which reads "by me every tongue shall swear") and the Christian affirmation that every tongue shall proclaim that *Jesus Christ* is *Lord*.

The middle phrase (line 11b) "to the glory of God the Father" eloquently witnesses to the Christian conviction that acknowledging Jesus as Lord in no way detracts from the Father's glory but rather adds to it (seeing that it is the Father's will and plan that Jesus be worshipped in this way).

The potent proclamation JESUS CHRIST IS LORD is universally acknowledged to be the earliest Christian declaration of faith in Jesus as God and loyalty to Him as Master. It was probably the profession of faith which an adult convert pronounced at his or her Baptism. As such it served as the springboard for all later Christian creeds.

We latter-day Christians are indeed indebted to St. Paul for incorporating this profound early Christian hymn into his appeal to the Philippians. Not only does it give us one of the earliest Christologies (understandings of Christ) in the New Testament; not only does it compel us to renew *our* efforts to make Jesus' attitude of sacrificial humility based on sacrifical love our own—it gives us a mystical insight into the Mystery of God, and thus calls us into a deeper relationship to the Father through Jesus in the inspiring presence of the Holy Spirit.

Having presented the strongest possible challenge to follow Christ's example, Paul goes on to mention some of the specific attitudes and actions which he hopes their discipleship will empower in them (2:12-18). His use of "anxious concern" (literally: "fear and trembling") in verse 12 does not refer to anxiety over the possible loss of one's salvation, but to the recognition of one's need of outside help. "Fear and trembling" is a stock phrase expressing the humility one feels when a task is too big for one. This is precisely the attitude to which Paul is calling the Philippians; they need to acknowledge the fact that they are fundamentally dependent upon God. After all, it is He who provides the inspiration and the motivation for further spiritual growth (v. 13).

Given the context of this letter, the "grumbling" and "arguing" mentioned in verse 14 are manifestations of the basic lack of unity within the Philippian Church. So, too, the lack of innocence and straightforwardness implied in 15a. These symptoms would disappear if the Philippians fully embraced the humility and love of Christ.

Paul balances his criticism and concern with praise in 15b. He tells his friends that they are already like stars, shedding light upon the darkened world around them. The overall impression one gets from this letter is that while there was a problem within the Philippian Church, it was still an eloquent witness to the transforming power of Christian faith. One is tempted to think that Paul rather exaggerates the case against them, like a parent who is especially severe with a small shortcoming in a favorite child.

The depth of Paul's affection and esteem for the Church at Philippi comes through in verse 16, where he states, in effect, that they are the high point of his lifework. Like the profitable servant in the parable of the talents (see Luke 19:11-26), he will not have to be ashamed when his Master returns and asks for an accounting of his activities.

He switches metaphors in verses 17 & 18, and likens his possible death to the drink offering which concludes ancient sacrifices. The image is a moving one: he represents the high quality of Christian living in the Church at Philippi as the substance of the sacrifice, and portrays himself merely as the "finishing touch." The thought of being able to serve them in this way (through his death) gives him great joy, because he knows that his further identification with the sacrificial love of Christ will draw them further into the mystery of their faith, and thus be a blessing to them.

Verses 19-30 concern Paul's sending Timothy and Epaphroditus to Philippi. Timothy was Paul's "right-hand man," his most trusted colleague, sharing in Paul's ministry to a unique degree. He had also helped Paul to found the church at Philippi; so he was the perfect person to stand in Paul's place.

Paul gives Timothy the highest recommendations. Compared to the depth and extent of his ministry, "Everyone is busy seeking his own interests rather than those of Christ Jesus" (v. 21). This complaint seems to imply that Paul's other trusted companions were not with him at this point and that the church in the city in which he was a prisoner was ignoring him. This, in turn, suggests Rome as the location of his imprisonment, since he had not founded the Roman Church and would probably be looked upon as an unwanted outsider.

Again, Paul's overriding intuition is that his imprisonment will end in release rather than death (v. 24). It is not wise to take a rigid stand on intuitions, however, and Paul expresses himself cautiously (v. 23).

Epaphroditus (vv. 25-30), a beloved member of the Philippian community, was sent to Paul to minister to his needs in jail. While doing this, he took ill and nearly died. Paul is deeply relieved at his recovery and sends him back to Philippi with a warm commendation.

*Questions for Personal Reflection/Group Discussion*

1. Please think of as many specific ways as you can in which friends have been instrumental in your continuing development as a Christian.

2. Think of several ways in which you experience solidarity with Christians whom you do not know personally.
3. Define the following:
   (a) *morphē*
   (b) *schēma*
4. Why does the author of the early Christian hymn in 2:6-11 use the word "likeness" in reference to Christ's human nature?
5. Render this hymn into your own words, trying to capture some of its nuances of meaning.
6. What does the phrase JESUS CHRIST IS LORD mean to you personally?

## Chapter 17:   Citizens of Heaven

*Please read Philippians 3-4.*   3:1 is simultaneously an attempted conclusion to the letter ("For the rest" means "finally," and "rejoice" is a customary "signing off" word in Greek) and the beginning of a whole new line of thought, a "postscript" which becomes as long as the preceding letter. Some scholars contend that this abrupt change signals the splicing together of two separate letters. It is more likely, however, that this is simply an example of that very common occurrence in letter-writing: jotting down new thoughts as fast as they come, with no regard for smoothness of transition. "These things" (1b) is really "the same things" and suggests that Paul is aware that he is about to repeat himself, restating things that they have already heard from him. He does this, however, for their safety—he does not want his friends to lower their guard against false teaching for even a moment.

Those against whom Paul is about to use some of the strongest language that we have in any of his letters are probably fanatical Jews who, much like himself before his conversion, are intent on eradicating the "heresy" of Christianity. As such they are avowed enemies of the Gospel, and Paul uses harsh language in an attempt to expose them as the impostors he considers them to be.

He begins by calling them "dogs" (3:2), which is supremely insulting given the fact that "dogs" was a common Jewish epithet for the Gentiles. This derogatory label probably derived from the fact that the Gentiles, making no distinction between "clean" and "unclean" in the matter of food, were considered to be like "dogs" who ate everything offered to them. At any rate, Paul inverts the term, implying that their unbelief in the Gospel has turned them into undiscriminating "dogs" who accept the garbage of inadequate teaching.

As if this were not enough, he calls them "workers of evil," and then throws in his ultimate insult, a pun on the word "circumcison" which reduces it to "mutilation" (2b). Circumcision, of course, was the hallmark of being a Jew: Paul could not have been more insulting if he had tried. He goes on and claims that it is the Christians who are observing the real meaning of circumcision, given the fact that real circumcision is a matter of Spirit-filled faith in the Gospel, and not external works (v. 3).

In order that no one be able to accuse him of speaking out of jealousy, he parades the full panoply of his Jewish credentials (3:4-6). The reference to his own circumcision (5a) is a boast that he was born into the faith (a "cradle-Jew," so to speak, and not a convert). "Being of the stock of Israel" (5b) witnesses to his ethnic purity; unlike so many of his Jewish contemporaries, he is not of "mongrel" stock. Coming from the "tribe of Benjamin" was considered to be a great honor; "a Hebrew of Hebrew origins" (5d) adverts to the fact that Paul was able to speak his native tongue. Finally, he was a Pharisee, a member of that elitist sect within Judaism which claimed, and was generally accorded, superiority in matters of faith and morals. Even among the Pharisees, he was a "Pharisee's Pharisee," excelling in zealousness and legal observance (6).

Following typical debating style, of which he was a master, Paul has gone to great length in building up a specious argument merely to see it fall the harder. He has pretentiously displayed his credentials merely to demolish them all the more forcefully. This he proceeds to do, declaring that all these things, which he formerly treasured, he now considers as liabilities (v. 7). Compared to his personal relationship with Jesus ("knowledge" has the connotation of intimate relationship in verse 8), he considers all these things as "rubbish" (the Greek is actually stronger and suggests the scrapings from a plate which are fed to the dogs).

Verse 9 is an eloquent summary of the "Gospel According to Paul." It condenses into a few words what his letters to the Galatians and Romans had taken pages to describe, namely the impossibility of self-salvation, the gift-nature of redemption, and the realization of this in relationship with Christ.

This powerful summation of his faith triggers in Paul a profound longing for an even closer solidarity with his Lord. This is a solidarity which, through the power of the Resurrection, will enable him to experience his own suffering and death as conjoined with the suffering and death of Christ (v. 10). The word which Paul uses for "formed into" is built on the root *morphē*, thus indicating, in this case, an *essential* conformity with Jesus' death.

Paul has been speaking of Christian perfection, a perfection which he yearns for mightily, but also a perfection which he knows is impossible of attainment this side of death. At this point he finds it necessary to make it clear that he is not making any false claims. Apparently some of the Philippians *were* making claims in this regard—that is, that they had already attained the fullness of Christian maturity. By sharing the fact of his own continuing quest with them, Paul hopes to persuade them to his point of view.

He uses the compelling image of a footrace to communicate the urgency of further growth in Christ (vv. 12-14). Conversion is not the end, but the beginning; being "grasped by Christ" (12b) propels one into the race. One's present relationship with Christ creates the desire for an ever-deepening relationship with Him. As in all races, it is essential not to look back if one is to win

(13b, 14). In a Christian sense this would mean clearing the twin pitfalls of enfeebling remorse over past sins or self-satisfaction over past achievements. The prize is so great—a truly fulfilled relationship with one's Lord and Maker—that any claim of having reached the goal already in this life is glaringly incommensurate with the person of Christ.

Paul is convinced that he is right on this issue (15a), that Christians must continue to strive for further spiritual growth. Since this is not a crucial matter of faith or morals, however, he will not force the issue (15b), trusting that prayer will resolve it. In his typical fashion, he throws in one last word (v. 16), a word which insists on spiritual development since it assumes various "stages" of growth.

There seems to be a shift, introduced in verse 17, from a critique of doctrinal error (3:2-16) to a critique of moral error. Granting this transfer of topics, a shift in adversaries would also seem to be indicated. The Jews tended toward self-righteousness, not moral laxity, and 3:17-21 seems to be dealing with loose morality.

Given the cosmopolitan nature of the times, even small cities like Philippi would be sure to contain a curious mixture of differing philosophies and religions. On one extreme would be a rigid form of Judaism very similar to Pharisaism; on the other would be a wild libertinism, probably related to the liberal wing of Gnosticism (which held that since the body was irredeemably evil it did not matter what one did with it). Having reminded the Philippians of one danger, he hastens to remind them of the other.

Paul offers himself and those who follow in his footsteps as examples worthy of being followed (v. 17). He does this not out of pride, but because he realizes the importance of modeling. A relatively immature Christian must be able to *see* Christian morality in action; without its embodiment in a person it would be too abstract. Paul is simply offering himself as a reliable guide.

Apparently a fair number of so-called "Christians" had given in to the temptation of immorality (v. 18), probably rationalizing it along the Gnostic lines mentioned above. In effect, they have rejected Christ as Lord and enthroned various carnal desires in His place (v. 19).

Paul reminds his friends that they are citizens of heaven (20a). By inference, this citizenship takes precedence over any other. His mention of heaven sparks in him an intense yearning for the return (the Second Coming) of Christ (20b).

This yearning, in turn, triggers a profound vision of what will happen when Jesus does come back (v. 21); this vision is part of Paul's longing. It is a vision of transformation: our mortal bodies will be dramatically changed in order to conform to His glorified body. This change will be not merely a change in outward appearance (*schēma*), but also a change in essential nature (*morphē*). It will be a change similar to the difference between Jesus' body before and after the Resurrection, as described in St. John's Gospel.

The last phrase, "by his power to subject everything to himself" (21a), celebrates Christ's cosmic sovereignty, and is reminiscent of Paul's contemplative vision of the cosmic Christ in Colossians and Ephesians.

"For these reasons" (4:1a) encompasses not just the immediately preceding, but the entire contents of the letter to this point. Paul is wrapping things up, and gathers together all his previous entreaties in one last round of admonitions (4:1-9). He is unreservedly affectionate, thinking of his friends in Philippi with love, longing, and joy. He calls them his "crown" (4:1b), alluding to the laurel wreath which went to a victorious athlete. Throughout the first nine verses of this chapter Paul speaks very much as someone whose love is so intense that it impels him to loving admonitions.

The first of these loving admonitions is to "stand firm in the Lord" (4:1c). The word which Paul uses for "stand firm" comes straight from the military, and evokes the image of unswerving steadfastness in the heat of battle. In the context of Philippians as a whole, the underlying idea is that life itself is something of a "battle" for Christians, a battle in which it is of paramount importance for them to resist the temptations of self-importance and self-sufficiency.

In verse 2 Paul functions as a Christian arbitrator, attempting to resolve a difference between two ministers whom he values highly by appealing to them in the name of their common Lord. He goes on to appoint an actual third party to help them resolve their dispute (v. 3). It is interesting that he does not mention this person by name. Either he was so well known as Paul's "dependable fellow worker" that his proper name could be considered superfluous, or the Greek for this can serve as a proper name in itself, much like Onesimus meaning "useful."

It is apparent from verses 2 and 3 that women were encouraged to be much more active in the ministry of the Church in Macedonia than they were in Greece. This is basically because of cultural reasons. In Greece proper "active" women were considered to be scandalous, whereas in Macedonia women were not expected to remain passively in the home. Thus, social behavior which would have brought a bad name to Christianity in Greece is encouraged in Macedonia, where conditions are substantially different.

Verses 4-9 form a veritable battery of admonitions. Paul's injunction to "Rejoice in the Lord always!" (4:4) at first seems like a blatant exaggeration. Underlying it, however, is his unshakable conviction of his—and every Christian's—absolute solidarity with Christ. Since not even death can break this solidarity, it is, indeed, possible for the Christian to rejoice *in the Lord* in any conceivable situation. Paul knows that what he has said is, at first sight, rather unfathomable; this is why he repeats himself: "I say it again. Rejoice!"

The word which the *New American Bible* renders as "unselfish" in 5a is a very difficult Greek word to translate. It has a strong nuance of not demanding one's due, of going beyond the boundary of a strict distributive justice. "Everyone" refers to all people, not just Christians. Consequently, there is a strong suggestion here that the "unselfishness," or "forebearance" of Christians should serve as a strong witness to Christ's transforming power.

"The Lord is near" (5b) is a variation on the early Christian theme of "O Lord, come!" (see I Corinthians 16:22b). While it is true that expectation of Jesus' imminent return gradually waned, it is also true that anticipation of the Lord's return never completely died out. It is actually fortunate that it lost some of its feverish intensity, for making Christ's Second Coming the focus of one's faith had a tendency to distort it (as we can still see in certain fundamentalist circles today). This loss in intensity allowed longing for our Lord's Return to become a vital companion to a vital faith.

Paul's exhortation to "Dismiss all anxiety from your minds" (6a) is based on the same underlying reality—a Christian's solidarity with Christ—as his previous admonition to "Rejoice in the Lord always!" (4a). On the surface, on our own, it is impossible; in relationship with Christ it becomes practicable.

The close connection between 6a and b in the original Greek, which reads as one sentence, not two, reveals that the key to dismissing anxiety is prayer. This is only to be expected, since prayer is the lifeblood of communication between the Christian and God. Paul describes prayer in terms of two essential elements: petition, through which we personally make our needs known to God, and gratitude, in which we personally thank God for the blessings He has already given us.

A causal connection is implied between prayer and "God's own peace," which Paul briefly describes in verse 7. In other words, prayer leads to peace of mind and peace of heart, a sense of wellness (at times even in the midst of stark brokenness) that transcends all attempts to understand it. This is God's special

gift—the gift of His abiding presence in Jesus—which He gives
to those who pray. This, more than anything else, is what enables
us to "Rejoice in the Lord always!"

In a flurry of comprehensiveness, Paul goes on to enjoin upon
his friends a list of virtues which they must strive to embody (v. 8).
"True," of course, is the opposite of false, and in this moral
context corresponds to a truthfulness in thought and behavior
which discloses rather than conceals reality. "Respect" means
deserving of veneration; "honest," just or fair in one's perceptions
and judgments; "pure" refers to unalloyed moral uprightness.
"Admirable" is more literally "lovable" and encompasses everything which is capable of inspiring love. "Decent" means "of
good report" and points to positive demeanor. "Virtuous" is a
comprehensive term meaning "all of the above," as is "worthy of
praise." These classic Greek virtues, plus the "classic" Jewish-
Christian ones which he has already mentioned in this letter,
namely, humility and sacrifice, pretty well cover the moral
dimension.

"Accepted" in verse 9 is literally "received" and adverts to
the living Tradition which Paul had shared with the Philippians
and which they had accepted when they accepted Christ. Paul
offers himself as a fitting example of Christianity-in-action. *"Then
will the God of peace be with you"* refers to a causal connection
between living the Christian life and enjoying the presence of the
"God of peace." Thus, action as well as prayer can open us to
God's presence. Or, from a more inclusive point of view, one
could say that each informs the other, and that both are necessary
components of a vital relationship with God.

At this point (4:10) Paul offers thanks for the monetary gift
that the Philippians had sent to him by way of Epaphroditus. This
is undoubtedly not the first word of thanks that Paul had given,
seeing that Epaphroditus had arrived several months earlier. One
gets the impression in reading this verse that he is much more
joyful concerning the loving sacrifice this gift implied than he is

about the money per se. He tactfully acknowledges their persistent poverty in 10b, when he refers to their prior lack of opportunity.

Lest this be taken as a complaint, he immediately goes on to affirm his self-sufficiency (vv. 11-12), not in himself, to be sure, but in the Lord (v. 13). "In him who is the source of my strength I have strength for everything," witnesses to a solidarity with Christ which is as profoundly practical as it is deeply personal. Returning to the topic of thanks in verse 14, the word which he uses for "share" presupposes their solidarity with him in his solidarity with Christ.

There is more going on in verses 15 and 16 than meets the eye. Paul makes it sound like the Philippians were the only ones who cared enough to give a gift in response to the priceless gift of the Gospel. In reality, Philippi was the only church which Paul trusted enough to accept money from. He made it a point—a bitterly contested point, as his letters to the Corinthians show—*not* to receive help from any other church, so that no one in that church would be able to accuse him of making a profit from the Gospel. His relationship with the Philippians is so close—on the order of a family relationship—that he does not have to set up this protective "fence" between him and them; he can accept their help knowing that they will not criticize him because of it.

In verses 17 and 18 Paul plays with some of the business jargon of his time. The "ever-growing balance" in their account (17b) is, in effect, the grace which they are receiving because of their generosity. In 18b he compares their liberality with a praiseworthy sacrifice.

Their generosity will open up the floodgates of God's generosity (v. 19); or, rather, since God is unfailingly generous, it enables them to participate more fully in God's superabundant grace, his "magnificent riches in Christ Jesus." This inspired thought triggers in Paul a short but powerful doxology (v. 20).

The letter concludes with an exchange of greetings. Paul, a close friend of many in the Christian community at Philippi, wisely refrains from mentioning only a few by name (v. 21). "Those in Caesar's service" (v. 22) can refer to anyone in the civil service, from the highest official to the "lowest" servant. The phrase witnesses to the fact that there were already Christians within the Roman government. As always, Paul's final words are a blessing (v. 23).

*Questions for Personal Reflection/Group Discussion*

1. In 3:4-6 Paul lists his credentials. Before he became a Christian he thought that these things made him superior in God's eyes. What are the things that you considered to be your religious credentials until you realized that what matters is relationship with Christ and not seemingly spiritual achievements?
2. *Expand* on 3:9— ". . . not having any justice of my own based on observance of the law. The justice I possess is that which comes through faith in Christ. It has its origins in God and is based on faith."
3. Paul is quite convinced that every Christian needs to be committed to a life-long process of spiritual development. How have you personally experienced your faith as a developmental process? In other words, what are some of the stages that you have grown through on your way to a deeper relationship with Christ?
4. Paul was not hesitant to offer himself as a model of faith. What are some areas in which you consider yourself to be a model of faith?
5. How would it be possible for you to "Rejoice in the Lord always" and "Dismiss all anxiety from your mind?"
6. What role does our Lord's Return play in your faith?

# *The Pastoral Epistles: Titus, I & II Timothy*

## Introduction

The controversy surrounding the authorship of the Pastorals is one of the fiercest debates in contemporary biblical scholarship. A slight majority of mainstream scholars favor the hypothesis that these letters are pseudonymous; that is, written by someone other than Paul—perhaps one of his disciples—who used Paul's name to establish his own credibility. The following are the three main arguments which those who posit the pseudonymity of the Pastoral Epistles use to substantiate their thesis:

1. The organization of the Church is too highly developed to reflect the Church of Paul's day.

2. The heresy which is combatted in the Pastorals appears to be Gnosticism, a school of thought which achieved its greatest influence in the second century.

3. The language and style of Titus and I & II Timothy are so significantly different from that of the rest of Paul's letters that the odds are against their having been written by the same person. Specifically: (a) many words occur in the Pastorals which do not occur elsewhere in Paul's writings; (b) many words and phrases which we would expect to find are not there; for example, Paul's favorite phrase "in Christ" does not occur; (c) "old" words appear with "new" meanings; for example, *faith*, which in his previous letters tends to mean a personal relationship of trust in God, has come in the Pastoral to signify *the* faith, the entire body

of Christian truths; (d) the style is noticeably different: the Pas-torals are less passionate and more literary than Paul's "authentic" letters.

Those, including this author, who accept the Pastorals as Pauline, offer the following counter-arguments:

1. The Ignatian Letters, written by Bishop Ignatius in Asia Minor from 110-117, reveal a much more highly structured Church than the Pastorals. The Pastorals would seem to reflect an *intermediate* stage of organizational development, a stage not inconsistent with that presupposed in Acts 20:17 & 28 and Philip-pians 1:1. Titus and Timothy as individuals possess a great author-ity; this authority, however, is derived from being Paul's official representatives, and not so much from holding an office, such as that of archbishop.

2. The heresy countered is not the fully-developed Gnosti-cism of the second century, but a proto-Gnosticism, with some significantly Jewish elements, such as that described in Paul's letter to the Colossians (which a large majority of scholars accept as authentic).

3. Concerning the differences in language and style between the Pastorals and Paul's previous letters: (a) For the first time in his literary career, Paul is writing at length concerning Church organization and administration. New topics demand new vocab-ulary; (b) Paul's emphasis on practical matters in the Pastorals pushes his more contemplative dimension into the background; (c) Paul realizes that his time is rapidly running out and wants to be sure, especially in the context of so much heretical opposition to true Christian teaching, that the faith is handed on intact; thus, the emphasis on *the* faith and Christian orthodoxy; (d) the less passionate style is that of an older person who has been somewhat worn out by controversy; given what we know of Paul's earlier missionary activities, it is not at all unlikely that he learned Latin; this would account for the more literary style of the Pastorals.

4. The extremely personal nature of some of the content

argues against pseudonymous authorship. A number of scholars maintain that these personal items are authentic fragments of Paul embedded in otherwise pseudonymous works.

As with so much debate of this type, the conclusions one reaches are largely contingent on one's interpretation of the evidence. The available evidence, in other words, can be argued both ways. Given the rather subjective nature of this debate, it is important that neither side ridicule the other or claim a more dogmatic certainty than the provisional nature of the evidence warrants.

Those who see the Pastorals as pseudonymous maintain that Paul met his death during the imprisonment in Rome mentioned in the book of Acts. Those who favor Pauline authorship consider the imprisonment mentioned at the end of Acts as his "First Roman Imprisonment."

The book of Acts ends ambiguously (see Acts 28:30-31). There is no mention of either Paul's death or his release. Roman law would have required, however, that Paul be freed after two years if no adequate case against him could be brought during that time.

Assuming this to be the case, those who claim Paul as author posit a "Fourth Missionary Journey," one in which Paul made the rounds of the eastern Mediterranean assumed in the Pastorals. According to this hypothesis, Paul designated Titus as his representative to the Church in Crete and Timothy as his representative to the Church at Ephesus.

His letter to Titus and his first letter to Timothy, written around the year 65, consolidate his instructions to them concerning the organization and administration of the Church. By this time the Emperor Nero has begun his persecution of Christians in earnest. Paul was recalled to Rome. It was during his "Second Roman Imprisonment" that Paul wrote his second letter to Timothy as a kind of "last will and testament." Tradition holds that Paul was martyred in Rome by order of Nero in 67.

**Titus**

## Chapter 18:    The Call to Correspondence
### between Faith and Action

*Please read Titus.*   By describing himself as a "servant of God"
(1:1a), Paul associates himself with some of the great heroes of
the Hebrew Scriptures, who are known by this designation. In
addition to being a "servant of God," he is also "an apostle of
Jesus Christ" (1:1b). "Apostle" is parallel to "servant" and Jesus
Christ is parallel to God; thus, Paul sees both his ministry and
the Christian faith as a continuation of the true faith of Israel.
He knows that his apostolate has been given, not for his own
glory, but for the sake of others (1:1c). Given the difficulty of
establishing a solid Christian community on Crete due to both
ignorance and heresy, Paul emphasizes his role as custodian of
the truth. He undoubtedly perceives that his ministry is gradually
drawing to a close, and wants to do everything he can to consolidate things. This is the major motivating force behind his instructions in the Pastorals.

In verse 2 Paul explicitly mentions hope of eternal life as
the reality empowering his ministry. This hope is not vague and
unsure, but concrete and certain because it springs from God's
promise, which cannot fail. This promise is so old (made in
"endless ages past") that it is, so to speak, part of God's very
nature. "In his own good time" (v. 3) alludes to the history of
salvation, the historical process through which God prepared the
way for the fulfillment of His promise in Christ Jesus. God's
promise of eternal life continues to be proclaimed in Paul's preaching.

His reference to Titus as his "own true child in our common
faith" (v. 4) probably recalls the fact that Paul was instrumental
in Titus' conversion. His reference to Christ as "Savior" rather
than the more common "Lord" is meant to underscore Jesus'
ability to save in spite of all obstacles.

Titus is serving as Paul's official representative in Crete; as such, Paul assumes that he will share in his apostolic authority. One of the purposes of this letter to Titus (which was to be read to the Church in Crete as a whole) was to remind the Cretans in writing of Titus' charge to organize and administer the Church there.

His first task is to appoint "presbyters," or elders, to oversee the various individual churches (v. 5). As far as we can tell, at this point in the history of the Church presbyters and bishops were synonymous terms. Verses 6-9 provide a detailed list of their qualifications. Notice the mention of "authentic message" and "sound doctrine" in verse 9. Paul considers the fundamental teachings of Christianity to have been firmly established. It is the duty of the bishop not to deviate from these teachings.

The background of this letter is one of controversy, and verse 10 makes it clear that the controversy centered in the battle between orthodox Christianity and the false teachings of certain Jewish Christians. These false teachers "must be silenced" (v. 11). The rest of the letter indicates that this silencing is to be accomplished, not through physical force, but through the powerful witness of true faith embodied in faultless Christian living.

The quotation in verse 12 is certainly not very tactful. Paul was not always known for his tact, and the inclusion of this sentiment in this letter can be seen as an indication of its authenticity. The point Paul was trying to make is that false teachings tended to flourish in Crete because the culture there was conducive to them.

The "Jewish myths" (v. 14) are probably fanciful genealogies of certain Old Testament characters which linked them to various heavenly intermediaries. This type of speculation, inspired by the proto-Gnosticism of the day, was very popular. On the surface, it seemed quite impressive intellectually. "Rules invented by men" refers to various elements of Jewish law (probably circumcision and dietary regulations) which these false teachers were trying to make binding on Christians.

Verse 15 could be an allusion to a teaching of Jesus (recorded in Mark 7:14-15 and Luke 11:39-40). The point is that moral purity is a matter of inward attitude (which, to be sure, expresses itself outwardly) and not simply a matter of external rules and regulations. The fact that the false teachers insist on these outward observances demonstrates that they are trying to earn their own salvation and are not really in a faith relationship with God (v. 16).

The first part of chapter two (2:1-10) consists of Paul's instruction to Titus concerning the proper behavior of various general classes of people within the Church, and a few words of admonition directed to Titus himself (vv. 1, 7-8). Paul's intent in this section is to elicit behavior from these various groups which is in conformity with the Gospel. In other words, he is calling for a correspondence between faith and action. This instruction is given to Titus who, in turn, is to instruct the following groups regarding conduct which is fitting for their particular station in life: older men (v. 2), older women (v. 3), young women (vv. 4-5), young men (v. 6), Titus himself (vv. 7-8), and slaves (vv. 9-10).

Paul's instruction is straightforward and nothing new. It needs no comment except to point out that the injunctions which he directs at women should be understood within the context of the time and culture. Christian women were given unprecedented freedom considering the repressive culture in which they lived. Paul is concerned lest they misuse their newfound freedom, become a scandal, and thus a further source of contention between Christianity and pagan society as a whole.

In 2:11 Paul alludes to the motivating power behind Christian morality. "The grace of God (which) has appeared" is a shorthand way of encompassing Jesus' Incarnation, Crucifixion, and Resurrection. This grace has been offered as a gift to all people. Accepting this gift and participating in the personal relationship with Christ which this entails, empowers one to live a Christian life, a life which Paul describes rather dryly in verse 12.

Christians live in the interim between Christ's first appearance (mentioned in v. 11), and His second, mentioned in verse 13. Like His life, death, and Resurrection, the joyful anticipation of His Second Coming is a source of moral empowerment for Christians. The *New American Bible's* "of the glory of the great God and of our Savior Christ Jesus" is an odd translation of the Greek which would much more naturally read "of the glory of our great God and Savior Christ Jesus." Not only is the latter better Greek, it better accords with the fact that in the rest of the New Testament, "appearing," in the sense of manifestation, is a characteristic applied to Christ, but not to the Father.

Verse 14 highlights Jesus' sacrificial death as the vehicle of our redemption. The phrase "a people of his *own*" witnesses to the special relationship which God's people share with Him. Again, this is a relationship which is open to all persons (see v. 11), but for it to become effective, for it to become a real relationship, a person must accept the grace of God which has appeared in Jesus Christ.

Paul is quite confident of his own authority in verse 15, and also quite confident that he has the competence to share his authority with Titus. Although bishops in a precise hierarchial sense did not yet exist, it is the experience of an apostle's sharing his authority in this way which was soon (in another fifty years or so) to give rise to the notion of "apostolic succession."

More instructions follow in 3:1-2, this time regarding obedience to civil authority and fulfillment of civic responsibilities. We know from other contemporary sources that the Cretans tended to be defiant and disputatious. Paul is concerned that conversion to the faith lead to transformed attitudes and actions. Christians should be model citizens, attracting others to Christ through their good example.

In this context—of what seems to many Christians today to be an excessive subservience to the state—we need to remember that Paul is assuming a situation in which the state is acting within its proper sphere of authority. If the state were to go beyond this, Paul would have seconded Peter's response to the Sanhedrin (the Jewish judicial council in Jerusalem): "We must obey God rather than men" (Acts 5:29, RSV).

Using a literary "we" to elicit the active imagination of the Church in Crete when this letter is read to them at one of its assemblies, Paul briefly describes the destructive nature of life without Christ in verse 3. He immediately contrasts this (vv. 4-8) with a joyful proclamation of the Good News.

"God our savior" (v. 4) probably refers simultaneously to both the Father and Jesus; the Father in the sense of taking the initiative in our salvation, Jesus in the sense of being the concrete manifestation of the Father's initiative. 5a succinctly states that we owe our salvation to God's mercy, and not to any accomplishments of our own. Christians have gained access to salvation through Baptism (the actual word in the Greek is "washing," an obvious reference to Baptism), which Paul describes here as a dynamic sacrament of sanctification and empowerment by the Holy Spirit (5b).

The gift of the Spirit is mediated to us through our faith in Jesus as Lord (v. 6). The total effect of all this is salvation and the promise of eternal life (v. 7). Because of their formal structure and cadence, some scholars consider verses 5-7 to be part of an early Christian baptismal hymn or confession of faith. 8a, "You can depend on this to be true," is Paul's way of saying "Amen" to the Gospel which he has just presented.

Knowing that he is about to bring his letter to a conclusion, Paul reminds Titus of the importance of the instructions contained within this letter (8b). He gives Titus a parting directive to studiously avoid the fantastic speculation and legalistic hairsplitting which were so much a part of his milieu (v. 9). His instructions concerning heretics (vv. 10-11) are intended to preserve the unity and dignity of the Church. The concept of self-condemnation with which Paul ends verse 11 is significant because it reflects

Paul's awareness of human responsibility for one's actions and one's beliefs. His thinking here is that a heretic has chosen to exclude himself from the Church.

If this letter were pseudonymous, one would not expect the unresolved issue of who to send to Crete to relieve Titus (v. 12); this verse reflects the casualness of a real life situation.

After reminding Titus of his duty of hospitality (v. 13), and throwing in one last instruction about the importance of Christians earning an honest living (v. 14), Paul exchanges greetings and ends his letter with a blessing (v. 15). This blessing is addressed not just to Titus but to all Christians under his care.

*Questions for Personal Reflection/Group Discussion*

1. Paul comes across as rather conservative in his letter to Titus. Do you see his conservatism as a positive or negative trait? Why?
2. What role does the promise of eternal life play in your own faith?
3. Paul simply assumes Titus' first-hand knowledge of the "authentic message" and "sound doctrine" of the faith. Based on your acquaintance with Paul's letters as a whole, summarize what you think he would see as the actual content of these categories.
4. Is the joyful anticipation of Jesus' Return (the Second Coming) a moral encouragement for you? If so, how? If not, why not?
5. What do you consider to be some examples within contemporary theology of fantastic speculation and legalistic hairsplitting?

# I Timothy

## Chapter 19:　On Managing the Church

*Please read I Timothy.*　Paul begins this letter by underlining his authority in an even more emphatic way than usual. He is an apostle "by command" (1:1). His reference to "God our savior" echoes the numerous instances in which the Father is described as savior in the Old Testament, a term which underscores His redemptive purpose. "Christ Jesus our hope" brings out the dimension of Christianity which abides in the future, hope alluding to the fulfillment which Christians anticipate with Jesus' Return.

Calling Timothy a "child" (1:2) is an idiom used to refer to a younger person in a close, but subordinate, position to oneself. Timothy, a young man (probably in his mid-thirties) and good friend of Paul's, who is now his official representative to the Church at Ephesus, fits this description completely. To his customary blessing of grace and peace, he adds the element of "mercy." Mercy, as a theological term, captures something of God's active and loving presence in the midst of unusually severe difficulties. Paul adds mercy to his blessing because he knows that Timothy, chief administrator of the strife-torn Church at Ephesus, greatly needs this particular grace.

The "false doctrines" mentioned in verse 3 are described in verse 4 as "interminable myths and genealogies." These are probably a bizarre combination of the occult meanderings of Gnosticism with the hero worship of Jewish mysticism. Paul is vehemently opposed to this approach because it issues in endless abstractions and not the "training in faith"—the application of Christian principles to real life—which is of the essence of Christianity. The concrete expression of love, and not "idle speculation," is the goal of the Christian faith (v. 5). The sure mark of a false teacher is the substitution of "meaningless talk" for purposeful action (vv. 6-7).

Paul's mention of the "law" in verse 7, where it was used in the context of "teachers of the law" (that is, catechists) prompts him to reflect on law in its Jewish sense in verses 8-11. His discussion here is reminiscent of his observations concerning law in his letter to the Romans. The whole point of the law is to force one to an awareness of one's sinfulness, and thus to a realization of one's need for salvation.

The overwhelming reality of his having been entrusted with the proclamation of the Gospel (v. 11) triggers in turn, a powerful section of praise and introspection (vv. 12-17). His thankfulness for his present calling causes him to remember his former state, and the discrepancy between who he was then and who he is now. The utterly frank way in which he describes his former self (v. 13) and calls himself the worst of sinners (15b) are strong indications of the authenticity of this letter—a disciple would hardly have portrayed his master in this negative way. The powerful statement "Christ Jesus came into the world to save sinners" (v. 15) is probably an early Christian maxim. Paul considers himself to have been so extremely sinful before he became a Christian that the reality of his conversion is proof positive that *anyone* can be saved (v. 16). This gladsome thought elicits a spontaneous prayer of adoration (v. 17).

Paul's "solemn charge" to Timothy (v. 18) is actually the various instructions which follow in the rest of this letter. This charge echoes those which Timothy received at his ordination, when he was the subject of the prophecies which Paul refers to in 18b and 19a. The content of these prophecies, which is probably tied up with the grace of ordination, should empower Timothy to be able to successfully integrate faith and morals (v. 19). Hymenaeus and Alexander are presented as examples of those who have lost their faith by losing their morals (19b-20a). They have been excommunicated in the hope that they "may learn not to blaspheme" (20b).

The next section, 2:1-8, concerns the role of prayer in God's saving plan. The thrust is on the necessity of prayer being offered for *all* (2:1), since God desires the salvation of everyone (2:2), and since Christ died for everyone (2:6).

The fourfold classification of prayer in 2:1 serves to underline the importance of prayer as a whole. "Petitions" are appeals centering on pressing material needs; "prayers" refers to prayer in general; "intercessions" are concerns offered for the sake of other persons; "thanksgiving" is the joyful acknowledgement that God does, indeed, hear our prayers.

Considering that the Church has been praying in this way for nearly two thousand years now, we tend to take it for granted that prayers should be offered for "all men." This insight was not nearly so obvious during the first few years of the faith, however. Jewish prayers of the time denounced or belittled persons outside the fold of Judaism; neither was there precedent for this type of universal prayer in the pagan religions of the time.

In short, prayer for "all men" was something radically new, something which the early Christians had to be taught and had to get used to. Paul's instructions that they pray "for kings and those in authority" (2:2) would have struck many Christians of the times as an unusual innovation. It was easy to see why one should pray for fellow Christians, but to pray for the "lost" was considered in many Christian circles to be a waste of time.

Paul's injunction to Christians to *pray* for their rulers actually goes beyond his directives in Romans 13:1-7, where obedience (in all legitimate matters) is stressed. As we have seen in the context of Romans 13 obedience is a rather passive, uninvolved response to governmental authority. Prayer, on the other hand, is an *active* response, reflecting something of the essence of what it means to be a Christian.

Verse 3 reveals the sacrificial nature of this type of prayer, since God's being pleased is His response to an acceptable sacrifice. The root meaning of sacrifice is "to make holy by making whole." This is what Christ has done for us (vv. 5-6), and this is what He wants us to do for others. Thus, praying for "kings and those in authority," especially if they are "enemies," is one concrete way in which a Christian is called to participate in the sacrifice of Christ.

2:4 is a clear statement of God's universal salvific will. His personal desire is that *all* people be saved. God wants to have a saving relationship with everyone. The only catch is that this saving relationship, to be real, or effective, must be *accepted* by the person to whom it is offered. This section (2:1-8) as a whole is calling Christians to become instrumental in enabling others to respond favorably to the Gospel. Through prayer, Christians simultaneously express their human solidarity with those for whom they are praying and their saving solidarity with Christ. Since prayer transcends time and space, it is able to make God's saving presence present to those for whom the prayer is offered.

The Source of the effectiveness of prayer is, of course, God; specifically God in the person of His Son, Jesus Christ. By taking our humanity upon Himself, and through His sacrifice of love, He was able to restore the bridge of relationship to God which has been broken (vv. 5-6). These verses, appropriately enough, are probably taken from an early Christian hymn. Given the importance of what he has just taught, Paul solemnly states his authority to teach these things (v. 7).

Verses 8-15 comprise various instructions concerning the proper roles of Christian men and women. Paul begins by asking that the men offer prayers in the traditional Jewish way, standing, with hands aloft and open (8a). More importantly, he insists on reconciliation within the Christian community as a prerequisite for valid prayer (8b). In doing this, he is probably consciously echoing Jesus' similar instruction in the Sermon on the Mount (see Matthew 5:23-24).

At this point Paul moves into a whole series of injunctions concerning women (vv. 9-15). These must be understood in their historical context. For a woman to do any of the things which

Paul forbids in these verses would have been to bring scandal upon the Church, given the prevailing culture. For example, for a woman to instruct a man would have been so unthinkable given the realities of both Greek and Jewish culture, that for either Greeks or Jews to witness such an event would most likely have led to their instant rejection of Christianity as destroying the very basis of society. Paul's exegesis, or interpretation, of Genesis 3 in verses 13 and 14 reads much more into the story of the fall than was originally intended.

Continuing his round of instructions, Paul considers the necessary qualifications for bishops (4:1-7), and deacons (4:8-13). These requirements are self-explanatory and attest the importance placed on congruence between a candidate's private life and his public image. The reference to "the women" in verse 11 can mean either "deaconesses" or deacon's "wives." Given the context, it probably refers to deaconesses.

Paul deems it prudent to state these things in writing, even though he expects to be visiting Timothy shortly (v. 14). This letter will serve as Timothy's blueprint for administering the church (v. 15). The phrase "God's household" testifies to the intimate, familial relationship which Christians share with God, and triggers Paul's contemplative flight in 15b-16.

The word "mystery" (16a) signifies a truth which is too big and too deep to be captured in words but which, nevertheless, demands description. Paul offers such a description of the mystery in 16b, which is a quotation from an early Christian hymn or creed centering on the person of Christ. "Manifested in the flesh" is a reference to the Incarnation; "vindicated by the Spirit," an allusion to the Resurrection; "taken up into glory" recalls the Ascension.

Returning to matters of administration and orthodoxy in chapter 4, Paul reminds Timothy that the apostasy which the Church in Ephesus is experiencing has already been anticipated (4:1). "The spirit distinctly says" is a reference to prophetic utterance.

The concept of the "later times" is indefinite, yet inclusive. It adverts to *all* time between the Ascension of our Lord and His Second Coming. Thus, we twentieth century Christians live in the "later times" in much the same way as did our first century counterparts.

Paul's citation of "deceitful spirits" and "demons" (1b) demonstrates that he regards heresy as intimately connected with demonic inspiration. We know from other contexts that he considers the devil to be a superhuman force of evil whose primary intent is to destroy what God has created. Heresy—departure from the true faith—is part of the devil's plan of destruction.

Just as God's Holy Spirit speaks through prophets, the devil speaks through human agents, in this case "plausible liars—men with seared consciences" (4:2). The forceful image of "seared consciences" describes the endpoint of the progressive deterioration in faith and morals that these persons have allowed themselves to undergo. "Seared" can also be translated as "branded," an allusion to their being the devil's possession.

The content of the particular heresy being perpetrated in Ephesus becomes clearer in verse 3; we know that it involved the denial of marriage and the abstinence from certain foods. These directives correspond exactly with those of the ascetic wing of Gnosticism, which held that the only way to overcome the evil of matter was to renounce it as much as possible.

This is diametrically opposed to true Christian teaching, which sees creation as fundamentally good because it is the expression of an all-good God (v. 4). Thus, all aspects of creation (in this particular case, food and sexuality) are capable of being made holy through God's sanctifying Word (v. 5). For Christians, wine can become the blood of Christ and marriage a sacrament.

Verses 6-11 are addressed specifically to Timothy and are intended to help him in the exercise of his administrative responsibilities. "The reading of Scripture . . . preaching and teaching" (v. 13) alludes to the three main parts of the early Christian

"Liturgy of the Word." In these days the Liturgy of the Word was separate from the Liturgy of the Eucharist. The gift referred to in verse 14, to use later theological language, is the gift, or grace, of ordination. If properly responded to, it will enable Timothy to carry out his ministry with the enthusiasm portrayed in verses 15 and 16.

Persisting in his compendium of instructions, Paul goes on to advise Timothy concerning his relationship with older men, younger men, older women, and younger women (5:1-2). What stands out is the essentially *family* nature of Christian relationships. He is to treat these various categories of people as fathers, brothers, mothers, and sisters respectively. Paul's vision of Christian community is dependent on the new family relationships which Christians share with one another through their solidarity with Christ.

At this point Paul presents detailed directions pertaining to the management of Christian widows (5:3-16). On the one hand, he is concerned that the Church not overextend itself in caring for widows who could more properly be taken care of by their own families. On the other hand, he is concerned that widows in real need receive assistance.

The mention of enrollment (vv. 9, 11) points to the fact that the Church in these early years sponsored an "Order of Widows." This was a formally established ministry—probably one of hospitality and visitation—through which a Christian widow was given her livelihood. The function and ministry of the Order of Widows was eventually subsumed by women's religious orders. Younger widows were forbidden to enroll (vv. 11-12) because of their tendency to remarry after a period of mourning. Since enrollment included a vow of celibacy, remarriage was considered tantamount to breaking a vow to Christ.

Paul goes on to consider the salary and the discipline of the presbyters (5:17-22). We do not know exactly what role these persons played in the early Church, although with the passing of the years it becomes apparent that this is the group from which the parish priesthood emerged.

The quotation of Deuteronomy 25:4 in verse 18, "You shall not put a muzzle on an ox when he is threshing the grain" refers to the fact that it was considered immoral to deny a work-animal the benefit of sustenance from its labor. The mention of laying on hands in verse 22 is ambiguous. It can refer to either or both of the nascent sacraments of ordination or penance. Haste is to be avoided in either case, since it implicates the celebrant in the shortcomings of the recipient.

The advice to "Stop drinking water only" (v. 23) is so personal that even those scholars who deny the overall authenticity of this letter maintain that this is a true fragment from Paul which has somehow found its way into this letter.

Verse 24 and 25 probably refer back to Paul's previous discussion concerning presbyters and/or penitents. The sense is that a person's true character will reveal itself sooner or later. Given Timothy's position of responsibility, it is wiser for him to wait for this revelation rather than to act precipitously.

Paul's teaching on slavery (6:1-2) is essentially the same as in his letters to the Colossians and to the Ephesians. It is characterized by the necessity of the Church being above reproach by the pagan culture in which it found itself. All Christians were called upon to be the best, in terms of attitude and action, of whatever they were. Thus, Christian slaves were expected to be outstanding slaves.

As we have seen, Paul has provided a rather comprehensive administrative directory in this letter to Timothy. It is, so to speak, his orientation manual for his position as Paul's official representative to the Church at Ephesus.

The false teachers are castigated in the next few verses (6:3-10). An already-established deposit of faith is assumed in verse 3. To depart from this deposit marks one as heretical. The fact that the false teachers were apparently charging hefty fees for their false teaching elicits a short sermon on the danger of the desire for wealth (vv. 6-10). "The love of money is the root of all evil" (10a) is a popular moral maxim which Paul uses as a homily illustration.

Beginning to bring his letter to a close, Paul admonishes Timothy to live up to the high calling which he has received as a true Christian (vv. 11-14). The "many witnesses" of verse 12 refers to the witnesses present at Timothy's Baptism. He would have been received into the Church as an adult, after thorough preparation and a profession of faith. Jesus' "noble profession before Pontius Pilate" (13b) was His willingness to die for the truth.

Paul's reference to the Second Coming in verse 14 inspires in him a profound outburst of adoration in verses 15 and 16. In applying to Jesus two of the favorite titles of the Roman emperors, "Kings of kings and Lord of lord" (15b), Paul is, in effect, claiming that these titles belong properly only to Christ.

Perhaps fearing lest his words against riches in verses 9-10 be taken as an absolute condemnation of wealth, Paul reapproaches this topic in verses 17-19. The substance of these verses is that wealth is not evil in and of itself, but provides the opportunity for generosity.

Again alluding to the entire deposit of faith which has been entrusted to Timothy, Paul closes his letter with a final admonishment to him to defend it (v. 20). Since the pronoun "you" in his concluding blessing is plural (v. 21), he intends this letter to serve as public instruction for the faithful at Ephesus, as well as for the personal instruction of his trusted friend and apostolic legate, Timothy.

*Questions for Personal Reflection/Group Discussion*

1.  What is the theological connection between faith and morality?
2.  Why is prayer for *all* people such an important aspect of Christianity?

3. How is prayer related to sacrifice?
4. Describe the difference between Gnosticism and Christianity concerning their understanding of creation and the created world.
5. Why is idle speculation so dangerous to truth and faith?


## II Timothy

## Chapter 20: Leavetaking

*Please read II Timothy.* If this epistle is a forgery, it is a brilliant one, for this letter comes across as the most consistently personal of any of Paul's letters. Deemed authentic, the context of this letter is Paul's "Second Roman Imprisonment," after his preliminary hearing, shortly before his martyrdom. As such it stands as his last will and testament.

The initial greeting (vv. 1-2) is rather unlike any of his others. The phrase "to proclaim the *promise of life in him*" (v. 1) is somber, yet hopeful. It captures the mood of a Christian in prison who knows that soon he will be executed, but who also knows that death is not the end. His address to Timothy as "my child whom I love" (v. 2) is more impassioned than usual. It hints of the yearning of remembrance, as well as loneliness.

The intensity of Paul's reminiscences comes out clearly in verses 3-5. Apparently Paul has been doing some reflecting on his own religious development. He sees where he is now, as a Christian, in continuity with where he was before, as a Jew ("the God of my forefathers whom I worship with a clear conscience"— 3a). The vigor and warmth of his prayer life stands out in 3b. Paul is no ascetic in regard to friendship; he candidly states his desire for Timothy's presence in verse 4. Thinking of Timothy causes him to remember the development of his faith in a way similar to the way in which he has just reflected on his own (v. 5). The whole tone of this section reminds one of the first part of his letter to the Philippians (Phil. 1:3-11); here he is even more poignant, addressing himself to an individual instead of a community.

Realizing that this probably will be his last letter, Paul takes the opportunity to admonish Timothy very much in the way a father would admonish his son who was to carry on the family tradition (vv. 6-14).

"The gift of God bestowed when my hands were laid upon you" (v. 6) refers to the grace of ordination. Paul does not see this particular grace (and, for that matter, grace in general) in an automatic way, but in a reciprocal way. In other words, the more a person *responds* to grace, the more it is stirred into flames. Verse 7 concerns the empowerment of the Christian through the indwelling presence of the Holy Spirit, a presence which enables the Christian to be courageous, to love to the point of sacrifice, and to be able to be the master of any circumstance.

Many *had* been ashamed of both the Gospel and of Paul; he hopes that Timothy will not join their ranks (8a). Suffering is a constituent part of living and proclaiming the Gospel, a part of the Gospel, however, which God Himself will enable the Christian to endure (8b).

Probably in response to the powerful way in which God has enabled him personally to bear his share of suffering, Paul breaks into praise in verses 9 and 10. Because of their majesty and measuredness, some scholars believe that he is quoting from a hymn sung at Timothy's ordination. Whatever the case, these verses are a moving declaration of God's initiative in salvation, an initiative which is part of His very nature, and a stirring celebration of the redemptive Incarnation of Christ.

Again, as one looking back over a long and incredibly rich ministry, Paul reflects on his pivotal role (v. 11), and considers his present adversity (12a). This leads to a profound affirmation of faith in 12b. Notice the extremely personal and relational nature of this affirmation. Paul's faith is no abstract assertion, but a trusting belief founded on a concrete relationship with a person. When he refers to "what has been entrusted to me," he is referring to two things: his own faith and the content of the faith of Christianity as a whole. The "Day" mentioned is the Day of Judgment. Thus, Paul is affirming his faith that God will preserve both his own faith and the faith of the Church until the end of time, when both he and the Church shall find their perfect consummation.

Returning to his task of admonishing Timothy, he enjoins him to follow his example of Christian faith and love (v. 13), and, like him, to be a defender of the faith (v. 14).

"All in Asia" (v. 15) probably refers to those from Asia (our Asia Minor) in Rome, all of whom deserted Paul at his trial. He singles out one notable exception, a certain Onesiphorus who stood by him through everything (vv. 16-18).

Referring to Timothy affectionately as his son (2:1), again Paul urges him to be strong. The frequency of these admonitions for strength has led some scholars to view Timothy as something of a weakling. Another way of looking at the evidence, however, would be to focus on Paul, considering the extraordinary effects of his ministry, and the intensity with which he must have been concerned that his ministry be carried on intact. 2:2 seems to confirm this interpretation, with its emphasis on faithfully handing on the Tradition which Paul himself has so faithfully taught. This is a foundational text for what the Catholic Church eventually came to teach as the reality of "apostolic succession," which involves just such a handing on of Tradition.

Using some of his favorite metaphors for ministry, Paul urges Timothy to be the best possible soldier, athlete, and farmer for the Lord (vv. 3-7).

Timothy's ultimate inspiration, of course, is Christ Himself. Paul presents him with a moving exposition of the Gospel in verses 8-13. He encompasses the three most important realities of Jesus' life in verse 8. The phrase "a descendant of David" adverts to the Incarnation, or Jesus' true humanity. Death refers to His sacrifice in the Crucifixion. The fact that he "was raised" points to the Resurrection. In verse 9 Paul contrasts his own imprisonment with the impossibility of constraining God's Word. Paul sees his suffering as a blessing for the entire Christian community (v. 10). On the one hand, his solidarity with Christ transforms his suffering into part of Christ's redemptive suffering. On the other hand, his solidarity with other Christians enables him to empower them through the gift of his sacrifical love.

Verse 11 is probably a quotation from an early Christian baptismal hymn, reflecting as it does the baptismal imagery of dying and rising with Christ. It may be that Paul complements this with a verse of his own reflecting martyrdom (12a). The statement "But if we deny him he will deny us" (12b) is based on the fact that in the coming Judgment, Jesus will respect what we have chosen to do with our human freedom. To force Himself upon us would be to "deny himself" (v. 13), because it is His nature to honor our choice. He remains forever faithful in the sense that He does everything in His power—with the single exception of force—to assure our salvation.

Having just summarized the essence of the Gospel—the Life, Death, and Ressurection of Christ, and the human freedom to choose either to be or not to be in a saving relationship with Him—Paul appeals to Timothy to "keep reminding people of these things" (14a); that is, the *essentials* of the faith. At the same time he is to "charge them before God to stop disputing about mere words" (14b). Paul sees these two complementary elements—the proclamation of the essential Gospel plus avoidance of theological infighting—as crucial for the continued well-being of the Church.

To the metaphors of soldier, athlete, and farmer previously mentioned, Paul now adds the metaphor of workman in verse 15. The image is one of Timothy's calling, like a good stonemason, to follow a "straight course"—to be absolutely impartial in his presentation of the Gospel.

Returning to the theme of pointless and destructive theological speculation in verses 16-21, Paul cites the case of Hymenaeus and Philetus. They had apparently adopted a Gnostic approach to Christianity, and were teaching that "the resurrection has already taken place" (in a spiritual way at Baptism), thus denying the fundamental doctrine of the Resurrection of the Body. Paul comes down harshly on them in 19a, implying that God does *not* know these two because of their false teaching; he seems, however, to be calling them to repentance in 19b. His metaphor of the different grades of household vessels in verses 20 and 21 is intended to inspire these, and other false teachers, to a change of heart.

The "youthful passions" which Paul admonishes Timothy to turn from in verse 22 are not primarily sexual passions (although these would not be excluded), but passions which would be disastrous in terms of administration, such as hypocrisy, favoritism, and argumentativeness. Returning yet again to the problem of theological quibbling (v. 23), Paul offers the model of the "servant of the Lord" (vv. 24-26), a model which is based on the servant songs in Isaiah, especially chapter 50, verses 4-5.

The notion of the "last days," which Paul mentions in 3:1, is inclusive. It covers the entire span of time between Ascension-Pentecost and the Second Coming. Timothy was living in the "last days"—and so are we. The long list of sins which Paul cites in verse 2-4 is just as descriptive of life in present-day America as it was descriptive of life in the Roman Empire of the first century.

What is most deadly about these sins is that certain "Christians" claim their compatibility with Christianity; in this way "they make a pretense of religion but negate its power" (v. 5). The power of Christianity is its power to transform a person's life. Claiming to be a Christian while refusing to undergo this process of personal transformation is a major threat to the integrity of the Christian faith.

Apparently one of the favorite tactics of the false teachers was the deception of credulous women (v. 6). The phrase "always learning but never able to reach a knowledge of the truth" (v. 7) describes a type of quasi-theological dilettantism which, if anything, is even more prevalent in our time than in Paul's. According to Jewish tradition, Jannes and Jambres were the names of Pharaoh's magicians who, to a certain extent, were able to produce the same effects as Moses (see, for example, Exodus 7:8-12). Just as their "power" was eventually shown up for the sham which it was, so too the counterfeit Christianity of the false teachers will also be exposed (vv. 8-9).

Using himself as an example of a person who has integrated his teaching and his conduct into a powerful whole (v. 10), and who has been attacked as a result (v. 11), Paul reminds Timothy that any real Christian can expect to experience persecution (v. 12). Such is the way of the world, that deceit (that is, a hypocritical division between belief and practice) is common currency.

Verse 14 reflects Paul's conviction on the importance of the leadership of the Church following an established teaching authority. His use of the aorist (in Greek, the tense used to describe something which is definitely past) for "learned" and "believed" suggests that Timothy has already received the definitive Christian faith, and that he is called to be faithful to the established content and conduct of this faith. Accredited teachers such as Paul and now, like Timothy, have a crucial role to play in the transmission of the true faith.

Complementing the living Word, communicated through teachers, is the written Word, communicated through the sacred Scriptures (v. 15). At the time Paul was writing this letter the term "scripture" referred properly to the Hebrew Scriptures, what Christians today call the Old Testament. Already at this time, however, the sayings of Jesus were given authoritative status, and it was only a matter of time before the Church enlarged its understanding of sacred Scripture to include the New Testament.

Paul goes on to affirm that "All Scripture is inspired of God"(v. 16). Notice that he does not deal with the question of *how* it is inspired, he simply affirms that it *is* inspired. The phrase "inspired of God" is literally "God-breathed," and communicates the fact that God is *present* in Scripture. We could say that God is present in Scripture in much the same way that Jesus is present in the Eucharist. Like the Eucharist, if the Christian approaches God's Word in faith, it can become a profound place of meeting between the believer and God.

Aware that he is about to pull this letter to a close, Paul takes the opportunity to exhort Timothy one last time (4:1-2, 5). This is the most solemn exhortation in any of Paul's letters. Given the circumstance of his impending death, this exhortation sounds like an empowerment; Paul seems to be formally handing on the essence of his ministry to Timothy. These verses read very much like one of the Old Testament Patriarchs solemnly giving his blessing to his first-born son, a blessing which simultaneously challenges and empowers.

Verses 3-4 stand as an aside; it is as if Paul began his blessing (vv. 1-2), paused momentarily to reflect on the terrible times he was leaving but in which his "son" would remain (vv. 3-4), then concluded the blessing (v. 5).

A libation was an offering of oil or wine—or blood—which was poured out as an act of worship. Paul describes himself as a libation in verse 6; he sees his imprisonment and death as his personal sacrificial offering to the Father. Viewed in this way his coming death is not meaningless, but becomes endowed with the highest meaning and dignity.

Using imagery from the games, Paul celebrates the entire span of his life as a Christian in verse 7. He is confident of his salvation; the "merited crown" is the gift of eternal life which God will give as the consummation of His relationship with Paul.

Returning to practicalities, he makes some random requests and observations (vv. 9-13). He would like Timothy to be with

him at the end (v. 9). Paul is obviously lonely; all except Luke
have either deserted him or left on other ministries.

It is likely that verses 14-15 reflect the series of events which
led to his imprisonment; Alexander is probably the person responsible for his arrest. Like Jesus, Paul was deserted by all his friends
at the initial hearing of his case; like Jesus (and Stephen), he
forgives them for their desertion (v. 16). Christ, however, did
not desert him. On the contrary, He empowered him to give a
magnificent defense of the Gospel, a defense so effective that
Paul is able to describe his preaching task as "completed" and
the message delivered to "all the nations" (17a).

Apparently Paul's defense earned him a reprieve: "That is
how I was saved from the lion's mouth" (17b). He is well aware,
however, of the temporary nature of this reprieve, and recognizes
that the Lord's final rescue will be simultaneous with his death
(v. 18).

Paul concludes his letter by asking Timothy to convey his
greetings to assorted friends (vv. 19-21). His final blessing (v. 22)
is in the singular, another indication that this letter is his personal
will and testament to Timothy.